W9-CMP-115

Motivation to Learn

SECOND EDITION

MOTIVATION TO LEARN

From Theory to Practice

Deborah J. Stipek
University of California at Los Angeles

Allyn and Bacon
Boston • London • Toronto • Sydney • Tokyo • Singapore

Editor-in-Chief, Education: Nancy Forsyth
Series Editorial Assistant: Christine Nelson
Editorial-Production Service: Spectrum Publisher Services
Cover Designer: Suzanne Harbison
Manufacturing Buyer: Louise Richardson

Library of Congress Cataloging-in-Publication Data
Stipek, Deborah J., 1950–
    Motivation to learn: from theory to practice / Deborah J. Stipek.
—2nd ed.
       p.   cm.
    Includes bibliographical references (p.) and index.
    ISBN 0-205-14697-X
    1. Motivation in education. 2. Achievement motivation in
children. 3. Learning, Psychology of. I. Title.
    LB1065.S82   1992
    370.15'4—dc20   92-26213
                                       CIP

Contents

Preface

Why do some children approach school tasks eagerly and work diligently on school assignments, while others work half-heartedly or avoid schoolwork altogether? Why do some children enjoy learning in and out of school and take pride in their accomplishments, while others rarely seek opportunities to learn on their own and are anxious and unhappy in school? These are motivational questions with important implications for learning.

Motivation is relevant to learning because learning is an active process requiring conscious and deliberate activity. Even the most able students will not learn if they do not pay attention and exert some effort. If students are to benefit maximally from the educational curriculum, educators must provide a learning context that motivates students to engage in learning activities.

The purpose of this book is to give readers a thorough understanding of motivation theories and an appreciation of the potential application of this knowledge in educational settings. The focus is on classroom learning, but the book also considers how strategies used to motivate students in school affect students' motivation to engage in intellectual activities outside the classroom. The book stresses the costs of individualistic, competitive learning environments that emphasize extrinsic rewards and punishment, and the benefits of learning environments that maximize students' intrinsic interest in learning. The primary goal of the book is to demonstrate how achievement motivation theory and research can help teachers develop autonomous, self-confident learners who enjoy learning activities both in and out of school.

Throughout the book terms are clearly defined so that a reader unfamiliar with psychological theory and the academic research literature can understand the concepts used. The book contains many specific examples of how principles based on research and theory might be applied in the classroom, making it especially useful to individuals anticipating a teaching career, as well as to practicing teachers. It would also be appropriate as a supplementary text in a course on educational psychology.

ORGANIZATION

The second edition retains the same organization as the first. The new edition, however, includes recent research and covers all the first edition's topics more thoroughly. Research is discussed in greater detail and measures that have been developed to assess motivation are described. Considerably more attention is given to the practical implications of motivation theory and research for instruction. Tables and appendices have been added to assist teachers in applying, in their own classrooms, the principles of motivation presented in this book.

Chapter 1 describes hypothetical children—Defensive Dick, Hopeless Hannah, Safe Sally, Satisfied Sam, and Anxious Amy— with motivational problems that are commonly encountered in classrooms. A profile of each student's behavior in the classroom makes these common motivational problems more vivid and less abstract. In subsequent chapters the hypothetical students briefly reappear as concrete examples that illustrate theoretical constructs and research findings.

Chapter 2 describes behavioral manifestations of motivation problems and suggests ways to identify them. A distinction, important in both theory and practice, is made between extrinsic or performance goals (e.g., a desire to earn a good grade or please the teacher) and intrinsic or learning goals (i.e., wanting to solve a problem, or increase mastery).

Chapter 3 reviews traditional reinforcement theory and gives examples of effective applications of reinforcement principles that can maximize student effort in the classroom. The potential negative effects of over-reliance on extrinsic reinforcement are also explored. Chapter 4 discusses social cognitive theory, in which cognitions are assumed to mediate the effects of reinforcement on behavior, and classroom applications (i.e., cognitive behavior modification).

The concept of intrinsic motivation is introduced in Chapter 5, and teaching practices that have been found to foster intrinsic motivation in the classroom are described in Chapter 6.

Chapter 7 discusses cognitive theories of achievement motivation, including Atkinson's expectancy x value theory, Rotter's concept of locus of control, and Weiner's attribution theory. Chapter 8 considers self-perceptions of ability in the context of Covington's self-worth theory and Bandura's self-efficacy theory.

The causes and consequences of achievement anxiety for learning and performance in achievement contexts are discussed in Chapter 9. The chapter also makes specific recommendations for alleviating the negative effects of anxiety in the classroom.

Chapter 10 suggests classroom practices that foster self-confidence, high expectations for success, and pride. Research on ways teacher expectations affect students' beliefs about competence is described in Chapter 11.

Chapter 12 summarizes the book's suggestions for maintaining motivation to learn by exploring remedies to the motivational problems of the hypothetical children in Chapter 1.

1

PROFILES OF
MOTIVATIONAL PROBLEMS

Like cold or flu symptoms, motivation problems come in many shapes and sizes. But some combinations of problems are more common than others. This chapter describes typical motivation "syndromes"—patterns of beliefs and behaviors that inhibit optimal learning. No child you will ever meet will look exactly like any of the five hypothetical children described here. Indeed, these children are in some respects caricatures. But these vignettes should remind some readers of real children they have observed or taught. Later chapters will discuss the causes of the kinds of problems described here and ways to improve the motivation and learning of children like these five.[1]

DEFENSIVE DICK

Dick is one of the worst students in his fourth-grade class. Poor performance, as far as Dick is concerned, is inevitable. So he puts his energy into preventing anyone from interpreting his poor performance as evidence of a lack of ability. Unfortunately, the kind of strategies he uses to avoid looking dumb do not lead to improved performance.

His strategies are clever and often missed by the teacher, who does not have time to monitor him closely. For example, one morning Dick is working on an assignment to answer ten questions about a story the children were supposed to have read. The teacher shifts her attention from one child to another, monitoring each student's work to the best of her ability while answering questions. Dick asks the teacher several questions, but he is careful to give her the impression that he is working diligently to answer most of the questions on his own. Actually, he receives the rest of the answers by asking classmates or by copying his neighbor's paper. Thus, Dick manages to complete the assignment without reading or understanding the story.

That afternoon the teacher asks students to take out yesterday's assignment, which required the use of a dictionary. Dick makes a show of looking through his desk for an assignment that he knows, his teacher knows, and his classmates probably know, he has not done.

During a social studies test Dick sharpens his pencil twice, picks up his eraser that falls to the floor, and ties his shoelaces. He makes no attempt to conceal his lack of attention to the questions. To the contrary, he seems eager for everyone to notice that he is not trying. The teacher publicly reminds him several times to get to work, giving Dick and his classmates the message that if he tried, his performance, which will otherwise inevitably be poor, might be better. This, of course, is exactly the interpretation Dick desires.

Dick's strategies serve their purpose at least in the short run. He manages to complete some assignments with a respectable, if not an excellent, level of performance. By fooling around while he is supposed to be taking tests (when other strategies, such as cheating, are not available), he at least avoids appearing dumb, the logical conclusion associated with poor performance and high effort. By not trying, he creates an alternative explanation for failure, leaving open the question of whether he would have done well on the test if he had tried.

The tragedy is that Dick's ingenious efforts to avoid looking dumb are self-defeating. He makes little progress in mastering the curriculum, and failure becomes increasingly inevitable. Eventually Dick will give up trying to preserve an image of himself as a capable person, and he will resign himself to the status of one of the "dumb" kids in the class. If he continues this self-destructive game, he will soon look like Hopeless Hannah, who does not even try to look smart.

HOPELESS HANNAH

Hannah has been sitting at her desk for nearly half an hour doing, as far as the teacher can tell, nothing. The teacher urges Hannah to try one of the arithmetic problems she is supposed to be working on. "I can't," claims Hannah without even looking at the problem the teacher is pointing to. She adds, "I don't understand it." The frustrated teacher replies, "But I just went over a problem like it on the board—weren't you listening?" "I don't understand," Hannah repeats. The teacher goes through a long division problem step by step, asking Hannah questions along the way. Hannah answers most of the questions correctly. She obviously has at least some understanding of the problem. "See, you know how to do these kinds of problems," the teacher observes. "Why don't you try one on your own now?" "I don't know how," Hannah stubbornly declares. "But you knew the right answer to my questions," the teacher responds. "I guessed," is Hannah's ready reply. Not to be fooled, the teacher concludes, "I think you know how to do these, and I want you to try some of the problems."

The teacher has the last word and turns her attention to another student, leaving Hannah alone with her arithmetic problems. Later, she passes by Hannah's desk and finds no progress. The scene just described is repeated, as it has been so many times that year, and the end result is an exasperated teacher and a student who interprets the teacher's despair as confirmation of her own lack of competence.

Hannah is a classic example of what researchers refer to as "learned helplessness." Her academic performance is uniformly poor, and she is regarded by her classmates as one of the "dummies." She has developed a firm view of herself as incompetent and unable to master any new academic material. Failure is inevitable, so "Why try?" she reasons.

Hannah makes little academic progress and is two grades behind in most academic subjects. But she is not disruptive. She is not socially integrated into the classroom and therefore is not tempted to spend her time socializing. She is not an aggressive child, and rather than acting out, calling attention to herself, or interfering with her classmates, she sits quietly, spending much of her time gazing into space. She also makes few demands on the teacher. Hannah perceives no reason to ask questions because she does not expect to understand or to be able to make use of the answers.

There are many variations of learned-helplessness students. Some of the children who have given up trying to gain respect through their academic performance turn to other domains for recognition. They may become the class clown, or bully, or tease. Or, especially as they approach adolescence, they may engage in more serious antisocial behavior to gain respect. It is unusual for the academically "helpless" child to turn to legitimate ways of demonstrating competence, such as athletics, music or other arts. For some children the feelings of incompetence are so profound that they assume that there is simply no domain in which they can excel.

School offers little joy for children like Hannah. Their days are characterized by hopelessness, despair, and probably, since they spend little time working on academic tasks, boredom. They are shunned by their classmates, and they are often ignored by their teacher. The teacher's response is understandable considering the recalcitrance of helpless students. Because they rarely try, they rarely succeed. Their repeated failures confirm their perceptions of themselves as incompetent. When they do succeed, they are quick to deny responsibility. They attribute their success to some variable over which they have no control—an easy problem, the teacher's help, or even luck. The logic is elegantly consistent; the consequences are devastating.

Luckily, pure cases of learned helplessness are rare; weak versions are more common. Learned helplessness is, however, the motivational problem most resistant to change by even the most clever and persistent teacher. Obviously, it is best to prevent it from developing. But teachers in later grades have no control over their students' experiences in earlier grades and, unfortunately, children like Hannah occasionally appear in their classes.

SAFE SALLY

In her senior year of high school Sally's SAT scores are in the top five percent. This does not surprise her teachers because she is a straight "A" student. In many respects, Sally is a perfect student—well-behaved, dependable, and highly motivated. A superficial look at her would reveal no motivational problems.

But despite Sally's academic performance she is an underachiever. She is motivated, but only to achieve high grades and the accompanying respect of her teachers. She perceives a "B+" as a disastrous blemish on her record, something to be avoided at all costs.

A careful look at Sally's perfect record reveals a series of courses that offered little challenge. She is in the high-achievement track for English, but the teacher of these courses is well-known for giving every student in the class an "A", as long as the work is done reliably. She took only the required science courses, and she enrolled in the calculus course but dropped it after getting a "B-" on the first weekly quiz.

Sally religiously follows directions for every assignment. She is tuned in to her teachers and has an astonishing ability to predict what material will be stressed on tests. She overstudies for every test, repeatedly reviewing the text and memorizing every possible fact that she might be asked to recall. She rarely reads anything that she is not required to read for a course.

Sally is anxious, but her anxiety is not debilitating within the context of the intellectual demands she allows herself. She is constantly reinforced by teachers for her achievements, and she appears to be academically self-confident. She enjoys the respect of her classmates and is socially active.

What is unfortunate for Sally is that she does not allow herself to be challenged. She systematically takes the safe route in all of her academic endeavors. And in her classes she learns only what she is told to learn, in ways she expects to be evaluated. The notion that learning has some intrinsic value aside from being a means to good grades and external recognition simply does not occur to her. Working methodically within the guidelines and structure given to her, she makes no effort to be creative.

Sally ignored the school counselor's suggestion that she take courses required for acceptance at a selective university. She lacks self-confidence in her academic skills and prefers not to risk failure. The self-confidence she displays in her own high school is, in a sense, illusory. She knows that she is "smart enough" to excel in the carefully chosen not-too-demanding courses she takes, but she is not at all sure she can handle a more challenging academic experience. She does not know the true boundaries of her competencies because she never allows herself to test them.

Sally will no doubt excel in college, and she will probably perform well in a responsible, albeit not intellectually challenging, job. But she will not, as an adult, stretch her knowledge and imagination. Learning, for Sally, is what you do in school. It has instrumental but no intrinsic value. It brings "As," but no joy or excitement. Learning means memorizing somebody else's ideas, not developing her own. Sally's potential for creative thinking will never be tapped.

SATISFIED SAM

Sam is the seventh-grade class clown. He is one of the first to arrive at school in the morning, and he often fools around with classmates on the school grounds long after school is over. He seems to enjoy school, is popular with peers, and only occasionally gets into trouble for his pranks.

He is a likable student, but has frustrated many of his teachers. Sam is a "C+"/"B-" student who could easily be earning "As." His scores on standardized aptitude tests consistently show him to be capable of achieving considerably beyond most of his classmates, and he occasionally demonstrates his unusual aptitude. On those rare days when he pays close attention, he is frequently the only student in the class who can answer a difficult question. His potential is also evident when he becomes seriously involved in a project, such as the prize winning model of the solar system that he presented to his science teacher after several weeks of intense effort.

More typically, Sam shows little interest in school work. Threats of bad grades have no effect because he is quite satisfied with a grade that requires little effort for him to achieve. He usually finishes his work, but he never does more than the minimum. He makes it a rule never to study for a test because he knows that he can pass most tests simply by paying marginal attention in class. He knows he is smart, but he is not inclined to show off. He is not interested in gaining his peers' respect by demonstrating academic excellence, and he is not at all interested in gaining his teachers' respect. He is motivated to stay out of trouble—at least most of the time. Consequently, he does what is required to keep teachers "off his back."

At home Sam spends hour upon hour working on his computer playing intellectually demanding games. Sam is also interested in science. He reads every book he can find on space, and often he surprises his science teacher with comments demonstrating sophisticated understanding—usually on topics that are not part of the science curriculum. His performance on topics that are covered in his science class is typical of his performance in all of his other courses—he does exactly what he needs to do without getting into trouble. Science fiction novels are another great love, and he has written a short novel himself. He has some talent for writing, but it has never been evident in any school assignment.

Sam's teachers know that he could do better in school. Each new teacher goes through essentially the same series of strategies. Noting his halfhearted effort on assignments, teachers first encourage him to spend a little more time on his schoolwork to achieve a higher grade. When holding out a carrot doesn't seem to be effective, they turn to the stick, threatening bad grades—worse than he is getting. But Sam is unresponsive to these strategies because high grades simply do not have the same value for him that they have for some other students and poor grades are not perceived as punishment, unless they dip below his "C+" threshold of acceptability.

Sam sees no reason to push himself on school-related work. He enjoys intellectual challenges, but on his own terms. If his current interests happen to overlap with course requirements, he excels. More typically, his intellectual life is outside of the classroom and his life in the classroom is not intellectual.

Students like Sam are seen at all grade levels, although they are commonplace in junior high school. They frustrate parents and teachers alike. In contrast to Hannah, who convinces her teachers that she really cannot learn, Sam's teachers know that he has the ability to excel. But conventional strategies to motivate students like Sam are ineffective.

ANXIOUS AMY

Amy is in the eighth grade. She is an average student in most subjects but she is doing poorly in math. All of her standardized test scores indicate that she has at least average aptitude in math, yet her performance on class exams is typically well-below average. Tests are often turned in with many problems unanswered. Sometimes correct answers have been written in and erased. Amy occasionally spends math period in the nurse's room, claiming a headache, a stomach ache, or some other ailment that miraculously disappears about the time her math class ends.

For the first few weeks of the semester, Amy's math teacher frequently asks Amy questions in an attempt to elicit her participation and to assess her understanding of the concepts the teacher is explaining to the class. But she usually refuses to participate, and the teacher, sensing that she is uncomfortable when questions are addressed to her publicly, stops trying to engage her in class discussion.

In contrast to her class performance, assignments that she can take home are often returned completed and mostly correct. The teacher knows from conversations with Amy's parents that she does her homework on her own. Her math teacher is puzzled by her reticence in class because she knows from Amy's homework assignments that she can figure out the answers if she tried.

Amy lacks self-confidence and apparently finds refusing to answer a question less threatening than risking a wrong answer. It is difficult for her to concentrate on math problems in class because she is distracted by her concerns about failure. However prepared she may be for a test, as soon as it is in front of her, she often panics. She cannot remember the simplest procedures that she knew well the evening before. When the teacher asks her a question in front of the class, she is conscious of the other students' evaluative gazes and she cannot concentrate on the question itself.

Amy will get through eighth-grade math with a passing grade, partly because she can compensate for her poor test scores and class performance with complete and correct homework. But she will take only the math courses required to graduate. And if she goes to college, she will major in an area that does not require any math. For the rest of her life she will claim, if the subject comes up, that she has no aptitude for numbers.

CONCLUSION

Much can be done to prevent children from developing the kinds of motivational problems described above; there are also ways to solve these problems when they appear. But solving motivational problems requires a good understanding of the underlying causes of the kind of maladaptive behavior manifested by these five children.

The following chapters place motivation problems in a theoretical context and discuss research that helps provide solutions to such problems. School learning is emphasized but attention is also given to how strategies used to motivate students in school affect their motivation to engage in intellectual activities outside the classroom. This book assumes that we want students to exert maximum effort on academic tasks in the classroom, but we also want them to engage in learning activities and to develop new skills outside of school. Indeed, we want individuals to value learning and to be motivated to seek learning opportunities throughout their adult lives.

2

DEFINING ACHIEVEMENT MOTIVATION

Achievement motivation theorists try to explain the initiation, direction, and intensity of an individual's behavior in situations in which performance can be evaluated according to some standard. The standard may be personal (i.e., achieving some predetermined goal) or it may be imposed by another individual, such as a teacher or parent. Opportunities for achievement occur in school, at home, on the playing field, on stage, and in many other places.

Some theorists conceptualize achievement motivation as a stable trait—something that an individual has either a lot or a little of and that is only modestly changeable. For example, McClelland (1961, 1971, 1978) claimed that achievement motivation is an unconscious trait that develops early in life as a consequence of parents' behavior toward children in achievement situations. Experiences in early childhood are assumed to play a continuing and pervasive role in individuals' responses to achievement situations.

Other theorists conceptualize achievement motivation as a set of conscious beliefs and values that are influenced primarily by recent experiences in achievement situations (e.g., the amount of success or failure) and variables in the immediate environment (e.g., the difficulty of the task). From this point of view an individual may have a strong motive to achieve in geography but not in algebra because of recent experiences in these particular classes, or she may be highly motivated to complete one task but not another.

The latter approach implies that teachers have considerable opportunity (and, therefore, responsibility) to maximize students' motivation to achieve in school. According to this view, students are not limited by the level of motivation inculcated in them by their parents. Parents are influential, but teachers control many aspects of instruction as well as the social climate of the classroom, and can therefore increase their students' motivation. To use this influence wisely, teachers need to know their students well.

BEHAVIORAL INDICES OF MOTIVATIONAL PROBLEMS

Teachers usually recognize the motivational problems of students who do not do well in school. In my experience, teachers believe that most children who do poorly in school have motivation problems and most children who do well are highly motivated. Motivation problems of relatively high-achieving children whose potential for intellectual development is not being fulfilled often go unrecognized.

That even high-achieving students can have motivational problems is demonstrated in a study by Phillips (1984; see also Phillips and Zimmerman, 1990). She studied 117 fifth-graders who were above the 75th national percentile on the Stanford Research Associates (SRA) achievement tests. Twenty-three of these students seriously underestimated their actual levels of performance, set low achievement standards for themselves, and persisted less on tasks than the high achievers in the sample who had high perceptions of competence. By setting low standards and by giving up easily, these high-ability students were, like Safe Sally, probably not living up to their learning potential.

It is easy to overlook relatively high-achieving students who are not performing at their capacity. Teachers who are burdened by as many as 25 or even 35 students in a class generally feel that their primary responsibility is to make sure that all students master the basic curriculum. As long as students consistently finish their work and are not disruptive, the fact that they finish assignments in half of the allotted time often goes unnoticed. This is especially true in classes where there are many students who are having difficulty mastering the assigned material and who require considerable attention. Thus, the "B+" student who could be getting "As," and the student who gets "As" without really trying, are less likely to be noticed or to be perceived as problems than students who are barely passing. It is, therefore, important to scrutinize all students for motivational problems.

Maehr (1984) describes five behavioral patterns that can be used as indices of motivation related to learning. First, he suggests that the *direction of an individual's attention and activity* is related to motivation. When students attend to one thing and not another, or choose to complete one task and not another, they presumably are motivated with regard to the former and not motivated with regard to the latter. Compare the child who works diligently on her math assignments to another child who socializes during math seatwork time. Both children are motivated, but they are motivated to engage in different activities. The first child's behavior may be explained by a motive to learn, or to please the teacher, or to obtain external rewards. The second child's behavior may be explained by a motive to be popular. Students who do not work hard on school tasks are not *unmotivated*; they are motivated to achieve different goals than those the teacher has in mind.

That children often have different goals than the teacher is illustrated in research by Wentzel (1989, 1991). She asked high school students how often they tried to achieve a set of 12 goals while they were in class at school. "Making or keeping friends" ranked the highest by students with average GPAs and second highest (after "having fun") by the lowest achieving students. Only the highest achieving students ranked "learning" above friends as a frequent goal in school.

Persistence is the second behavior Maehr (1982) associates with motivation. The length of time a person engages in an activity, especially a difficult task, is often used as a behavioral index of his or her motivation. Students who give up easily when they encounter difficulty are presumably less motivated than students who persevere.

Third, the *activity level* of the individual is a behavioral index of motivation. Individuals can work intensively or they can work halfheartedly on tasks. The level of intensity is to some degree related to their level of motivation.

A fourth behavior is what Maehr refers to as *continuing motivation*. Individuals who return to a task without apparent external incentives, who do a task "on their own," are apparently highly motivated. Examples include reading at home or during free time about subjects discussed in school, or solving math problems that the teacher does not require.

Performance is the fifth behavioral index of motivation, although it is to some degree a consequence of the four factors described above. A student who works intensely on a task, persists when the task is difficult, and engages in the task without external incentives will undoubtedly learn more and perform better than a student who avoids tasks, works half-heartedly, or gives up easily. Nevertheless, because there is not a perfect relationship between motivation and performance (some children do poorly despite considerable effort and others do well without really trying), motivation must be assessed independent of performance.

IDENTIFYING MOTIVATION PROBLEMS

How do we know when students are performing or learning below their capacity? One approach that is used to identify "underachievers" is to give aptitude tests. Students whose performance in class is below the level that would be expected from their performance on an aptitude test may have motivation problems. However, standardized tests alone do not provide sufficient information. We do not have tests that measure pure aptitude, and tests are no substitute for a teacher's own observations.

The questions in Appendix 2-A can be used to guide teacher observations. Teachers should observe all students, including those who are achieving relatively well. Teachers should also observe the same student in different subject areas, in a variety of contexts, and doing a variety of tasks. Some students work diligently in small groups but never finish tasks that are designed to be done individually; some students work best in structured learning situations, others in unstructured situations, and so on. These differences will not be identified if students are observed in only one learning context. Motivation levels may also vary systematically depending on the type of task. Observations of these variations can contribute a great deal to a teacher's understanding of motivational problems and to finding solutions.

Although essential, even careful observations are often insufficient to diagnose problems and need to be supplemented with discussions with students. Discussions with individual or small groups of students can be revealing if teachers encourage and do not penalize students for honesty and openness. Teachers are often surprised to hear some of their high-performing students say that they do not like schoolwork and work hard only to achieve extrinsic rewards or avoid parental sanctions. Some poor-achieving students whom teachers perceive to be unmotivated occasionally confess to being discouraged or fearful of failure.

The importance of going beyond observable behavior is demonstrated in a study by Peterson and Swing (1982), in which some elementary school-age students who looked as if they were attending faithfully to a math lesson on probability reported in subsequent interviews that they were actually thinking of other things. They claimed, for example, to be worrying about whether they would be able to solve the problems and whether they would be one of the last to finish. Students' responses to questions about their thoughts during the time they were supposed to be working on the task predicted their achievement better than observers' judgments regarding their level of attention. Not surprisingly, children who claimed that they were thinking about strategies to solve the problems performed better than those who claimed to be thinking about whether they could solve them.

This finding should not be surprising. What adult has not been guilty of feigning attention at a teachers' meeting or during a sermon at church or synagogue while planning the evening's dinner menu or fantasizing about an upcoming vacation? What college student has not pretended to be taking notes in a lecture while writing a letter to a friend? Adults sometimes have elaborate strategies for looking attentive, and so do children. With a large group of students to observe, it is often difficult for the teacher to see through these ruses. Since we cannot observe children's thoughts, the most careful observations of a student's work habits will not be sufficient to identify motivational problems.

One of the purposes of this book is to help teachers identify and remedy motivational problems stemming from unobservable thoughts and feelings, such as levels of self-confidence, expectations for success, interest in academic work, feelings of autonomy, achievement anxiety, and fear of failure. Even if motivational problems are apparent from overt behavior, remedies require accurate diagnoses. Observational and other methods to assess these variables will be described in later chapters to help teachers in this important process.

GRADE DIFFERENCES IN MOTIVATIONAL PROBLEMS

Underachievement in the early elementary grades (i.e., kindergarten and first grade) usually has different causes than it does in later grades. Most young children's failure to work effectively on school tasks is a consequence of immaturity or poor socialization. Young children usually have not had experience in formal academic settings. Some have difficulty sitting at a desk for more than a few minutes. They may also be distractible, either because they are not accustomed to the stimulation of many other children and activities or because they have attention difficulties associated with immaturity. Some young children, who are used to being able to choose their activities, do not accept the formal educational settings' necessary constraints on their activities.

Although children in the early grades have some difficulty following directions and completing tasks, nearly all are eager, self-confident learners (although not necessarily on the tasks the teacher provides). Young children typically have very high (sometimes unrealistic) confidence in their ability to succeed (Stipek, 1984a, b). In one of my own studies we asked children in kindergarten, first, second, and third grade to rate how smart they were on a 1–5 scale, with "5" representing the smartest child in their class (Stipek and Tannatt, 1984). Nearly every kindergartner and most of the first-graders gave themselves a 5, including some who were actually performing very poorly compared to their classmates. By second or third grade some students lose self-confidence, become anxious in learning contexts, and consequently engage in activities that inhibit rather than facilitate learning. Thus, although the kinds of adjustment problems very young children have usually disappear with time and experience in a school setting, other problems emerge.

The older the child, the more serious are the consequences of motivation problems. For the first six to nine years of school, students have little choice in their educational curriculum. Because there are not many tasks they can avoid, children's motivational problems are often revealed in low effort expenditure, poor attention, or acting out. High school students have more choice in the type and difficulty level of the courses they take, and in whether they remain in an educational context at all. Older students can, like Safe Sally, avoid certain courses, or even school itself. Thus, while the younger child who lacks self-confidence in math may "forget" to do her homework every day, the older student may simply not take any courses in math. Or, if the older child's self-confidence is very low, she may drop out of school altogether.

STUDENTS' GOALS

Recently motivation theorists have focused as much on students' goals—their *reasons* for engaging in achievement tasks—as on their behaviors in achievement contexts. This work is based on the belief, well-supported by research, that the benefits of working on academic tasks vary as a function of the reasons for task engagement.

Motivational researchers have categorized goals as *intrinsic* and *extrinsic*. Satisfied Sam is intrinsically motivated inasmuch as he works only on tasks he enjoys or tasks that develop skills he cares about, or tasks that give a sense of personal mastery. Task engagement is, in effect, an end in itself. Brophy (1986, 1987b) refers to this kind of engagement as "motivation to learn." Safe Sally, in contrast, is motivated for extrinsic rewards, especially good grades and social approval;

for her, task engagement is a means to another end. Other extrinsic reasons for working are to get stickers, please a parent, gain social acceptance among peers, meet a minimum GPA that is required to play on the football team, or gain entrance into a prestigious university. Hopeless Hannah doesn't engage much on tasks at all, and might be considered "amotivated" with regard to school tasks.

Task/Learning/Mastery Goals versus Ego/Performance Goals

This distinction between engaging in tasks for extrinsic reasons (i.e., to achieve some goal unrelated to the task itself) and engaging in tasks for intrinsic reasons (for enjoyment or to develop competency) relates to a distinction theorists currently make between **learning goals** (referred to by some researchers as "**mastery**" or "**task**" goals)—which concern mastery and developing understanding—and **performance** goals (also referred to as "**ego**" goals)—which concern doing better than others, demonstrating more intelligence, and winning approval (Ames and Archer, 1988; Nicholls, 1983; Maehr, 1984; Meece, 1991).

Dweck (1986) proposes that learning goals and performance goals have very different implications for how students behave in achievement settings and how they interpret performance outcomes (see also, Dweck and Elliott, 1983; Dweck and Leggett, 1988; Elliott and Dweck, 1988; Lepper, 1988; Nicholls, Cobb, Yackel, Wood, and Wheatley, 1990). According to Dweck's theoretical analysis, students with learning goals—regardless of whether they perceive themselves to be relatively high or low in ability—seek challenging tasks that provide opportunities to develop new competencies and see their teacher as a resource or guide in the learning process, rather than as an evaluator. When they encounter difficulty, they assume that their current strategy is inappropriate and needs to be changed, or that they are not trying hard enough. Accordingly, they analyze their strategy and redouble their efforts. For students with learning goals, judgments of competence are based on the amount of effort expended and real learning or mastery achieved.

Students with performance goals, in contrast, want to look competent, like Safe Sally, or avoid looking incompetent, like Defensive Dick. Dweck proposes that these students see the teacher as a judge or rewarder/punisher, rather than as a resource, and their judgments of competence are based on performance relative to others or to external feedback, not on real gains in understanding or mastery. Those who are confident in their ability choose moderately difficult tasks to allow them to display their competence, and because they are confident that they will succeed when they encounter difficulty they, like students with learning goals, engage in effective strategies. Because their goal is to *look* competent (as opposed to *be* competent), however, they may use shortcuts which achieve their immediate goal but do not actually foster learning (Nicholls, 1983).

Students like Defensive Dick, who have performance goals but lack confidence in their ability, choose easy tasks to avoid displaying incompetence. When they encounter difficulty they either engage in self-defeating strategies to avoid being seen as low in ability, or give up because they don't believe they can demonstrate competence.

Studies have supported Dweck's claim that a task- or mastery-orientation is associated with moderate risk-taking and willingness to engage in challenging tasks. In one study children who were task-oriented were more likely than performance-oriented children to select a task described to them as difficult but that would promote skill development (Elliott and Dweck, 1988). Most performance-oriented children selected a task they were told would not teach them anything new, but on which they could demonstrate their competence. In another study students who perceived their classroom as relatively mastery-oriented claimed that they would prefer a science project that would be difficult but result in new learning over an easy project (Ames and Archer, 1988; see also Nicholls, 1984).

Task versus ego goals also have implications for students' attention while they work on tasks. Nicholls (1979b, 1983) claims that students focus on the process of completing the task when they are motivated to learn or master—when they are **task-oriented**. Performance goals are associated with attention on the self, and especially on external evaluations of the self, referred to as an **ego-orientation**.

This distinction is illustrated in Peterson and Swing's (1982) study, mentioned above. One of the students they observed looked as if she were paying attention throughout the math lesson they observed. Nevertheless, when subsequently asked what she thought about during the lesson, she commented that her first thought was: ". . . since I was just beginning, I was nervous, and I thought maybe I wouldn't know how to do things . . . " (p. 486). After a later lesson segment, she responded: "Well, I was mostly thinking . . . I was making a fool of myself" (p. 486). In contrast, a task-oriented child responded to the same question by describing in some detail the strategies she used to solve the problems.

Csikszentmihalyi (1975) refers to the intense involvement associated with a task-orientation as **flow**. Individuals experiencing flow are so intensely attentive to the task that they may lose awareness of time and space. Most great artists and scholars report that they experience flow when working in their field. People who are known for their creativity have reported that they were in a flow state when they did their best work (Nicholls, 1983).

A task orientation is also associated with the use of effective problem-solving strategies. In one study, students scoring high on a measure of task orientation in science reported relatively greater use of active "metacognitive strategies" (e.g., reviewing material not understood, asking questions as they worked, making connections between current problems and past problems), and less use of "superficial engagement" (copying, guessing, skipping questions) than children who claimed to be relatively more ego-oriented [Meece, Blumenfeld, and Hoyl (1988); see Pintrich and Schrauben (in press), for further evidence on associations between goal orientation and cognitive learning strategies]. Ames and Archer (1988) found, similarly, that the more students perceived their junior high school classroom to support mastery rather than performance goals, the more they reported engaging in active learning strategies (planning, organizing material, setting goals) that are known to facilitate learning. Finally, Nolen (1988) found that the higher the task orientation of junior high students, the more they used deep processing strategies (e.g., discriminating important information from unimportant information, trying to figure out how new information fits with what one already knows, and monitoring comprehension) to understand a passage from a science magazine.

Researchers have demonstrated the advantages of a task orientation on problem-solving strategies both by experimentally manipulating subjects' attention and by observing subjects in regular classroom tasks. They have, for example, demonstrated that interventions creating a self-focus (e.g., placing a mirror or video camera near subjects) impair performance on cognitive tasks (Brockner, 1979; Elliott and Dweck, 1988).

The research is consistent with Dweck's (1986) proposal that an ego- or performance-orientation undermines effective problem solving for children who have doubts about their competence, more so than for self-confident children. Elliott and Dweck (1988) experimentally induced performance or learning goals by emphasizing either the benefits of learning or the importance of performance. They also manipulated children's perceptions of skill on a task. When performance-oriented children who had low self-confidence encountered difficulty, their problem-solving strategies deteriorated. This did not occur for performance-oriented children with high self-confidence. Learning or mastery-oriented children's strategies were not affected by whether they had high or low confidence in their ability. Brockner (1979) found, also, that the video camera and mirror resulted in impaired performance only for subjects who had low self-esteem, and Elliott and Dweck (1988) found that children who had relatively low perceptions of their ability showed the most impaired performance in the performance-goal condition.

Task orientation is also associated with more constructive beliefs about what causes success or failure. In the Ames and Archer (1988) study, students who perceived their classroom to be mastery-oriented tended to attribute success to high effort and effective learning strategies, while students who perceived their classroom to be more performance-oriented tended to attribute failure to low ability. The latter students are disadvantaged because children who attribute failure to low ability have no reason to exert effort in the future (see Chapter 7).

Nicholls, Cobb, Wood, Yackel, and Patashnick (1990) found that a task orientation was also associated with more constructive beliefs about the cause of success. The second-grade students in their sample who were relatively more task-oriented were more likely to believe that success was caused by interest and effort to understand, whereas students who were more ego-oriented believed that success was caused by efforts to compete with classmates.

Students' perceptions of the role of effort also vary as a function of students' goals. For students with mastery goals, more effort is associated with greater feelings of competence. Individuals with performance goals typically measure success in normative terms, that is, by their performance relative to classmates. In studies conducted by Jagacinski and Nicholls (1984), students were asked to imagine or recall times that they had succeeded with high or low effort under task-involving or ego-involving conditions. When students imagined ego-involving conditions, they judged their ability higher and claimed that they would feel better if they completed a task by applying *low* effort and others needed high effort than if they applied high effort and others used low effort. The opposite was found under task-involving conditions; high effort was associated with judgments of high ability. This effect was observed presumably because failure following high effort is likely to be attributed to incompetence when individuals are ego-oriented, whereas the cause of failure following low effort is ambiguous (Covington and Beery, 1976; see Chapter 8).

Individuals are also believed to experience greater pleasure and greater emotional involvement when they are task-oriented. In the Ames and Archer (1988) study mentioned above, the more students perceived their classroom as supporting mastery goals, the more they liked the class. Elliott and Dweck (1988) report that many of the children in a performance-oriented condition who had low perceptions of their ability spontaneously expressed negative feelings about the task with comments like, "After this (problem), then I get to go?" or "This is boring," "My stomach hurts" (p. 10). Children who were task-oriented rarely made such comments, whether or not they believed that they were competent at the task.

Finally, goals affect what students learn. This is demonstrated in a study by Benware and Deci (1984), who asked two groups of college students to learn material from an unfamiliar passage on neurophysiology. To create different goals, they told one group that they would be tested on the material and another group that they would be teaching the material to other students. Both groups spent the same amount of time learning the material. The two groups did not differ in their rote learning, but the group that was told that they would teach the material to others demonstrated greater conceptual understanding than the group that expected to be tested. Thus, the manipulated goal influenced how the material was learned. In another study, fifth- and sixth-grade students were manipulated to be ego-involved (by claiming that performance was diagnostic of problem-solving ability) or task-oriented (by claiming that the task would be challenging and fun). Compared to students who were primarily concerned about mastering the task, subjects who were ego-oriented showed poorer word recall at deep processing levels (having to do with meaning) but not at shallow processing levels [having to do with the sound of the word; Graham and Golan (1991)].

Given the important implications of students' reasons for working on tasks, teachers need to attend carefully to students' goals. Strategies for assessing these goals are discussed next.

Assessing Students' Goals

Several researchers have developed measures of students' goals. Harter (in press) asks students to rate the truth value of a series of statements that reflect different goals. Some of the goals they are asked to rate are *extrinsic*, such as pleasing parents or avoiding negative sanctions from parents (e.g., "If I don't do my schoolwork my parents will be mad or annoyed at me"), pleasing a teacher, obtaining good grades, avoiding negative sanctions in school (e.g., "If I don't do my schoolwork, I'll get in trouble with the teacher"), or obtaining tangible rewards (e.g., "I'll get something extra or special from my parents if I do my schoolwork"). Other goals are *intrinsic* (e.g., ". . . because a lot of what we learn is really interesting"; "I enjoy figuring things out"; ". . . because it's challenging").

TABLE 2-1 • Behaviors Associated with an Ego Orientation

1. Uses short cuts to complete tasks (tries to get them done without going through steps that would contribute to learning)

2. Cheats

3. Seeks attention for good performance

4. Only works hard on graded assignments

5. Hides papers with low scores/grades

6. Compares scores/grades with classmates

7. Is upset by low scores/grades

8. Copies classmates' papers

9. Chooses tasks that are most likely to result in a positive evaluation

10. Is uncomfortable with assignments in which criteria for evaluation are not clear

---

Nicholls and his colleagues developed a measure to assess children's task versus ego orientation to schoolwork, and a third goal, which he refers to as "work avoidance." The following are examples of what children are asked to rate. To indicate the strength of their *task orientation* is the statement, "I feel really pleased in school when I solve a problem by working hard"; for *ego orientation* "I feel really pleased in school when I know more than the others", and for *work avoidance*, "I feel really pleased in school when I don't have to work hard."

Students also reveal their goals through their behavior. Table 2-1 includes behaviors that are typically associated with an ego orientation. Students who manifest these behaviors may be more concerned about doing well or looking good than they are about developing skills or mastering problems.

Parents' Goals

Ames and Archer (1987) have measured parents' goals for their children. They classified mothers as having mastery or performance goals by asking them whether they would prefer to have their child (1) demonstrate effort by working hard in school even if he or she doesn't do very well, or (2) demonstrate performance by doing well in school even if he or she doesn't have to work very hard. About 60 percent of the mothers chose the mastery goal and about 40 percent chose the performance goal. The mothers who stressed performance as a goal preferred that their children be given tasks that assured their success rather than tasks that challenged their current skill level. Parents' goals are important because they affect how parents respond to their children's performance in school. Some parents punish children for bad grades, regardless of whether they have made progress. Others reward their children for progress, regardless of their grades. Parents with different goals give different messages to children (e.g., "The only thing that is important is that you do your best," versus, "You really have to get more 'As' next time"). Parents' goals undoubtedly influence children's goals, and the more teachers know about the messages parents give their children, the better they will understand their students' motivation.

Teacher Effects on Students' Goals

Although students enter a classroom with tendencies toward learning or performance goals developed from experiences in previous grades and at home, teachers have enormous influence on children's goal orientations in their classrooms. The teacher who stresses learning over performance, gives the message that mistakes are a normal and acceptable part of learning, and encourages risk-taking and personal improvement will foster a task orientation in children. The teacher who emphasizes performance, conveys the message that mistakes are bad, and encourages competition will foster a performance orientation.

Ames and Archer (1988) developed a measure of students' perceptions of their own classroom. Some of the questions refer to teacher or classroom practices that support mastery or learning goals (e.g., "In this class, making mistakes is a part of learning"; "In this class the teacher makes sure I understand the work"). Other questions refer to practices that are more likely to foster performance goals (e.g., "In this class students compete to see who can do the best work"; "In this class the teacher favors some students more than others"). Giving this measure to students can reveal to their teachers specific behaviors and instructional strategies that they use which inadvertently foster goals other than those they intend.

The match between the student's and the teacher's goal is also important. A student like Satisfied Sam who is primarily intrinsically motivated may not work hard in a classroom in which the teacher stresses extrinsic goals. The threat of a bad grade may be very effective for the extrinsically motivated child, but not for a student like Sam. Students like Safe Sally who are oriented toward extrinsic rewards may not initially work hard in a class in which the teacher stresses a mastery orientation. I found this to be true when I first began teaching college students. In an effort to orient students' attention toward the joy of learning about child psychology, I did not give grades for class partici- pation or papers. I found very quickly that my own goal orientation was initially incompatible with the goal orientation of the students. Rather than studying to understand child development, they studied to get good grades in their *other* classes and came to my class unprepared. This realization forced me to try different strategies in the hope of increasing student effort in my course without giving in to their per- formance orientation. Teachers need not capitulate to students' goal orientations, but they should be aware of them and of possible conflicts between their classroom practices and their students' orientations. Strategies for influencing students' goals will be discussed in some detail in Chapter 6.

VALUES

Related to students' goals are their values. Individuals at all age levels forego opportunities to engage in achievement-related activities, not because they expect to fail but because they simply do not value suc- cess. Feather (1988), for example, found that college students' percep- tions of the value of math versus English was a strong predictor of course enrollment decisions. Values also affect how much effort people put into activities, how they feel about outcomes, and ultimately how they view their lifelong professional commitments. For example, chil- dren who value athletic performance more than academic performance may exert more effort on the field than in the classroom, experience greater pride and shame as a consequence of performance in athletic competitions than as a consequence of report card results, and aspire to an occupation requiring athletic skills. Similarly, some children learn to value musical or other artistic competencies, popularity among peers, or serving the community. And within the academic domain, there is variation in the degree to which children value competence and success in different subject areas.

Values also affect individuals' self-esteem. A study reported in Harter (1987) demonstrates that perceptions of low competence in domains that children valued highly had more negative effects on their self-esteem than perceptions of low competence in domains that they valued less.

Eccles (1983) proposes three kinds of values relevant to achievement:

Attainment value is the subjective importance of doing well on a task or in an achievement domain, determined by how the task or the domain fulfills the individual's needs. Attainment value concerns the relevance of an activity to an individual's self-concept. Children presumably engage in activities and develop competencies that are consistent with their concept of themselves (e.g., as feminine, musically talented, socially deviant).

Utility value concerns the usefulness of a task as a means to achieve goals that might not be related to the task itself. For example, a good grade in chemistry would have considerable utility value for a college student hoping to be admitted to medical school.

Intrinsic value is the immediate enjoyment one gets from doing a task. When a task has intrinsic value it is engaged in for its own sake, rather than for some other purpose.

A fourth way to conceptualize value that is not specifically addressed by Eccles is in terms of anticipated emotions. Individuals seek opportunities to experience pleasurable feelings, such as pride, and to avoid situations in which they are likely to experience unpleasant feelings, such as shame or embarrassment (Weiner, 1980b). Achievement situations expected to generate pride, therefore, are perceived to have more value than situations believed likely to produce feelings of shame.

Most of the research on attainment and utility value has focused on gender differences. Research suggests, for example, that with age, males increasingly value achievement in school and females become more concerned about potential conflicts between academic and social goals (Sherman, 1979). Theorists have claimed that gender-typing of some domains as "masculine" and some as "feminine" influences the attainment value of performance in different domains for males and females, and thus influences their behavior on tasks related to particular domains. Eccles (1983) proposes, for example, that the attainment value of math achievement is low for those females who perceive math courses as a masculine activity and who feel a need to avoid masculine activities to affirm their femininity.

The evidence for an effect of sex-typing on females' perceptions of the attainment value of math *courses* is, however, weak. Females are actually less likely than males to see math courses as a male achievement domain, and females usually do not characterize participation in math activities as unfeminine (Eccles, 1983). It is possible, however, that although females do not see math courses as a male domain, they do see math-related *occupations* as unfeminine. Eccles suggests that if females are less likely to aspire to a profession in mathematics, math courses would have less utility value for them than they would for males. Sex-typing of careers, therefore, may be a more important mediator of sex difference in the perceived value of advanced math courses than is sex-typing of the courses themselves. Consistent with this claim, a study by Stevenson and Newman (1986) found that tenth-grade boys had higher expectancies than girls for success in a career that required mathematical ability and boys perceived math to have greater utility in daily life than girls.

CONCLUSION

This chapter makes it clear that diagnosing motivation problems and finding solutions are very complex tasks. Low motivation is not synonymous with low performance. Some children perform poorly relative to peers regardless of their effort; others do well without really trying. Even careful observations of behavior can be misleading. Children's reasons for their effort, the goals they are trying to achieve, and their achievement-related values all have important implications for motivation and learning. Teachers, therefore, must be careful observers of their own and of their students' behavior and they must engage students in discussions and use other strategies to understand students' goals and values.

TABLE 2-2 • Summary of Terms

Term	Definition
Task/Learning/ Mastery Goals	Goals involving learning, mastery, or developing competencies
Ego/Performance Goals	Goals are to demonstrate competence or avoid demonstrating incompetence, to gain social recognition or approval
Task orientation	Attention is on strategies needed to complete a task or to develop understanding or skill
Ego orientation	Attention is focused on the self, especially others' evaluation of the self
Flow	Intense task involvement
Attainment value	The subjective importance of doing well on a task or in an achievement domain
Utility value	Perceived usefulness of a task as a means to achieve goals that might not be related to the task itself
Intrinsic value	The immediate enjoyment one gets from doing a task

3

REINFORCEMENT THEORY

Reinforcement theory was developed to explain *all* human behavior, not just achievement-related behavior. But a great deal has been written about the application of reinforcement theory to classroom learning. Indeed, for many years a reinforcement model of motivation dominated the educational psychology literature.

THE THEORY

Operant conditioning theorists assume that behavior is caused by events external to the person, and they claim that behavior can be understood in terms of simple laws that apply to both human beings and animals. According to the **law of effect**, behavior is determined by its consequences. Responses become more probable as the result of some consequences and less probable as the result of others. Thorndike (1898) derived this principle from his observations of food-deprived cats placed inside a box with food outside. In their attempts to escape, the animals would, by accident, eventually operate a device that released the door, allowing them to consume the food. The animals subsequently operated the device more and more rapidly upon being placed in the box. Thus, an accidental behavior that originally had very low probability occurred with increasing frequency as a result of its consequence.

Skinner (1974) elaborated upon the law of effect proposed by Thorndike by systematically manipulating consequences and studying their effects on behavior. He defined consequences that *increased* the probability of behaviors they were made contingent upon as **positive reinforcers**, and consequences that *reduced* the probability of behavior as **punishments**. **Negative reinforcement** refers to consequences that increase the probability of a behavior by taking something away or reducing it in intensity.

Although originally derived primarily from research on animals, reinforcement theorists assume that these principles apply to human beings as well. Consider, for example, a teacher who wants to increase the amount of attention a child pays to his or her directions. This child likes **social reinforcement** (e.g., teacher smiles, verbal praise) and dislikes missing recess. If the teacher praises the child (positive reinforcement), or stops frowning (negative reinforcement) when he pays attention, he is more likely to pay attention in the future. If the teacher cancels his recess (punishment) when he is *in*attentive, his inattention will decrease.

Reinforcers and punishments are defined strictly in terms of their effects on behavior and cannot be identified independently of these effects. What is a positive reinforcer for some may, therefore, be punishment for others. An opportunity to perform in front of the class may be a real treat for an outgoing, self-assured child, and would serve as a positive reinforcer. The same "opportunity" may be punishing for a shy child or a child who lacks self-confidence.

Consequences can become reinforcing by being linked to other consequences that are already reinforcing. Consider grades, for example. Grades have little effect on most kindergartners who have not learned their value. But kindergartners who bring home "As" are likely to be praised by their parents and possibly even given tangible rewards. As a result of being paired with consequences that are already reinforcing, "As" take on—independent of the rewards they were originally paired with—reinforcing qualities.

This process also works for punishment. A child who is teased or rejected by his friends for being the teacher's pet may cease engaging in behaviors that win teacher approval. What once served as a positive reinforcer therefore becomes punishment by being linked to an undesirable consequence.

If a previously reinforced behavior ceases to be reinforced, its rate of occurrence decreases; the desired behavior becomes **extinguished**. Thus, for example, if the attention of the boy described above is not reinforced he will stop paying attention (i.e., attention will be extinguished).

Although a reinforcer needs to be contingent upon a behavior from time to time to avoid extinguishing the behavior, reinforcers are not *always* necessary to maintain behaviors. In fact, behaviors that are reinforced **intermittently** or partially (rather than every time the desired behavior occurs) take the longest amount of time to extinguish when reinforcement ceases altogether.

Another operant condititoning principle explains the conditions under which behavior that has been reinforced will occur. Skinner found that unrelated external cues became signals for the availability of reinforcement or punishment. Thus, for example, if a rat is reinforced for pushing a lever only when a particular type of light is on, the rat will begin to push the lever when the light is turned on, and will not push it without the light. The light, according to Skinner, serves as a **discriminative stimulus**, and the lever-pushing response is under **stimulus control**. Thus, according to the principle of stimulus control, stimuli that become associated with consequences can occasion behavior itself, and the behavior may occur only in the presence of those stimuli. The stimuli that are present when reinforcement occurs serve as a "signal" for the consequences to the behavior.

The principle of stimulus control applies to humans as well as rats. For example, a teacher standing in front of the classroom may cause children to pay attention if, in the past, children were rewarded for paying attention or punished for not paying attention when the teacher stood in front of the class. A change in the stimulus, such as a substitute teacher or a student standing in front of the class, may not cue children to pay attention because persons other than the teacher were not previously associated with positive reinforcers or punishment. This principle may explain why discipline sometimes deteriorates when the teacher leaves the room for a few minutes or when a substitute takes over a class.

Fortunately, it is not necessary to positively reinforce *every* desired behavior. The effects of positive reinforcement on one response **generalize** to similar responses. In essence, reinforcement for a particular behavior affects not only that behavior but also a class of behaviors. Thus, for example, the probability of a child paying attention during a social studies lesson may be increased by rewarding him for paying attention during math. A child who is punished for disrupting the class by throwing paper airplanes may, as a consequence, be less likely to disrupt the class by other means as well as by the specific behavior for which the punishment was received.

Reinforcement theory is considered "mechanistic" because no reference is made to such unobservable variables as choice, beliefs, expectations, or emotions. The emphasis is exclusively the environment and observable behaviors. A strict reinforcement theorist, such as Skinner (1974), assumes that a person's behavior at any given time is fully determined by his or her reinforcement history and the contingencies in the present environment. Thoughts and feelings are irrelevant. According to the theory, we should look only at the environment to understand behavior, and we should ignore inner thought and emotional processes, such as self-perceptions of competence, expectations for success, fear, or anxiety.

Strict reinforcement theorists, therefore, would not consider motivation as a characteristic of the individual. Individuals would be considered "motivated" only inasmuch as they exhibit behaviors that are believed or known to enhance learning, like paying attention or working on assignments. Faced with a child who is not working in school, a reinforcement theorist asks, "What's wrong with the environment?" rather than "What's wrong with this child?" The only way to change a student's behavior is to change the reward contingencies (consequences to behavior) in the classroom.

IMPLICATIONS FOR EDUCATIONAL PRACTICE

The educational implications of reinforcement theory for maximizing desired learning behaviors are straightforward. The teacher makes positive reinforcers contingent upon desired behavior and punishments contingent upon undesired behavior. The simplicity of the theory is no doubt a major reason for its long-standing central role in educational psychology, and its widespread classroom application. [See Sulzer-Azaroff and Mayer (1986), for a detailed discussion of the use of behavioral strategies in the classroom.]

The teacher's first task is to determine what constitutes rewards and punishment for any given child. Most teachers try to make different consequences contingent on behavior, observe students' responses to each, and continue to use those that increase desired behavior and decrease undesired behavior. Rewards that are common in American classrooms include praise, good grades, public recognition, and privileges. Disapproval, bad grades, public humiliation, and staying after school are commonly used as punishment. I have also observed teachers make the opportunity to clean the blackboard, do extra challenging math problems, and read a poem to the class contingent upon some desired behavior. In one kindergarten class I visited the teacher explained that the children were being especially good because homework was only given to the students who behaved well that day!

Teachers sometimes make positive reinforcers and punishment contingent on the whole class behaving or not behaving in a particular way. This can produce peer pressure for desirable behavior. For example, a teacher might make a popcorn party on Friday afternoons contingent upon the class' meeting some achievement standard, and make a shortened recess for the whole class a result of too many students' failure to complete their assignments.

Reinforcement affects a particular behavior only if it is contingent on *that* behavior. The teacher must, therefore, reinforce only desirable behavior and ignore or punish undesirable behavior. Clearly, if maximum learning is the goal, behaviors that enhance learning need to be reinforced and behaviors that inhibit learning need to be ignored or punished. Accordingly, students should be reinforced for paying attention to the teacher or the task at hand, persisting on tasks that are difficult, selecting challenging tasks, completing tasks, and other behaviors that enhance learning. Such behaviors as inattentiveness, giving up quickly, selecting very easy tasks, or turning in incomplete assignments, should be ignored or punished.

Rewards and punishment might be used to change the behavior of some of the children described in Chapter 1. Safe Sally is presumably being positively reinforced for her cautiousness. She desires teacher approval and good grades, and these are probably made contingent upon good performance, regardless of the difficulty level of the task. Sally is, therefore, reinforced for avoiding challenging tasks. A teacher who wants to increase Sally's risk-taking should, according to reinforcement theory, make positive reinforcers contingent on her approaching challenging learning situations rather than on performing well. The teacher might, for example, praise Sally for selecting a difficult book for her English assignment, and not show approval for relatively high performance on an assignment that, for Sally, is not particularly challenging. To the degree that approaching a challenge is positively reinforced, and success achieved without much effort is ignored, the probability of risk-taking should increase, and Sally's choice of tasks on which success is guaranteed should be extinguished.

A different approach would be required to get Hopeless Hannah to complete her assignments. For Hannah, rewards need to be contingent upon effort itself. If Hannah likes to draw, drawing time might be made contingent upon her finishing assignments. A classroom responsibility is sometimes particularly reinforcing for children, like Hannah, who receive little positive social attention. Being chosen to take attendance or to deliver a note to the office is often highly valued, and, if the privilege is made contingent upon Hannah's completion of assignments, it should increase the probability of effort in the future.

This approach can only work, however, if Hannah actually completes an assignment. What can a teacher do if a desired behavior never occurs? The problem is particularly serious for students who almost never engage in desired behavior. Individuals using reinforcement methods have developed a strategy called **shaping**. The strategy was used by Skinner to teach pigeons to play ping-pong. Needless to say, if Skinner had waited for his pigeons to begin a game of ping-pong to allow him to reinforce the behavior, he would have had a long wait! Instead, he began by giving a pellet of food for the first behavior in a chain required for playing Ping-Pong. When that behavior began to occur with some frequency, he was able to reinforce the pigeon for the first and second behavior in the chain, and so on.

This same strategy can be used to shape behavior in children. The teacher first makes clear to the child what the desired behavior is, and then begins reinforcing any behavior that *approximates* it. If a troublesome student looks in the teacher's direction, the teacher may praise him for paying attention. Presumably the student will, as a result of the reinforcement, look more often in the teacher's direction. The teacher may then praise the student for maintaining a gaze in the teacher's direction for more than a minute and gradually increase the length of time required for reinforcement. Thus, the teacher "shapes" the student's actions in the direction of the desired behavior—paying attention to the teacher for an extended period of time.

Shaping would probably be necessary to get Hopeless Hannah to finish assignments because she has become completely disengaged from classroom activities. The teacher might begin by praising her for opening her book and taking out her pencil after an assignment is given. This should, according to the theory, increase the probability of her preparing to work on assignments. The teacher could then praise Hannah only for actually beginning the assignment (e.g., doing a few problems), and then "up the ante"—praise her for persisting on an assignment. If praise serves as a positive reinforcer for Hannah, she should eventually complete an assignment—which the teacher can then reward.

Token Economies

In some classrooms teachers have developed elaborate token economies—formalized systems for administering extrinsic rewards. The essential components of a token economy are (1) tokens (that can be exchanged for a reward), (2) target behaviors, (3) rules for earning and losing tokens, and (4) "backup consequences" for which tokens can be exchanged. Tokens that have commonly been used include points, play money, chips, stars, and check marks. Tokens can be anything that is easily counted. They have no inherent value; rather, their worth is based on their ability to be exchanged for a "backup consequence," which is valued. Although token economies have been used primarily to improve social behavior—such as talking out of turn, being out of seat or off task, and poor attendance—they have also been used to improve assignment completion and accuracy. A token economy can be implemented with one student, a small group of students, or the whole class.

For programs designed to reduce undesirable behaviors (e.g., talking out of turn), students are initially given a set of tokens and have to give up a prespecified amount for engaging in the undesirable behavior. In programs designed to increase desirable behaviors (e.g., completing assignments), students are given tokens for exhibiting the target behavior.

All programs include specific rules for earning or losing tokens, which may be simple or complicated. Systems can be created to increase a single behavior or a combination of behaviors. For example, the teacher who desires to increase both task completion and task accuracy may allow students to earn one token for completing an assignment and two for completing it with 80 percent accuracy. Or a variable number of tokens may be earned for different degrees of accuracy. Backup consequences that tokens can be exchanged for have included material objects—such as candy, toys, trinkets, and money—and activities—such as extra recess, and movies.

A program developed by Cohen (1973) for a difficult group of adolescent boys in a residential home illustrates how token economies are implemented. Most of the students in Cohen's study had dropped out of school and many had been found guilty of crimes. These boys were given points that could be exchanged for goods, services, and special privileges, such as recreational time in a lounge, books, magazines, extra clothing, mailorder supplies, a private shower, or a private room for sleeping and entertaining. (This list demonstrates the importance of tailoring reinforcers to the particular individuals whose behavior one desires to change!) Reinforcement was made contingent upon academic achievement and, presumably, behaviors which enhance achievement. Despite a long history of failed attempts to increase the motivation of these boys, their academic achievement improved dramatically under this token economy system.

Another form of a token economy is illustrated by Alschuler's (1968) performance contracting. In one program, students were advanced $2,000 in play money. Students determined their own performance goals which they indicated on a written contract. The higher the goals, the greater the payoff. Students lost money, however, for not meeting their goal, or for turning in late assignments. Consequently, unrealistically high goals generally resulted in losses and unnecessarily low goals resulted in very low payoffs. The system, therefore, encouraged moderate risks which should produce the greatest amount of learning. In one study of fifth-graders, Alschuler observed an average gain of three years of growth on standardized mathematics tests in one academic year.

Different procedures for implementing token economies are required for students of different ages. High-school age students may be able to comprehend complicated systems and to delay exchanging tokens for the backup consequence for a relatively long period of time. Young children cannot understand or keep in mind complicated systems, and they are likely to lose interest in the tokens if the exchange is delayed more than a few days. I discovered the importance of frequent exchanges when I tried to implement a token economy to motivate my five-year-old to get dressed for school in the morning. She was allowed to put a star on a calendar each day that she was dressed by 7:30. I explained that when she earned 20 stars I would take her to a toy store and she could pick out a toy. The implementation of the star system had an immediate and dramatic effect on her behavior, but after about a week she lost interest in the stars and we returned to our daily conflict. Twenty days without linking the stars to a tangible reward was simply too long.

Historically, token economies were begun—often as a procedure of last resort—with clinical, frequently institutionalized populations. In the last decade or two they have also been applied to less severely disturbed populations and to children in regular classrooms. Studies have examined the effectiveness of token economy programs in changing behavior, such as attention and persistence on tasks. Most studies find that tangible rewards, systematically applied, can produce major behavior change, even in the most recalcitrant subjects (Kazdin, 1975; O'Leary, 1978).

Research on the maintenance and generalization of desired behaviors in token programs is less positive. O'Leary and Drabman (1971) and Kazdin and Bootzin (1972) review data assessing how well behavioral changes are maintained after token programs are withdrawn, and how well the desired behaviors generalize to other settings in which tokens are not administered. They conclude that removal of the tokens usually leads to a rapid return to baseline behaviors (behaviors preceding the implementation of the token economy program). They also report that behavior outside of the setting in which the tokens were given (sometimes referred to as "transfer") is generally not affected by the token economy. These and other limitations of external reinforcement are discussed next.

PROBLEMS WITH REWARD AND PUNISHMENT

Teachers usually find that the promise of a reward or the threat of punishment can affect most children's behavior in the classroom, at least in the short term. Behavioral methods have been particularly successful with children who behave extremely maladaptively in school settings. The problem is that teachers sometimes use reinforcement inappropriately or rely too much on rewards and punishment to control behavior. Inappropriate application of reinforcement principles can adversely affect behavior; dependence on rewards and punishment to influence achievement behavior has long-term negative effects on student motivation. We turn now to a summary of some of these problems.

Finding an Effective Reinforcer

Consider first the problem of finding an effective reward. Aside from praise, which may be reinforcing for most children from the time they enter school, traditional rewards used in most American classrooms are not universally effective. Grades, for example, are ineffective with some children in early elementary school who have not yet learned the cultural value placed on high grades. Furthermore, unless the value placed on grades by teachers is reinforced by parents and peers, students are unlikely to work for such a symbolic reward. For some children, even when grades are valued, good grades are not sufficiently desirable to inspire high effort, and for others, high grades are perceived as unobtainable, regardless of their level of effort. Satisfied Sam is an example of a child who is satisfied with a grade that requires a level of performance below what he could achieve with effort. Hannah is an example of a student who does not believe she can earn a good grade even if she tries hard. The teacher who perseveres in offering good grades as a reward for positive achievement behaviors, and in threatening bad grades for negative ones, will not obtain desired behaviors in students like Sam and Hannah, or in students who might never have learned to value good grades.

The effectiveness of grades as reinforcers may decline for some individuals in adolescence. In early adolescence peer approval becomes increasingly important and adult approval less critical. Unless peer acceptance is to some degree associated with good grades, grades may lose their value. Indeed, among some rebellious or alienated adolescents for whom success in school is explicitly devalued, high grades may be perceived as an embarrassment, and thus a punishment, rather than as a reward. Recall that Cohen (1973) used private showers, magazines, and clothing to reinforce achievement behavior among delinquent boys. In a residential center, such rewards may be available and appropriate, but in most regular schools they are not. Alternatives to grades—such as candy and even money—have been used, but there are obvious problems with using such controversial reinforcers in regular school, regardless of how effective they might be.

There are many situations in which teacher and student perceptions of what constitutes a reward are completely at odds. As one example, any form of teacher or peer attention, including negative attention (e.g., threats, nagging, teasing), serves as positive reinforcement for some children. For these children, reprimanding, which the teacher believes is punishment, actually positively reinforces undesirable behavior.

Availability of Positive Reinforcers

If grades are based on competitive criteria (and they usually are), high grades will not be available to all students. Normative grading usually means that a "C" is given to students whose performance is average, a "D" to students whose performance is below average, and a "B" or an "A" to students whose performance is somewhat or well-above average. By definition, all children cannot be above average. Moreover, students begin classes with varying levels of preparation, and some students learn new concepts more quickly than others. A few students, like Hannah, will find that they cannot get a high grade, regardless of how hard they work. Others, like Sam, will find that they can get a respectable grade with little effort. The threat of a bad grade will not affect the behavior of students who believe that bad grades are unavoidable, whatever they do. The promise of a good grade will not affect the behavior of students who believe that they will achieve a good grade whether or not they exert effort. This principle holds for any reward that can be earned easily by some children and only with great difficulty (or not at all) by others.[1]

Unavailability of positive reinforcers explains why teachers often get a false impression that a student does not desire conventional rewards. Teachers often express dismay at a student's apparent unwillingness to engage in behaviors that will be positively reinforced. I have heard teachers complain: "I have told him over and over that if he would just put a little effort into his work he could get good grades; he just doesn't seem to care one way or the other." Careful observations of these troublesome students often reveal that they virtually never receive positive reinforcement, even when they do exert a little effort. They would, in fact, be quite happy to receive teacher praise or good grades. They perceive neither of these positive reinforcers as available. It is not uncommon for such students to resort to alternative, often undesirable, means of gaining recognition. Misbehaving to get negative teacher attention is not their preferred mode of operation; it is used as a last resort.

If the teacher's goal is to obtain maximum effort and performance from children, then effort must be rewarded. One strategy that can be used to make rewards realistically available to all students is to make them contingent upon students reaching absolute standards. The standard can be the same for all children, but in most classrooms, in which children vary in their skill levels and the speed with which they achieve mastery, children should be given as much time as they need to achieve the standard. Alternatively, standards can vary among children according to their present skill levels. Thus, performance that earns an "A" for one child might earn a "B" for another. Both of these approaches have the advantage of making rewards realistically available to all children. But they can also cause problems. Having the same standard for all children may result in a lot of wasted time for high achievers who have to wait for low achievers to meet the standard. Varying standards can engender resentment in high achievers, who may perceive as unfair a system that requires a high level of performance for them to achieve the same grade that some of their classmates achieve with a lower level of performance.

The most effective strategy that I have seen is to reward *improvement*, or a combination of improvement and meeting a standard. The advantage of this strategy is that positive reinforcement is realistically available to relatively low achievers, and it requires some effort on the part of high achievers—which is often not true of normatively-based or mastery-based systems of allocating rewards. (See Chapter 10 for a discussion of the criteria for grading.)

But what about a troublesome student who appears not to care about conventional rewards? A combination of ignoring misbehavior and shaping positive behaviors can sometimes be used to change the way such children operate. Admittedly, it is difficult to ignore misbehavior and the most difficult children are the least likely to engage in desired behavior that can be reinforced. It is usually possible, however, to ignore all but the most disruptive behavior, and to find something to praise in a difficult child. I have observed dramatic improvement in the behavior of troublesome children as a consequence of fewer negative reactions to undesirable behavior, and praise and other rewards made contingent upon behaviors that approximate what the teacher desires.

Application of Reinforcers

Another problem with relying on reinforcement is that only observable behavior can be reinforced. Some "behaviors," such as attention, are not entirely observable. As mentioned in Chapter 2, students can look as if they are intensely engaged in intellectual tasks while they are actually reliving the home run they made at recess or planning their strategy for getting a particular boy to ask them to the junior prom. The teacher can directly reinforce students for looking in her direction, but it is difficult to reinforce students for *listening* or *thinking* about the information. The teacher can also reinforce observable outcomes, like good performance on a test, that seem to be associated with paying attention. But if the student had cheated or guessed on the test, the teacher will inadvertently reward cheating or guessing behavior by rewarding the good performance.

Another common problem with the application of reinforcers is being aware of consequences that affect students' behavior in unintended ways. A fifth-grade teacher once complained to me that her students spent too much time fooling around during seatwork periods and many didn't finish their assignments. She criticized them often for not finishing, but her complaints had only a momentary effect; they were not effective as punishments. It appeared, rather, that recess, which directly followed seatwork, was serving as a reinforcement for the behaviors (fooling around and not finishing assignments) the teacher wanted to extinguish. When she later made recess contingent upon completing assignments, completion rates increased dramatically.

Teachers are also sometimes unaware of inconsistencies between the behavior they desire and the contingencies in their classroom. A teacher once told me that he valued individual initiative and creativity and was disappointed that his students were passive and conforming. It turned out that his grading system was incompatible with his values. Students lost points by failing to follow arbitrary rules, and their grades were determined almost entirely by accuracy. There were no rewards for personal initiative or creativity. To the contrary, students could be punished for straying slightly from, or even going beyond, the teacher's directions.

It is useful for teachers (and parents) to reflect upon the kinds of rewards and upon the punishments they use, the behavior upon which these consequences are contingent, and the degree to which they are available to all children. Appendix 3-A is designed to help teachers in this reflective process, which will occasionally reveal inconsistencies between values and actions.

Negative Effects on Behavior

In several studies rewards have been shown to have a negative effect on individuals' willingness to attempt challenging tasks. In one study, for example, some children were offered an extrinsic reward for correct answers and others were not. Subjects who were offered extrinsic rewards chose significantly less difficult problems than subjects who were not offered rewards for correct answers (Harter, 1978b). Thus, under the reward condition children were less likely to select a challenging problem.

Extrinsic rewards may also affect teachers' behavior. Garbarino (1975) describes a study in which sixth-grade children served as tutors for first-grade children. Tutors who were offered a reward for their success in tutoring exhibited a more "instrumental" orientation toward their pupils. They were more demanding and critical and created a more negative emotional atmosphere in the tutoring setting than tutors who were not offered a reward. The reward presumably focused these sixth-grade tutors' attention exclusively on their students' performance. Tutors consequently neglected behaviors like nurturing and giving encouragement that may have seemed unnecessary, but actually would have helped them accomplish their goals.[2]

Short-Lived Effectiveness

A fifth problem with external reinforcement is that its effectiveness is often short-lived. Rewards may be effective in eliciting desired behaviors, but if the only reason for engaging in a behavior is to obtain a reward, the behavior will occur only under reward conditions. Indeed, evidence discussed in Chapter 5 suggests that under some circumstances when a reward is given and then later withdrawn, the desired behavior occurs *less* frequently than it would have occurred if no reward had ever been offered.

This limitation in the use of external reinforcement becomes increasingly important as children advance in grade in school. The curriculum in the early elementary grades is generally broken down into small units with frequent opportunities for positive reinforcement. Most assignments are completed in less than half an hour and are reviewed by the teacher soon after. In the upper grades assignments are generally larger, less frequent, and span a longer time period. Compare, for example, typical language arts assignments for elementary versus high-school students. The younger students may, in one day, be given as many as three short assignments for which they can receive reinforcement (e.g., a grade, a star, or teacher praise). High-school students are more likely to be asked to write a theme based on assigned reading once every week or two. Consequently, while young children can be reinforced for every subcomponent of an academic task, older students must go through many steps without any rein-forcement (i.e., they must read the assigned literature, think about it, make an outline, write, and perhaps rewrite the theme). The older stu-dent is not rewarded for the several intermediate tasks that are required to complete the assignment.

For students who enter college, many rewards (e.g., obtaining a degree, getting into graduate school, getting a good job) are far removed from the immediate situation requiring achievement behav-iors. Even within a given course, a midterm and a final examination are often the only "products" of a semester of academic labor that the professor sees and, consequently, the only opportunities students have to be reinforced. The promise of such distant rewards will not be effec-tive for students who are accustomed to being reinforced daily for every academic effort.

Providing positive reinforcements for all intellectual activities can, ultimately, undermine students' desires to be involved in *any* non-school-related learning activity. I once gave a copy of *Tom Sawyer* to a boy in junior high school. He graciously accepted the gift, but added that he had already written a book report for his English class that semester so he wouldn't be reading the book until the next semester. It apparently did not occur to him that a book could be read for reasons other than getting a good grade in school. Safe Sally is another exam-ple of a student who has learned to participate in learning activities only for extrinsic rewards. She does not engage in learning activities outside of the classroom unless products are graded or are likely to bring some kind of social recognition. Even the novels she reads are on the high school reading list and may be included in the English curricu-lum the next year.

Reinforcing behavior also conveys the message that the behavior is not worth doing for its own sake. Consider the different messages given by the teacher who tells students that they will be *allowed* to spend 15 minutes at the computer if they finish their math assignment versus the teacher who announces that students who have not put in their 15 minutes on the computer will not be able to go to recess. The former teacher is much more likely than the latter to foster the perception that computers are fun. This is why I particularly favor using interesting and challenging academic activities as rewards. It doesn't always work, but there is considerable value in giving the message that intellectual tasks are fun and worth doing for their own sake, and this will not be achieved by rewarding them for engaging in such tasks.

Effects of Punishment

When the carrot approach is ineffective, it is natural to turn to the stick. Fear of punishment, such as public humiliation or low grades, can motivate positive work behaviors. But it can also cause severe anxiety, which is well known to hinder learning. Many children, like Defensive Dick, spend considerably more energy trying to avoid punishment than they do trying to understand material or learn new skills. For example, they avoid asking questions or volunteering answers for fear of revealing their ignorance. Or, they turn in completed assignments with answers that they know are incorrect rather than trying to figure out the right answers, because they have learned that punishment is more severe for not turning in an assignment on time than for poor performance. Other students, like Anxious Amy, become paralyzed by their fear of humiliation or low grades.

Astute classroom observers have described these and other more elaborate measures that some children take to avoid punishment (Covington and Beery, 1976; Holt, 1964; see also Chapter 8). Most of these behaviors accomplish the student's immediate goal, but they are self-defeating in the long run because they do not promote learning.

Punishment can also have negative consequences if it is applied inappropriately. Consider, for example, the child who works hard, but for reasons beyond her own control (e.g., poor English proficiency, poor preparation for school), performs poorly compared to her peers. She receives a low grade despite her efforts. If the child aspires to high grades and considers low grades undesirable, the low grade she receives serves as a punishment. She is, in effect, punished rather than rewarded for her effort. Teachers generally try to reward children for effort, even when the outcome is poor compared to other students. In practice, however, it is often difficult to distinguish poor performance despite high effort from poor performance caused by low effort. As a consequence, for some children, punishment follows high effort and, as reinforcement theorists claim, their effort decreases.

Students need to be made accountable for their work, and there should be some consequences for low effort. But punishment has to be used judiciously for the positive effect to outweigh the negative. And to the degree possible, punishment (public humiliation, low grades) should not be given for poor performance if there is evidence that the student has done his or her best.

SUMMARY

Reinforcement techniques are used in virtually all classroom settings. When teachers praise students, give grades or gold stars, put students' papers on public display, or require students to stay after school for disruptive behavior, they are applying principles of reinforcement theory. The same is true for parents who praise children for cleaning their room and deny privileges for breaking rules. The basic notion—that positive reinforcement increases the frequency of desired behavior and punishment decreases the likelihood of undesirable behavior—underlies all of these techniques.

But, as we have seen, there are costs for over-reliance on reinforcement as a means of motivating behavior. The next chapter describes new classroom applications of reinforcement theory that are designed to maximize the benefits of reinforcement while minimizing these costs.

TABLE 3-1 • Summary of Reinforcement Theory Terms

Term	Definition	Example
Law of Effect	Principle of operant conditioning theory in which behavior is assumed to be determined by its consequences	Children complete assignments because this behavior is rewarded
Positive reinforcer	A consequence that increases the probability of a behavior that it is made contingent upon	Good grade; star; teacher praise; teacher attention
Negative reinforcer	A consequence that increases the probability of a behavior if terminated or diminished	Teacher's angry stare; social isolation
Punishment	A consequence that decreases the probability of a behavior	Bad grade; loss of privilege
Social reinforcement	Positive reinforcer linked to social approval	Praise; smile

Term	Definition	Example
Extinction	The termination of a behavior as the result of terminating positive reinforcers	Students stop doing homework when teacher stops grading it
Intermittent (partial) reinforcement	The reinforcement of some but not all occurrences of a response	Teacher praising some, but not all correct answers
Discriminative stimulus	A stimulus that acquires the ability to control behavior because of its association with reinforcement or punishment	Teacher standing in front of the classroom
Stimulus control	Behavior is influenced by the presence of a stimulus that has previously been associated with reward or punishment	Children quiet when the teacher moves to the board where checks for misbehavior are made
Generalization	The principle that behavior will occur or not occur because a similar behavior has been positively reinforced or punished	A child who is praised for neatness on a math assignment writes her spelling words neatly
Shaping	Providing reinforcement for behaviors that increasingly approximate the desired behavior	Praising a child for opening a book, then for beginning, and then completing assignments
Conditioned Response	A behavior that occurs in the presence of a stimulus that has been paired with a positive reinforcer or a stimulus that naturally causes the response	Children line up for recess when the bell rings
Token Economy	A system in which children receive or lose tokens that can be exchanged for a reward	A poker chip is earned for every assignment completed, and later exchanged for added recess

ENDNOTES

1. An analogous argument could be made for merit pay for teachers. If it is available to only a small percentage (e.g., 5 percent), most teachers would not perceive merit pay to be realistically available. Therefore, it would not serve to motivate most teachers. Reinforcement must be perceived by individuals to be genuinely available to them for it to have any positive effect on their behavior.

2. It is possible that rewards to teachers made contingent on the achievements of their students can also result in an "instrumental" orientation—a focus on behavior directly and obviously related to achievement (like drill and practice), and a neglect of variables, such as a positive social environment, that enhance achievement indirectly, but in the long term may be extremely important.

4

SOCIAL COGNITIVE THEORY

In contrast to strict reinforcement theorists such as Skinner, most current motivation theorists—even those who focus on observable behavior and its consequences—refer to cognitions (thoughts, beliefs) to understand and influence behavior. This chapter discusses theories in which the effects of reinforcement are assumed to be at least partly mediated by thoughts. The chapter also describes applications of reinforcement theory designed to help students learn to control their own behaviors. Finally, principles for the use of praise—one of the most extensively used positive reinforcers in the classroom—are summarized.

Bandura (1977a, b, 1986) recognized the powerful effects of reinforcement and punishment on individuals' behavior, but objected to the notion that individuals are entirely regulated by external forces— that they are passive respondents to environmental contingencies. As an alternative to strict reinforcement theory, he developed a social cognitive theory in which cognitions are assumed to mediate the effects of the environment on human behavior. According to Bandura, whether individuals *expect* to be reinforced for a behavior is more important than whether they have previously been reinforced for it. He claims, furthermore, that reinforcement history does not have a direct effect on individuals' cognitions. Rather, it is filtered through personal memory, interpretations, and biases. Social cognitive theorists, therefore, portray individuals as actively processing events and developing expectations regarding reinforcement, rather than as automatically behaving according to previous reinforcement contingencies.

Evidence for the importance of expectations and beliefs comes from studies finding that when individuals are not aware of the contingencies of reinforcement, their behavior is not affected by it (Dulany, 1968), and if individuals are led to believe that previously reinforced behavior will not be reinforced in the future, they will not engage in the behavior (Estes, 1972). *Beliefs* about future reinforcement appear to be more important determinants of behavior than actual reinforcement histories.

Social cognitive theorists assume that personal experience with reinforcement and punishment are not required for behaviors to be manifested. This assumption solves the problem strict reinforcement theorists have in explaining new behavior. According to operant conditioning theory, individuals' behavior is determined by their own reinforcement history. Children attend to the teacher and complete assignments because they have been reinforced for this behavior, or because they have been punished for alternative behaviors, in the past. Operant conditioning theorists rely on the principle of shaping to explain how children learn new behaviors—behaviors that have not previously been reinforced. But this explanation is not entirely satisfying because it would be too cumbersome for every new behavior to be shaped by reinforcing successive approximations.

Bandura and Walters (1963), therefore, proposed that individuals exhibit behaviors that have not been previously reinforced as the result of observing another individual being reinforced for the behavior— referred to as **vicarious learning**. This principle is illustrated in a classic study by Bandura (1965). Children were shown one of three versions of a 5 minute film that depicted aggressive responses to toys, including hitting and throwing objects at a Bobo doll. In the version shown to one group of children, the child was rewarded by an adult for the aggressive behavior; in another version the child was punished, and in the third version there was no adult reaction. After they had viewed a version of the film, children were secretly observed in a room that contained the toys shown in the movie. Children who viewed the rewarded model were most likely to repeat the model's aggressive behavior; children who viewed the punished model were least likely to repeat the behavior, with the third group falling in between. Thus, the likelihood of their demonstrating the behavior was a function of the reinforcement contingencies of the child they had observed in the film.

Note that all children were equally capable of reproducing the aggressive behavior; they had, therefore, learned the behavior. But they differed in the degree to which they actually manifested the behavior.

This distinction between *acquiring* a behavior and *manifesting* a behavior in action—between *learning* and *performance*—is made by social cognitive theorists, but not by traditional reinforcement theorists.

Principles of vicarious learning are used frequently in early elementary school classrooms. It is common for teachers of young children to reinforce one or a few children for a behavior that they desire in all children: "I like the way Jackson got to work on his assignment right away"; "Table 5 is quiet and may go to recess." The effect can be dramatic. Before the children from table 5 reach the door, children at the other tables are likely to have ceased talking and put on their most angelic expressions.

Bandura (1986) also stresses the importance of personal evaluation and self-satisfaction as positive reinforcement. He claims that most people value the self-respect and the self-satisfaction derived from a job well done more highly than material rewards. Thus, achieving a personal goal or meeting a personal achievement standard, and the accompanying self-satisfaction, can serve effectively as reinforcement.

Goals or intentions also play a central role in the theory. One way to influence children's behavior is to influence their goals. When individuals commit themselves to a goal, discrepancies between what they do and what they intended to do create self-dissatisfaction that serves as incentive for enhanced effort.

According to Bandura (1977b, 1986), the capacity to use symbols—especially language—provides humans with a powerful tool for dealing with their environment and a means of controlling their own behavior. Environmental influences have lasting effects on behavior because they are processed and transformed into symbols. These cognitive representations of behavior and its consequences serve as a guide for future behavior. For example, children in the classroom in which the teacher dismissed the quietest table first may quiet down quickly before recess in the future because they have a cognitive representation of the teacher's reaction.

The cognitive capacity for symbolic representation and forethought (e.g., of goals and expectations) also allows people to sustain efforts over a long period of time. Thus students who aspire to mastering a skill or to obtaining high grades can, by keeping their goal in mind, continue to exert effort without regular reinforcement.

Representational abilities allow human beings to have more control over their own behavior than animals have—more control than is assumed by strict reinforcement theorists. One way human beings exercise self-control is by arranging the environment in a way that produces the behavior they desire. Setting an alarm clock to wake up at a particular time is a simple example. Making a reward (e.g., a pizza) contingent upon a particular behavior (e.g., finishing a homework assignment) is another way of regulating one's own behavior. Individuals shape their own experiences, including the frequency and nature of reinforcements in academic contexts by choosing which courses to take, which assignments to do, or which strategies to use to complete an assignment.

Social cognitive theory has inspired the development of a variety of techniques that can help individuals regulate their own behavior. These techniques are usually referred to as **cognitive behavior modification**. Most cognitive behavior modification researchers are reinforcement theorists in the sense that they believe that ultimately behavior is determined by its consequences (i.e., reinforcement and punishment). Nevertheless, like Bandura, they believe that cognitive processes mediate the influence of the external environment on behavior, and that individuals can manipulate the stimulus conditions which influence their own behavior. Thus, individuals can arrange the environment to maximize the chance that desired responses will occur.

The techniques described next have grown primarily out of social cognitive theory. Reinforcement theorists have also used them, but they explain their effectiveness in the context of the principles of operant conditioning rather than in terms of cognitive mediators.

COGNITIVE BEHAVIOR MODIFICATION

More so than traditional behavior modification approaches, cognitive behavior modification (CBM) involves students in regulating their own behavior. Hallahan and Sapona (1983) define it as "the modification of overt behavior through the manipulation of covert thought processes" (p. 616). It is similar to approaches based on strict reinforcement theory in that it is designed to change overt behavior and because reinforcement principles are assumed to be operating. It is different because the treatment involves modifying a person's cognitive operations in order to achieve a change in his or her behavior. When CBM approaches are used, the teacher is not the only determiner of reinforcement contingencies or the sole dispenser of rewards, as is the case in behavior modification programs such as token economies. Rather, cognitive behavior modification requires children to take more responsibility, either by monitoring their own behavior, setting their own goals and standards, or administering their own rewards (Meichenbaum, 1977).

Personal involvement is believed to have a number of advantages over external monitoring and reinforcement. First, there are problems with external reinforcement that personal responsibility can resolve. It is difficult for teachers to monitor and reinforce many students' behavior at one time, and students are less likely than teachers to miss their own reinforcement opportunities. Students will also better understand the relationship between environmental events and behavior if they develop strategies for monitoring and controlling their own behavior rather than relying on teachers who maintain all the control. Furthermore, when rewards and punishment are always administered by an external agent, the agent may become a discriminative stimulus, and thus a necessary cue for the performance of the desired behaviors. The behavior, therefore, will not occur when the external agent is absent. As mentioned in the previous chapter, this is why classroom discipline can break down the moment the teacher steps out.

Desirable behaviors should be maintained longer after contingent rewards are withdrawn when students are involved in regulating their own behavior than when they are not involved. Personal involvement should also result in more generalization outside of the setting in which the rewards are given. In general, CBM is believed to result in less reliance on external agents to control behavior with reinforcement and punishment (Mace and Kratochwill, 1988), although reinforcement theorists claim that ultimately all behavior is controlled by the contingencies of external reward or punishment (Mace, Belfiore, and Shea, 1989). Below is a summary of some of the CBM strategies that have been developed and studied.

Self-Recording

One simple method that has been used to help children begin to take responsibility for their own behavior is to have them keep a record of it. Self-recording itself has been found to influence behavior, even without tangible reinforcements—an outcome referred to as **reactivity** (Mace et al., 1989).

Children may be asked to record the duration of an activity, frequency of a particular behavior, task completion, or the level of performance (Mace and Kratochwill, 1988). For example, students may record how long they read at home each evening, each time they take their homework home, how often they begin an assignment without asking the teacher to repeat the instructions, or how frequently they complete an assignment on time. Or they may record how many arithmetic problems they finish or get right on assignments, how many spelling words they practice or spell correctly on quizzes, or how many pages they read. Time-sampling methods have also been used. Glynn, Thomas, and Shee (1973), for example, had a class of second-grade students self-record on-task behavior every time a tape recorded series of intermittent beeps (which varied randomly between one and five minutes) were heard.

What is recorded depends on the problem. A child who is not doing assignments at all might benefit from keeping track of assignments completed and not completed. A child who usually finishes assignments but not carefully should record error rates or some other index of quality. Children's competencies for self-recording must also be considered. For example, duration may be too difficult for young children to monitor.

Self-recording can be done in a variety of ways. One of the simplest is to have students make a mark on a sheet of paper every time they engage in some behavior (e.g., bring back a completed homework assignment) and endeavor to increase the number of marks from week to week. Some CBM researchers have taped paper on to children's desks to record behavior. Shapiro (1984) describes "countoons"—simple stick figure drawings that represent the specific behavior to be self-monitored. Children place a tally mark next to each picture when the behavior occurs. Alberto and Troutman (1986) describe a classroom in which children at their seats were instructed to "give themselves a point" if they were working when the teacher made a noise with a noisemaker while she worked with a reading group.

However self-recording is done, researchers have found that students need to be thoroughly trained. They need a clear and simple definition of the target behavior, clear instructions, and a demonstration of the self-monitoring procedure. Teachers need to assess children's understanding of the procedures before children are asked to implement them (Mace and Kratochwill, 1988).

A predetermined performance standard has been shown to enhance the effectiveness of self-monitoring (Kazdin, 1974), presumably because it gives children a particular goal to work towards. A few researchers have also found that self-monitoring is more effective in increasing desired behaviors than in decreasing undesirable behaviors (Litrownik and Freitas, 1980).

It is sometimes useful to have students graph their "scores" [Thoresen and Mahoney (1974); see Shapiro (1984), for examples]. Some children are encouraged and excited when they see the line in the graph going up or down, depending on whether they are trying to increase or decrease the behavior. The line going in the "wrong" direction could focus the child's attention on his or her inappropriate behavior and, ideally, stimulate the child to try to improve.

Teachers can encourage personal responsibility by allowing students to set their own goals for improvement. Students may, for example, decide how many math problems they will do each day or how many spelling words they will get right on the next spelling test. Students may even choose the area in which they would like to improve their behavior. Personal choice and goal setting engages students' involvement and interest and makes them feel more responsible for their own behavior.

Personal goal setting also helps students learn how to set realistic goals—an important skill in achievement settings. Many students begin by setting goals that are either too easily achieved or too difficult. Initially, teachers usually need to help students adjust their goals. Charting goals along with actual behavior shows them how close their progress is to their goal. If they are working hard but not meeting their goals, they may need to make them more realistic.

If the goal is set too high, students will simply become discouraged when they do not reach it. Teachers should encourage students like Hopeless Hannah, who are doing very poorly in school, to set modest goals at first, such as simply remembering to take their homework home or getting more than half of the spelling words right. Once they have met the modest goal, the standard can be raised. Better performers like Safe Sally and Satisfied Sam may need encouragement to set ambitious goals. Research has shown that maximum learning occurs when standards are gradually raised as a function of students' past performances (Masters, Furman, and Barden, 1977).

O'Leary and Dubey (1979) point out that self-recording may be effective primarily for students who already want to engage in the desired behavior, but who for some reason have difficulty controlling their behavior. Evidence for this comes from a number of studies on smoking behavior. Lipinski, Black, Nelson, and Ciminero (1974), for example, found that self-recording decreased smoking in subjects who volunteered for an experiment to reduce smoking, but not for subjects who volunteered for a general experiment that involved smokers. Self-recording may, therefore, only be effective for students who genuinely desire to change their behavior. It may, for example, help an easily distracted student who is motivated to finish assignments, but not a student who does not care whether she completes her work.

Self-Reinforcement

Another way to help students control their own behavior is to involve them in selecting and administering their own reinforcement. According to social cognitive theorists, self-reinforcement increases performance mainly through its motivational function. By making self-reward conditional upon attaining a certain level of performance, individuals create self-inducements to persist in their efforts until their performance matches the prescribed standard (Bandura, 1977b). Self-reinforcement is an example of "reciprocal determinism" in social cognitive theory. Individuals exercise control over the environment, which, in turn, influences their own behavior. Examples of self-reinforcement are promising oneself a chocolate chip cookie for finishing some predetermined amount of work, or a vacation for not smoking for a specified length of time.

Children have also been taught to engage in self-reinforcement. For example, in a study by Bornstein and Quevillon (1976), the experimenter modeled self-reinforcement by initially taking M & M's for appropriate behavior (e.g., paying attention), and then by praising himself, "I'm doing a good job." Masters and Santrock (1976) found that when children were told to verbalize pride in their work, they persisted longer on a task than when they were told to utter neutral statements.

A practice common in elementary school classrooms is to give children opportunities to engage in desired activities (e.g., playing a puzzle or game, using a listening center, or playing with the pet gerbil) when they finish their assigned work. This is a form of self-reinforcement when children choose the specific activity and administer their own reward. A problem with this practice is that the reward may only be realistically available to a small subset of relatively fast workers. As a consequence, it will be motivating only for these students. The approach could be adapted, however, to make the reward genuinely available to all. For example, the amount and level of difficulty of the assignments can be individualized so that all students can finish them in time to engage in attractive activities if they work diligently.

Another potential problem with making one set of activities contingent on completing another is that it gives an implicit message to students that the assignment that is reinforced is undesirable, and the activities that serve as reinforcement are desirable. As noted in Chapter 3, the teacher who tells students they can read, play with the gerbils, or work on the computer when they finish their math assignment gives the message that the math assignment is not interesting or worth doing in its own right. As with all reinforcements, such possible side effects need to be kept in mind.

A few classroom studies in which children determined the standards for their self-reinforcement have found that children tend to select lenient performance standards (Rosenbaum and Drabman, 1979; Wall, 1983). If self-reinforcement is used, it might be necessary to have some incentive for selecting stricter standards. Research also suggests that publicly stated standards are more effective than private ones (Hayes et al., 1985). Studies have also documented a fair amount of cheating [e.g., administering unearned rewards; Speidel and Tharp (1980)]—suggesting that some monitoring is required.

Self-punishment can also be used. For example, a child could make himself do ten extra math problems for not completing the previous day's homework. But research suggests that self-reinforcement is more effective (Humphrey, Karoly, and Kirschenbaum, 1978), and in practical terms, it is more realistic.

Self-Instruction

Meichenbaum (1977) suggests that speech can be used to regulate one's own behavior or to solve problems. Adults, for example, might talk out loud to direct their own behavior on a new or difficult task, such as learning to drive a car or preparing a complicated dish. The notion that language can be used to control one's own behavior—a key assumption in social cognitive theory—is based on Russian psychologists' theories of cognition and behavior. Vygotsky (1962; 1978) and Luria (1961) believed that language is responsible for human beings' abilities to control their own behavior. Unlike animals, human beings can use language to plan and direct their actions *before* implementation.

A number of researchers have observed that children with learning problems often lack two kinds of skills: metacognitive skills (awareness of what capabilities, strategies, and resources are needed to perform a task effectively), and self-regulation skills (e.g., planning, evaluating effectiveness of ongoing activities, or remediation; Hallahan and Sapona, 1983). These skills can be enhanced by teaching children to verbalize instructions. Swanson and Scarpati (1985, p. 30), for example, taught students to use a set of written instructions with prompts to improve their learning strategies: (a) "How do I understand the passage before I read it? First, I need to look at the title, then skim the passage for new words and circle them. Second, I need to underline people's names and words that show action"; (b) "I need to ask myself, Who, What, Where, and How? before I read."

Although the results of research on self-instruction are mixed, some studies have shown that when self-instruction is encouraged as a supplement to reinforcement, children are more likely to engage in the desired behavior and the behavior is more likely to generalize to other situations and to persist after the external reinforcement is withdrawn (e.g., Robertson and Keely, 1974; Meichenbaum and Asarnow, 1979). Some researchers have suggested that self-instruction strategies may be particularly appropriate for learning-disabled children. Kauffman and Hallahan (1979) claim that behavior modification based on strict reinforcement theory may contribute to learning-disabled children's attention problems because the external reinforcement increases the likelihood of a passive learning style. They recommend a CBM approach because it engages children in the intervention process and provides them with strategies to improve their own performances.

Summary

Social cognitive theory and CBM represent a significant departure from strict reinforcement theory and approaches to changing children's behavior. The word "cognitive" is the key to the difference. Recall that strict reinforcement theorists do not consider cognitions as mediators of behavior. Proponents of cognitive behavior modification claim that cognitions do mediate behavior, and an effective way to change behavior is to intervene in children's cognitions—to help them become self-conscious, to "think about" their behavior.

The CBM procedures described above are designed to deal with some of the practical problems related to the use of reward and punishments in educational settings. The developers of these techniques hoped that they would free teachers to spend more time teaching skills and that they would assure the maintenance of the desired behavior when children were not being monitored by adults and when external reinforcement was not available.

Research implementing CBM procedures has found, for the most part, that although they may be superior to behavior change programs that rely entirely on external reinforcement, they are usually not very effective unless accompanied by contingent reinforcement. Thus, they are more a complement to, rather than a substitute for, external reinforcement.

But, as mentioned in the previous chapter, reinforcement produces desired behavior only if it is applied properly. We turn next to a discussion of effective use of a type of reinforcement that is commonly used in classrooms—praise. Although the final section of this chapter focuses on social reinforcement, most of the recommendations for the effective use of praise apply to other forms of reinforcement as well.

PRAISE

Brophy (1981) defines praise as ". . . teacher reactions that go beyond simple feedback about appropriateness or correctness of behavior . . . " (p. 5). Simply indicating to a child that his or her answer is correct would not be considered praise. Congratulating the child for a right answer, or saying, "you're really good at this" or "good job" are examples of praise. Praise serves as a reinforcer for most students, especially very young children. And according to the principles of reinforcement theory, behaviors followed by praise should increase in frequency.

Praise is not, however, universally valued by psychologists. Kamii (1984) suggests that praise, as it is commonly used, may discourage children from developing personal criteria for judging their own work and may lead to dependency on adult authority figures. Others have claimed that because learning is intrinsically rewarding, praise is at best superfluous and can interfere with the natural disposition to learn (Montessori, 1964; see also Chapter 6). Another objection concerns the differential status it creates between the person giving the praise and the person receiving it, which teachers who desire a more egalitarian relationship want to avoid (Brophy, 1981). The remainder of this chapter discusses ways to minimize such negative effects by using praise effectively.

To be effective, praise, like any other positive reinforcer, must be *contingent* on the behavior the teacher desires to maintain or increase. Brophy (1981) claims that praise is often not contingent on good performance or even on high efforts, especially among teachers who have low expectations for student learning and toward students who are typically poor performers. Anderson, Evertson, and Brophy (1979) found, for example, that the rate of praise following reading turns containing mistakes was slightly higher than the rate of praise following errorless reading turns. No doubt, teachers use praise to encourage poor performing children to try harder. But if praise is not contingent on high effort or good performance, it will not increase the likelihood of either one. If poor performance is just as likely to be praised as good performance, or if students are praised regardless of their efforts, students learn that praise is not based on anything they do and they discount it.

Praise must also be *credible* to be effective. Praise that is not contingent on effort or good performance, or that is not backed up, or is contradicted by nonverbal, expressive behavior, is not believable. Brophy et al. (1976) found that troublesome students sometimes received as much verbal praise as successful students. Aspects of the teachers' nonverbal behavior, such as stern or distracted expressions on their faces, however, often indicated that they were expressing negative emotion or were not really paying attention while they were praising a student.

Praise given noncontingently and praise lacking in credibility can, under certain circumstances, actually have negative effects on students' self-confidence. Praise for succeeding on a very easy task, for example, may be interpreted as an indication that the teacher has a low perception of the student's ability (Meyer, 1982). This interpretation is understandable in light of evidence that teachers tend to reward high effort (Covington and Omelich, 1979b). Thus, if a teacher praises a student, presumably he or she believes the student exerted some effort, and high effort on an easy task suggests low ability.

In contrast to older children and adults, who sometimes see negative implications in praise, research suggests that young children are more oriented toward pleasing adults, are more responsive to praise, and tend to accept it at face value. In a study by Meyer et al. (1979), many ninth-graders and adults believed that praise after success at an easy task implied low ability, and criticism for failure at a hard task indicated high ability. But third- and fifth-graders tended to interpret praise as an indication of high ability regardless of the difficulty level of the task.

Thus, praise may be interpreted differently by different age children. Students in the first few grades of elementary school accept praise at face value even when other information concerning their performance (e.g., grades, number incorrect) is negative (see Stipek, 1984a). This was demonstrated in a study by Meid (1971) in which six- and ten-year-old children were given either high-, medium-, or low-objective information (i.e., scores) for their past performance, and either praise, no comment, or a mildly negative comment. The younger children's expectations for performance on a subsequent task were based entirely on the social, verbal feedback, even when it conflicted with the objective feedback. Thus, for example, young children who were praised for a low score had higher subsequent expectations than young children who received a high score but were not praised. The older elementary school-age children took both objective feedback and social feedback into account in their expectancy statements.

Although children in the elementary grades do not assume that praise on easy tasks is evidence that the individual praising them has a low perception of their ability, young children who are praised when they have not exerted some effort will learn that effort is not necessary for reinforcement. There are, therefore, negative consequences to indiscriminate praise, even for very young children.

Praise can also be used to inform students of the teacher's standards and to focus their attention on particular aspects of their performance. The elementary teacher who says "I like the way your letters are all in between the lines," or "What nice, neat handwriting" is providing information on what she desires. This information function is best accomplished with praise that is *specific and informative*. A general, "good job," is appreciated by most students. But more informative praise (e.g., "Your paper is well-organized, clearly written, creative, persuasive, well-researched, neat . . . ") provides information on the teacher's standards and guidance for future assignments.

Praise can also orient students to particular *kinds* of standards. Praise that *focuses students' attention on their own improvement or effort*—e.g., "Your handwriting has improved"; "You obviously put a lot of time in on this"; or "I think you are really beginning to understand this material"—is better than praise that encourages social comparison—e.g., "This is one of the best papers in the class." The former, in essence, sets a high personal standard that all students can achieve. All children can improve, and if they are praised for improvement, they must continue to progress to receive further praise. Children who are praised for

---

TABLE 4-1 • Guidelines for Effective Praise[1]

Effective Praise

1. Is delivered contingently

2. Specifies the particulars of the accomplishment

3. Shows spontaneity, variety, and other signs of credibility; suggests clear attention to the student's accomplishment

4. Rewards attainment of specified performance criteria (which can include effort criteria)

5. Provides information to students about their competence or the value of their accomplishments

6. Orients stuaents toward better appreciation of their own task-related behavior and thinking about problem solving

7. Uses students' own prior accomplishments as the context for describing present accomplishments

8. Is given in recognition of noteworthy effort or success at difficult (for this student) tasks

9. Attributes success to effort and ability, implying that similar successes can be expected in the future

10. Fosters endogenous attributions (students believe that they expend effort on the task because they enjoy the task and/or want to develop task-relevant skills)

11. Focuses students' attention on their own task-relevant behavior

12. Fosters appreciation of and desirable attributions about task-relevant behavior after the process is completed

---

1. From Brophy (1981)

Continued

TABLE 4-1 • *Continued*

Ineffective Praise

1. Is delivered randomly or unsystematically

2. Is restricted to global positive reactions

3. Shows a bland uniformity which suggests a conditioned response made with minimal attention

4. Rewards mere participation without consideration of performance processes or outcomes

5. Provides no information at all or gives students information about their status

6. Orients students toward comparing themselves with others and thinking about competing

7. Uses the accomplishments of peers as the context for describing students' present accomplishments

8. Is given without regard to the effort expended or the meaning of the accomplishment (for this student)

9. Attributes success to ability alone or to external factors such as luck or easy task

10. Fosters exogenous attributions (students believe that they expend effort on the task for external reasons—to please the teacher, win a competition or reward, etc.)

11. Focuses students' attention on the teacher as an external authority figure who is manipulating them

12. Intrudes into the ongoing process, distracting attention from task-relevant behavior

---

relative performance need to continue to perform better than class-mates—which for some children is impossible and for others requires neither effort nor improvement.

Praise for outcomes that are achieved with little effort gives students the message that effort is not valued. This is unproductive because optimal performance requires effort. Praise should, therefore, be given only for outcomes that required some effort to achieve, and it should sometimes be given for effort alone, regardless of outcome.

Students should be encouraged to work for their own purposes, not to please the teacher or for external rewards. Comments such as, "You're really getting good at figuring out these problems," are better than "I'm really pleased at how well you are doing." The first focuses the student's attention on skill development, the latter on external approval.

Table 4–1 is Brophy's (1981) summary of effective versus ineffective ways to use praise. Most of these principles apply to any form of external reinforcement, not just praise.

It is difficult for teachers to monitor how they use praise because it is usually given spontaneously in the context of complex interactions in the classroom. It is, therefore, useful for teachers to have an aide, or another teacher, or a parent, observe them and give feedback. The form in Appendix 4–A is provided to help in this process.

CONCLUSION

Reinforcement and punishment have important effects on children's behavior in the classroom. The strategies for helping students control their own behavior that have evolved out of social cognitive theory help minimize some of the many problems that arise when another individual has complete responsibility and control over students' behavior. But the effectiveness of even these new strategies is limited, and they do not solve all of the problems created by relying primarily on external consequences. In the next two chapters we discuss an alternative motivational system that has many advantages over external reinforcement.

TABLE 4-2 • Summary of Terms	
Terms	*Definition*
Vicarious learning	Engaging in a behavior as a result of observing the consequences to another individual engaging in it
Cognitive Behavior Modification (CBM)	Strategies for changing behavior that involve changing beliefs and expectations and assigning a more active role to the person whose behavior is being changed
Reactivity	Behavior change that occurs as the result of self-recording of behavior

5

INTRINSIC MOTIVATION

Picture a group of four-year-olds sitting around a table in a preschool. Two children are drawing a picture with markers; another is carefully gluing a cotton ball to a rabbit she has just cut out. Two others explain that they are making a hotel out of legos. The children work intensively and appear to enjoy these activities which, in addition to being fun, help them develop fine-motor and other important skills.

A strict reinforcement theorist would explain these children's efforts by their reinforcement histories: in the past these or similar behaviors must have led to social approval, or maybe even tangible rewards. Or perhaps alternative behaviors (e.g., failing to engage in one of these teacher-sanctioned activities) were punished. A social cognitive theorist would add that the children may have *observed* other children being reinforced for these activities, and that in this situation they *expected* to be reinforced for their efforts or punished for alternative behaviors.

Intrinsic motivation theorists offer another explanation. They claim that human beings are naturally disposed to develop skills and engage in learning-related activities; external reinforcement is not necessary because learning is inherently reinforcing; individuals learn best when they see themselves as engaging in learning behavior for their own intrinsic reasons—because they *want* to rather than because they *have* to. Working on tasks for intrinsic reasons is more enjoyable, and results in more learning, than working on tasks for extrinsic reasons, such as pleasing a person in authority, obtaining a reward, or escaping punishment.

This chapter discusses four perspectives on intrinsic motivation. The first three perspectives are all based on the premise that human beings have natural inclinations that render some tasks intrinsically motivating. According to these three views, human beings (1) are innately disposed to seek opportunities to *develop competencies*; (2) are naturally *curious* about novel events and activities that are somewhat discrepant from their expectations; and (3) have an innate need to feel that they are *autonomous* and engaging in activities by their own volition. The fourth perspective stresses the role of adults in socializing certain achievement-related values. Theorists focusing on socialization assume that some children engage in tasks in the absence of external reinforcement because they *learn to value academic work*.

These four perspectives on intrinsic motivation are not mutually exclusive. To the contrary, they are compatible and to some degree overlapping. Each is discussed below.

COMPETENCE MOTIVATION

In 1959 White published a now-classic paper presenting evidence that human beings have an intrinsic "need" to feel competent and that such behaviors as exploration and mastery attempts are best explained by this innate motivational force. White claims that the underlying need to feel competent explains behaviors as diverse as an infant examining an object visually, a two-year-old building a tower out of blocks, a nine-year-old playing a computer game, and an adolescent playing bridge.

White's defense of an intrinsic **competence motive** rests partly on this motive's evolutionary adaptive value, since it impels the organism to deal more effectively with the environment. He points out that human beings, unlike lower animals, have few competencies innately provided and need to learn a great deal about how to deal with the environment. Thus, a drive or innate disposition to develop competence has considerable value for adaptation.

Piaget (1952) similarly claims that, from the first day of life, human beings are naturally inclined to practice newly developing competencies (what he calls "schemes"), and that practicing new skills is inherently satisfying. For the very young infant, the "skill" may be as simple as being able to make sense out of a visual stimulus (e.g., recognizing a face). Other early skills practiced by infants include sucking and grabbing: infants usually attempt to grasp nearly any object that is close to them and, as a consequence of practicing this skill in different contexts and with different objects, they become more adept at grasping differently shaped objects.

As children develop they practice different and more varied skills and consequently become more effective in their interactions with the environment. For example, toddlers can develop their spatial abilities by doing increasingly difficult puzzles. Adolescents can become more adept at thinking hypothetically by playing games like dungeons and dragons, chess, or bridge.

Piaget's theory provides an explanation for children's repetitive, and occasionally annoying, behaviors that appear to serve no purpose. For example, when children begin to learn to take off their own shoes they repeatedly remove them. Children also turn door knobs without any apparent desire to open the door, and they open and shut cupboards with little interest in the cupboards' contents. Older children may make the same cookie recipe over and over until they have perfected it, listen to the same record until they have "mastered" every note and word, or play the same video game until they consistently "beat the machine."

To be sure, behaviors that children engage in to increase competence sometimes also result in tangible reinforcement. Most children enjoy eating the cookies they bake. But the feeling of competence that is derived from making a successful batch of cookies is often more rewarding than the good taste. Furthermore, infants and children are encouraged in some mastery activities and praised for their successes (unless, for example, children remove their shoes just as the parents are leaving to take them outdoors). But children often practice developing skills without any reinforcement from the environment. Indeed, they engage in some activities that develop competence even when the activity results in some form of punishment. Consider the one-year-old who is frequently "punished" by painful falls for practicing walking. I have yet to see a child stop trying to walk as a consequence of such punishment.

Principle of Optimal Challenge

Competence motivation explains children's efforts only on challenging tasks—tasks that are moderately difficult and on which their efforts will increase their competence. Children are not intrinsically motivated to engage in activities that are easy and that will not lead to increased skills or understanding. Once they have mastered a skill, children will no longer practice it, except as a means to another end. Thus, once toddlers have mastered the skill of opening doors they won't turn a knob unless they want to open a door.

A study by Danner and Lonky (1981) demonstrated children's preference for tasks that allow them to practice newly developing skills. Children were given experience with three classification tasks of varying levels of difficulty and then told that they could spend time working on any of the three tasks. Children spent the most time with and rated as most interesting the tasks that were one step ahead of their pretested level of classification skill. Additional evidence for the value of moderately difficult tasks comes from Boggiano, Pittman, and Ruble (1982), who found that when a reward was not made contingent on their performance children preferred to work on tasks of intermediate difficulty [see also Shapira (1976) for a study using college students]. Similarly, McMullin and Steffen (1982) found that when subjects worked on puzzles that got slightly more difficult on each trial, they displayed more subsequent intrinsic motivation than when the difficulty level remained constant.

Emotional Reactions to Mastery

According to White and Piaget, the increasing competence that results from practicing newly-developing skills and mastering challenging tasks engenders a positive emotional experience, which White refers to as a *feeling of efficacy*. This feeling of efficacy, or competence, is evident in children's smiles when they achieve some goal—completing a puzzle or drawing, or even a difficult arithmetic problem. It is this positive emotional experience that makes mastery behavior self-reinforcing.

Consistent with the principle of optimal challenge, several studies have confirmed that children's emotional responses (i.e., joy, pride) are most intense when they master moderately difficult tasks. Studies of infants as young as eight weeks have shown that smiling is associated with processing novel visual stimuli (a form of mastering the environment for an infant) more than with processing familiar stimuli. As infants get older, they smile at increasingly complex stimuli, presumably because simple stimuli are no longer challenging (Shultz and Zigler, 1970).

Harter systematically studied positive emotion (smiling behavior) in elementary school-age children's responses to mastery attempts. In several studies, Harter (1974, 1978b) gave anagrams (letters that can be arranged into words) to children, and observers rated the intensity of pleasure children expressed at the moment they solved each puzzle. When the problems were extremely difficult and required an unusual amount of time and effort to solve, they expressed little pleasure and reported feeling annoyed and frustrated. Easily solved anagrams did not produce very much smiling either. Tasks that required some effort but were not extremely difficult (i.e., were challenging but solvable) resulted in the most positive expressions.

A little self-reflection should make it clear that solving challenging tasks produces the most feelings of efficacy or competence. Finding the correct answer to a simple arithmetic problem does not, for example, engender the strong feelings of competence that result from finding the successful solution to a more difficult problem (e.g., finishing the *New York Times* crossword puzzle). Competence motivation and the principle of challenge explains why adults get little pleasure from beating someone who is not very skillful at tennis, or why people are compelled to try a steeper hill after mastering a ski run. Success at a challenging task, a situation which is most likely to lead to improved competence, results in the most positive emotional experience.

Effects of the Social Environment

Competence motivation has been presented as a biologically-based "drive" compelling individuals to engage in activities that result in increased competency to deal with the environment. While there are merits to this view it is important to recognize the role of the social environment.

As children get older they increasingly require adult feedback to determine whether they have mastered tasks. Infants usually do not need an adult to tell whether mastery has been achieved. Their mastery attempts are, for the most part, directed at affecting the environment in some way, and the feedback comes directly from the objects they manipulate; if the shoe comes off or the door knob turns, they know they have been successful. Feedback is also intrinsic to some tasks for older children. A child who makes it around the ice rink for the first time without falling will feel efficacious regardless of whether an adult congratulates her. But an adult or older child is often needed to inform a child that her swimming stroke has improved, or the theme she wrote for her English class is well-organized or vivid, or her solutions to a set of arithmetic problems are correct. Adults also influence *standards* of achievement by encouraging and praising particular outcomes. Thus, a parent who praises only certain kinds of drawings might influence a young child's artistic standards, and thus which drawings engender feelings of competence. Depending on others' reactions, 85 percent correct or a grade of "B" will generate feelings of competence and pride in one child and incompetence and shame in another.

Subtle classroom practices can affect students' standards for achievement as well. Putting only papers with 100 percent correct answers on the bulletin board may undermine feelings of competence in children who achieve lower, albeit respectable, scores. Grading competitively (i.e., based on a normal curve) can deny feelings of competence to children who cannot outperform classmates, even when their own performance has improved. Many children do not enjoy school and schoolwork because it fails to provide the feelings of competence and mastery they need to sustain intrinsic interest. Redefining what constitutes mastery can give these students an opportunity to succeed and to find intrinsic value in school tasks. We will return to this topic in Chapter 6, which addresses the effects of the educational context on intrinsic motivation.

To summarize, it is assumed that individuals engage in tasks, in part, for the purpose of developing competence and experiencing the positive feeling of *efficacy* or competence associated with successful mastery attempts. In some cases, competence is defined by the task. In others, it is defined by parents, teachers, or peers. In all cases, no extrinsic reward is necessary. If an extrinsic reward is provided, it is superfluous or, as discussed below, even harmful.

Accordingly, learning contexts that increase a sense of competence will enhance intrinsic motivation, and situations that engender feelings of incompetence will dampen intrinsic motivation. This relationship between perceived competence and intrinsic interest is apparent in studies showing that children who believe they are competent at a task enjoy it more; students who believe they are competent academically are more intrinsically interested in school tasks than those who have a low perception of their academic ability (Boggiano, Main, and Katz, 1988; Gottfried, 1990; Harter, 1981a; Harter and Connell, 1984). A study by Mac Iver, Stipek, and Daniels (1991) suggest a causal relationship between perceived competence and intrinsic motivation. These investigators assessed, at both the beginning and the end of the semester, junior and senior high school students' perceptions of their competence and intrinsic interest in a subject they were studying. Analyses revealed that interest changed in the direction that perceived competence changed. That is, students whose perception of competence increased over the course of the semester rated the subject more interesting at the end of the semester than at the beginning, and those whose perception of competence decreased rated the subject as less interesting at the end of the semester.

For some children who feel incompetent, just a few success experiences can rekindle enthusiasm. I observed this effect in my daughter's experience on a little league baseball team. At her first game she failed twice to make it to first base. Despite considerable praise for her efforts, she wanted to go home. Fearing that I would never get her back again (and knowing that all she needed was to feel competent), I insisted that she stay. A subsequent hit and tour of the bases was all it took to create such enthusiasm that it was I who, in the end, had to beg her to leave. In Chapter 6 we consider specific ways in which competence experiences can be promoted in learning contexts.

CURIOSITY

Theorists emphasizing the second perspective on intrinsic motivation portray human beings as information processors. Berlyne (1966), Hunt (1965), and Kagan (1972) claim that we are predisposed to derive pleasure from activities and events that provide us with some optimal (intermediate) level of surprise, incongruity, complexity, or discrepancy from our expectations or beliefs. This theory may explain why infants a few months old look longer at a novel stimulus than at a stimulus they have seen before (Hunter, Ames, and Koopman, 1983), why an eight-month-old likes to look at things upside down, or why a two-year-old will call herself by a wrong name and then laugh hysterically at the discrepancy she created between her real and her made-up name. It may also explain why so many children like cartoons, science fiction, and video games.

According to information processing theorists, pleasure is assumed to derive from creating, investigating, or processing stimuli that are *moderately* discrepant. Stimuli that are not at all discrepant or novel will not arouse interest, and stimuli that are too discrepant from the individual's expectations will be ignored or cause anxiety.

The information-processing approach is similar to Piaget's and White's competence motivation approach, which assumes that individuals seek tasks that challenge their skill levels. A novel stimulus offers a challenge, just as a task might. The individual must exert more effort to process or understand novel stimuli discrepant from their expectations or experience than to process expected or familiar stimuli. Competence motivation and information-processing theorists also agree that once individuals encounter a novel event or challenging task, they need to reduce the discrepancy. In the first case the discrepancy is between their expectation and the novel stimulus; in the second it is between their current skill level and the skill level required to complete the task.

Deci describes human beings as engaging in a perpetual process of seeking challenge and novelty and then "conquering" it. People seek novel situations which challenge their current level of skill or understanding and then they strive to achieve mastery—to conquer the challenge and experience feelings of competence or understanding.

AUTONOMY

A third perspective on intrinsic motivation stresses autonomy. DeCharms, Deci, Ryan, and other achievement motivation theorists claim that, in addition to a need to be competent, human beings have a natural need to feel *self-determining*: they want to believe they are engaging in activities by their own volition rather than to achieve some external reward or avoid punishment (deCharms, 1976, 1984; Deci, 1975; Deci and Ryan, 1985). They argue that individuals are intrinsically motivated when they perceive themselves as the cause of their own behavior or, to use the language of motivation theorists, when they perceive themselves as the **locus of causality**. Individuals are extrinsically motivated when they believe they are engaging in behavior because of rewards, constraints, or a desire to please another person; that is, when the locus of causality is external.

Thus, the very same activity is assumed to be more motivating and pleasurable when someone *chooses* to engage in it than when it is done for some external purpose. A common distinction between reading that is required for school or work and reading done by choice illustrates this principle. When I was in college, books that were not required for a class were referred to as "pleasure reading." The phrase conveys clearly the notion that books required for a course were, by definition, *not* fun to read. I doubt that anyone would have noticed the irony in two roommates reading the same book—one by choice (and therefore enjoying it) and one because it was required (and therefore not enjoying it).

Many factors affect the perceived locus of causality, including the level of control exerted by others and the availability of rewards. Thus, someone who chooses to engage in an activity and is not rewarded for doing so is more likely to have an internal locus of causality than someone who is required or forced to engage in the activity or told that he will be rewarded for it. Despite the important effects of these and other variables, theorists stress that a person's *perception* of causality is more important than any objective index of causality. Thus two individuals in the same situation can have different ideas about how much choice they had to engage in a particular behavior or activity.

LINK BETWEEN INTRINSIC AND EXTRINSIC MOTIVATION

Intrinsic motivation and motivation based on extrinsic rewards are, to some degree, in competition with each other. Research has shown that under certain circumstances, offering extrinsic rewards for engaging in tasks actually *undermines* intrinsic motivation. Two classic studies illustrate this effect of extrinsic reinforcement. Deci (1971) enlisted college students to participate in a problem-solving study over three sessions. In the first session, all of the students were asked to work a series of interesting puzzles. In the second session, half of the students were told that they would be given an extrinsic reward (money) for correctly solving a second set of puzzles; no mention of a reward was made to the other half of the students. During the third session the experimenter left all of the students with the puzzles, telling them that they could work on the puzzles if they wanted, or they could look at current issues of *Time*, *The New Yorker*, and *Playboy*, which were placed near the students. In this last session, like the first, no students were offered extrinsic rewards.

Students were observed through a one-way mirror in order to assess the effect of the reward on the amount of time they chose to work on puzzles. In the second session, students who were offered a reward for working on the puzzles spent more time working on them than students who were not offered a reward. Thus, the extrinsic reward had the immediate effect of increasing the amount of time subjects engaged in the task. In contrast, in the third session, when no reward was offered to anyone, students who had previously been rewarded spent *less* time working on puzzles than students who had never been offered a reward. The rewarded students lost interest in the task when the reward was withdrawn.

Lepper, Greene, and Nisbett (1973) conducted a similar study with preschool-age children. One group of children was offered a reward for playing with Magic Markers, and another group was not. The reward was a "Good Player Award" consisting of a big gold star and a bright red ribbon on a piece of paper that had their name on it. A third group of children was given a reward at the end of the experiment, but they had not been told about it before. When the reward was withdrawn, children who had played with Magic Markers and expected to receive the external reward did not spend as much subsequent free time on the activity as children who were never given a reward or those who were unexpectedly offered the reward. The quality of the rewarded children's pictures also declined markedly once the reward was withdrawn.

According to Morgan's (1984) review, 70 or 80 published studies have used a paradigm similar to these two studies to examine the effects of reward on subsequent engagement in various activities. [See also reviews by Bates (1979); Deci and Ryan (1985); Notz (1975); Lepper (1983); Pittman, Boggiano, and Ruble (1983); Ryan, Connell, and Deci (1985)]. These studies suggest that external rewards can *undermine* intrinsic interest in a task.

This observed effect of extrinsic rewards seems contrary to reinforcement theory. According to reinforcement theory, a reward made contingent on a behavior will increase the frequency of the behavior. When it is withdrawn the behavior should return to baseline (its level of frequency before the reward had been given), but it should not dip below baseline, as was found in these two and other studies.

Intrinsic motivation theorists assume that the negative effect the reward had on the target behavior after it was withdrawn can only be explained by cognitive processes. "Self-attribution" theorists propose that when a reward is offered, an individual perceives the reward as the reason for engaging in the activity, even though the individual would have been intrinsically motivated to do the task without the reward. The person, therefore, ceases the activity when the reward is withdrawn.

This effect of rewards on motivation is related to what theorists refer to as the **discounting principle**. According to the discounting principle, if one possible explanation for an individual's behavior is salient, all other explanations will be "discounted." An external reward for performing an activity is usually more salient than intrinsic reasons. Thus, an individual may originally perceive intrinsic interest as the reason for doing a task, but if a desired extrinsic reward for the behavior is offered, intrinsic interest is discounted and the more salient extrinsic reward is perceived to be the cause.

The discounting principle and the undermining effect of rewards are illustrated by an anecdote about an old man who was bothered by the noisy play of boys in his neighborhood (from Casady, 1975). The old man called the boys together and told them he was deaf and asked them to shout louder so he could enjoy their fun. In return he would pay each of them a quarter. The boys were delighted and on the first day the old man was provided with a considerable amount of noise for his money. On the second day, he told the boys that he could only afford to pay twenty cents. The pay rate dwindled day by day and eventually the boys became angry and told the old man that they certainly were not going to make noise for nothing!

While self-attribution theorists focus on individuals' interpretation of events after they have occurred, *cognitive evaluation theorists* believe that the effect of rewards involves processes that occur at a deeper level than thoughts and prior to or during, as well as after, task engagement. Deci and Ryan (1985) claim that rewards cause individuals to shift from an internal to an external locus of causality; rewards create a *feeling of being controlled* and interfere with a feeling of self-determination. Cognitive evaluation theorists conceptualize motivation on a continuum rather than in terms of an internal-external dichotomy. Thus, intrinsic motivation is proportional to the *degree* to which individuals perceive their behavior as self-determined or volitional rather than controlled by others, by rewards, or by intrapsychic forces, such as guilt, or a sense of obligation (Deci, Vallerand, Pelletier, and Ryan, in press; Ryan and Connell, 1989; Ryan and Stiller, 1991).

Whether locus of causality is conceptualized as a dichotomy or as a continuous dimension, it is affected by the availability of rewards and other aspects of the social context. Rewards, however, can be used in different ways and for different purposes, and their effects on locus of causality, and thus on intrinsic motivation, are determined by *how* they are used as much as by whether they are used.

Controlling versus Information Function of Rewards

Lepper (1981), Deci (1975), and Bandura (1982b) all distinguish between two uses of rewards in classrooms—as an *incentive* to engage in tasks (that is, to control behavior) and as *information* about mastery (Deci and Ryan, 1985; Ryan et al., 1985). Rewards used to control behavior as well as other instructional practices (e.g., close monitoring of performance) that shift students away from a perception of autonomy and personal causation and toward a perception of external causation undermine intrinsic motivation. Rewards used to provide information vary in their effect, depending primarily on whether the information is positive (suggesting competence) or negative (suggesting incompetence).

When the teacher makes recess (a reward) contingent upon students' finishing their math assignment, the reward contains no information about students' level of mastery. In this situation the reward is being used to *control* or constrain students' behavior. It will, therefore, engender an external locus of causality, and ultimately children will complete their math assignments only so long as the reward is expected, even if they were previously interested in the task without any reward contingent upon it.

This kind of **task-contingent reward** (based on engaging in the task) is nearly always experienced as controlling. Deci and Ryan (1985) point out that **performance-contingent rewards** (based on achieving a specified level of performance), in contrast, can be perceived as controlling or informational, depending to some degree on the interpersonal context or the message that is conveyed. Praise, for example, can be worded so that it will be experienced as either informational or controlling, and research suggests that praise that is interpreted as informational (e.g., "good job, your paper is well-written") maintains rather than undermines intrinsic interest (Pittman, Davey, Alafat, Wetherill, and Kramer, 1980; Ryan, 1982).

Several studies have shown that subtle differences in the way rewards are administered have implications for their effects on intrinsic motivation. In an experimental study by Ryan (1982), for example, intrinsic motivation was not undermined when the experimenter simply said "good." It was, however, undermined when a simple phrase to convey control ("You're doing as you *should*") was added. In another experimental study, Ryan, Mims, and Koestner (1983) administered monetary rewards in either an informational or a controlling manner. Controlling rewards were given contingent upon success, but experimenters also emphasized that subjects who received the rewards were doing what the experimenter wanted (thus focusing attention on the experimenter's desire to control the subject's behavior). Although informational rewards were also success contingent, the controlling function was not emphasized. The controlling reward undermined intrinsic interest in the task, whereas the informational reward actually enhanced it. (See also Enzle and Ross, 1978; Pittman et al., 1980; Rosenfield, Folger, and Adelman, 1980; Harackiewicz, 1979.)

Other practices that have been shown to undermine intrinsic interest, presumably by creating an external locus of causality, include close monitoring (Lepper and Greene, 1975; Plant and Ryan, 1985), deadlines (Amabile, Dejong, and Lepper, 1976), evaluation (Hughes, Sullivan, and Mosley, 1985; Maehr and Stallings, 1972), imposing goals (Mossholder, 1980; Manderlink and Harackiewicz, 1984), and competition (Deci, Betley, Kahle, Abrams, and Porac, 1981; Vallerand Gavin, and Halliwell, 1986). Extrinsic rewards, therefore, constitute one among many classroom practices that can foster the perception of an external locus of causality, which interferes with intrinsic motivation.

Practices that foster an ego-orientation, that is, concerns about demonstrating competence, can also undermine feelings of self-determination and consequently hinder intrinsic motivation. In a study by Ryan (1982) subjects who were told that their performance on a task reflected creative intelligence (and were thus ego-involved) displayed less subsequent intrinsic motivation than task-involved subjects (to whom the statement about intelligence was not made). In an experiment by Butler (1987) with fifth- and sixth-graders, evaluation in the form of global praise (e.g., "very good") and normatively distributed grades resulted in greater ego involvement, less task involvement, and lower interest and desire to engage further with the activity than task-oriented evaluation involving comments containing both reinforcement and goal-setting (e.g., "You thought of quite a few ideas; maybe it is possible to think of more unusual, original ideas").

Ryan (1982; Ryan and Stiller, 1991) explains that ego involvement represents a kind of internal control or pressure that people apply to themselves; being pressured by these internal constraints (i.e., a feeling that it is necessary to do well to prove one's self-worth) undermines intrinsic motivation in the same way that external pressures do.

A few researchers have suggested that competition can heighten an individual's perception of external control, even though it also provides information about competence. To demonstrate this effect experimentally, Deci, Betley, Kahle, Abrams, and Porac (1981) gave college students puzzles to complete with two different sets of instructions. One group was told to try to win (solve the puzzles faster than the other person) and the other to work quickly. Subjects were subsequently left alone in a room with similar puzzles. The results indicated that subjects who had previously competed spent less time on the puzzles during this free-choice period than subjects who had not competed. In a classroom-based study, Fry and Coe (1980) found a negative association between the level of competitiveness in junior and senior high schools and students' ratings of their enjoyment in learning.

Brophy (1987c) points out that competition is not always bad, and can, under some circumstances, make a task more exciting. He adds, however, that competition will only have positive effects on a class as a whole, if (1) all students have an equal chance of winning and (2) the emphasis is on what is being learned rather than on who won or lost. He suggests team competition and handicapping systems (described in Chapter 10) to equalize everyone's opportunity to win.

Effects of Rewards Conveying Information

Rewards made contingent upon a specific level of performance provide information about levels of mastery and are less likely than task-contingent rewards to undermine interest—they may even enhance it (Boggiano and Ruble, 1979; Karniol and Ross, 1977; Rosenfield et al., 1980). The competence feedback implicit in social reinforcement is presumably why praise, although external, does not reduce intrinsic motivation [Anderson, Manoogian, and Reznick (1976); Blanck, Reis, and Jackson (1984); Deci (1971 and 1972); Dollinger and Thelen (1978);

Swann and Pittman (1977); see Arkes (1978) for a review]. The exception to this principle appears when the controlling function of praise is emphasized, as mentioned above.

One problem with performance-contingent rewards is that they maintain or enhance intrinsic motivation only if the feedback is positive (Boggiano and Ruble, 1979; Rosenfield et al., 1980; Ryan et al., 1983). Rosenfield et al. (1980) report, for example, that performance-contingent rewards enhanced intrinsic motivation when they conveyed high competence, but not when they conveyed low competence. Negative feedback about competence undermines intrinsic motivation.

The student's history of rewards may also influence the degree to which rewards conveying competence are perceived as informational versus controlling. This is suggested by a study by Pallak, Costomiris, Sroka, and Pittman (1982). They found that "good-player" awards (certificates) were interpreted informationally (and thus increased intrinsic motivation) by children in schools where symbolic rewards were used regularly to signify competence, whereas they were interpreted controllingly (and thus decreased intrinsic motivation) when given to children in schools where they had not been typically used.

Summary

The research discussed here suggests that the effect of rewards and other methods of controlling students' behavior is not straightforward. Rewards undermine intrinsic interest to the degree that they are perceived to be controlling, and the controlling function can be conveyed in varied and subtle ways. When the information value of rewards is salient, rewards can actually increase intrinsic motivation, but only if they convey competence.

INTERNALIZED MOTIVATION

Some children seem to work hard on assigned tasks that are not intrinsically interesting and for which no reinforcement is expected (e.g., an ungraded assignment); they simply do what the teacher says—however boring and unchallenging the tasks. Adults, too, sometimes read books and take courses, not because they enjoy them, but because they want to be well-informed. What is driving this behavior? Neither reinforcement theory nor intrinsic motivation theory seems to offer a satisfactory explanation.

A few motivation theorists have proposed that individuals engage in academic activities that are not intrinsically interesting and for which they are not positively reinforced because they have *internalized* achievement values. Children learn from parents and other significant adults that achievement behaviors are valued in our society. They take on these values as their own and behave in ways that are consistent with them.

The more children accept the values of their social surroundings as their own, the more they will experience socially sanctioned behavior as self-determined. As mentioned earlier, Ryan, Deci, and their colleagues conceptualize motivation as a continuum from extrinsically controlled to self-determined. At one end of the continuum are externally controlled behaviors and at the other end are intrinsically motivated behaviors (i.e., that give pleasure). In the middle of the continuum are behaviors that were originally regulated by external contingencies (**extrinsically regulated**) but became transformed to be experienced as self-determined, or **self regulated** (Ryan and Connell, 1989; Ryan et al., 1985; Ryan and Stiller, 1991); that is, they come to be adopted by the self as valuable and worth doing.

Self-regulation of achievement behavior is believed to result from a process of internalization in the same way that all other behavior valued in the child's social environment come under self-regulation, including moral behavior (e.g., not stealing) and social behavior [e.g., sharing; Aronfreed (1969)]. Children at first need to be externally reinforced for certain behaviors that are not intrinsically interesting. Thus, a child at first may do boring homework assignments only to earn a star on a public chart or to avoid punishment.

Gradually children begin to internalize rules; they judge themselves for engaging in a behavior in the same way that their parents or teachers have judged them for engaging in the behavior in the past. This internalization results in emotional reactions to compliance and noncompliance—what Ryan et al. call **introjected regulation**. Thus, a child may finish her homework because she will feel anxious or guilty if she doesn't, or she may spend time with her grandmother out of feelings of obligation. Although external forces (the promise of a reward or the threat of punishment) are not present, introjected regulation is associated with feelings of being controlled or coerced more than with feelings of self-determination.

Ultimately, children accept as their own some of the values underlying the behaviors for which they were previously reinforced—a motivational level referred to as **identification**. In this case, behavioral regulation has been integrated into one's self; the individual experiences volition without a sense of pressure or coercion. For example, a student might explain that she studies vocabulary words because she wants to be able to write and speak well. She experiences herself as self-determining—engaging in the activity because she *wants* to—even though she may not find the activity interesting or enjoyable and she is not reinforced for it. Thus, identified regulation is extrinsic in the sense that the individual is not intrinsically interested in the activity, but it is experienced as volitional.

The least coercive and salient forms of extrinsic reinforcement are the most likely to facilitate identification with adults' values (as opposed to introjected regulation). Thus, children are more likely to integrate parents' and teachers' values if they are *socially* reinforced (e.g., praised) than if they are given tangible reinforcement (e.g., money, toys, candy). Both social and tangible reinforcements give the message that the activity is valued. But tangible reinforcement is more salient and gives children the additional message that the activity is not intrinsically interesting and they are not expected to engage in the activity unless they get something for it. This "minimal but sufficient" principle for rewards is derived in part from work comparing the effects of mild versus severe threats of punishment on children's ability to prohibit themselves from engaging in prohibited activities (Lepper, 1973). Presumably salient rewards, like severe punishment, focus children's attention on the external reasons for a behavior more than less salient rewards.

Children who have an internalized "school-work ethic" are no doubt the easiest to teach. Teachers are not obliged to make tasks intrinsically interesting, nor do they need to offer an external reward for effort, or threaten to punish such a child for not working. Nevertheless, even children who work because they have internalized the value of hard work and good performance in school occasionally need to be reinforced for their efforts. It is unlikely that valuing academic work could sustain effort without a social environment that rewards effort. It is also unlikely that effort will be sustained on tasks that are not at all intrinsically interesting and do not result in feelings of competence.

Individual Differences in Intrinsic and Internalized Motivation

Three of the four perspectives on intrinsic motivation described above assume that intrinsic motivation is innate. Why then does achievement behavior vary so much among students in the same achievement context? Why do some students approach new tasks with enthusiasm while others seem totally uninterested?

There are many explanations for variation in students' behavior in achievement contexts. For example, the degree to which tasks are challenging may vary among students in the same classroom. Tasks that are optimally challenging for some students may be too easy or impossibly difficult for others. Only those students who find the classroom's tasks moderately difficult will experience competence motivation.

Also, despite the innate origins of competence motivation, relatively stable individual differences in mastery behavior may develop as a consequence of differences in the behavior of parents and other significant adults. Harter (1978a) has speculated that some social reinforcement from early infancy is necessary to sustain a child's mastery attempts. Social reinforcement for attempting, as well as mastering, tasks enhances mastery behavior, while punishment for attempting, or for failing to master, tasks inhibits intrinsic interest in achievement tasks.

Parents and other adults also have a role in the development of internalized motivation; adult reactions to children's mastery efforts convey their own values regarding hard work and learning. Adults teach children what *kinds* of mastery behaviors or products are valued. The student who internalizes his parents' value of athletic skills may demonstrate considerable mastery motivation on the football field, but little in the classroom. The student who learns to value artistic competency may work hard to develop competencies as a musician, but not to master algebra. One student is not necessarily less intrinsically motivated than the other. Rather, the domain in which each manifests his or her motivation is different.

Individual differences along these lines may also develop as a consequence of past experience with achievement tasks. For example, children may develop a preference for easy work because they have failed in the past and therefore underestimate their ability, or because their parents punished failure and they do not want to risk the failure that sometimes occurs when initially attempting a moderately difficult task. Children who are dependent on the teacher for help may have had overintrusive parents and thus failed to develop self-confidence in their ability to complete tasks on their own. Previous experiences in achievement settings can have enduring effects on children's behavior that are resistant to teachers' efforts to change.

Measures of Individual Differences in Motivation

Several researchers have developed measures of stable individual differences in children's intrinsic and internalized motivation to do schoolwork. Harter (1981b) developed a measure designed to assess stable individual differences on five dimensions related to intrinsic

---

TABLE 5-1 • Sample Items from Harter's Intrinsic Motivation Scale[1]

Really true for me	Sort of true for me			Really true for me	Sort of true for me
		Preference for challenge	*Preference for easy work*		
4	3	Some kids like to go on to new work that's at a more difficult level	Other kids would rather stick to assignments that are pretty easy	2	1
		Pleasing teacher/ getting grades	*Curiosity/ interest*		
1	2	Some kids do extra projects so they can get better grades	Other kids do extra projects because they learn about things that interest them	3	4
		Dependence on teacher	*Independent mastery*		
1	2	When some kids get stuck on a problem they ask the teacher for help	Other kids keep trying to figure out the problem on their own	3	4
		Reliance on teacher's judgment	*Independent judgment*		
1	2	Some kids think the teacher should decide what work to do	Other kids think they should have a say in what work they do	3	4
		Internal criteria	*External criteria*		
4	3	Some kids know whether or not they're doing well in school without grades	Other kids need to have grades to know how well they are doing in school	2	1

1. A copy of the scale and a manual for scoring and interpreting results is available from Professor Susan Harter, Department of Psychology, University of Denver, University Park, Denver, CA 80208.

motivation: (1) preference for challenging work versus preference for easy work; (2) learning motivated by curiosity versus learning done to please the teacher; (3) desire to work independently versus dependency on the teacher for help; (4) independent judgment about selecting tasks versus reliance on teacher's judgment; and (5) internal criteria for success or failure versus external criteria (e.g., grades, teacher feedback). Harter's measure has been tested on hundreds of elementary- and junior-high-school-age students. Table 5-1 provides examples of statements students are asked to respond to when they fill out the questionnaire.

Gottfried (1985, 1986, 1990) developed the Children's Academic Intrinsic Motivation Inventory (CAIMI), which assesses intrinsic interest in specific subject areas (reading, math, social studies, science), and in school in general. One version is for children in the lower elementary grades and the other is for children above the third grade. Studies have revealed some stability in children's scores over a two-year period.

It is useful to assess intrinsic interest in different academic domains because there is considerable variation in children's intrinsic interest in various school tasks. In addition to using the questionnaires discussed above, teachers can assess students' intrinsic motivation for tasks by observing their behavior in different task situations or by asking them to rate their interest in specific kinds of routinely given tasks. Behaviors that are associated with high intrinsic interest are summarized in Table 5-2. An example of a rating scale a teacher might create to assess students' intrinsic interests on tasks that are frequently given in his or her own classroom is shown in Table 5-3.

Harter's (in press) questionnaire, mentioned in Chapter 2, contains a subscale that assesses *internalized* motivation. The questionnaire contains 24 items to assess three motivational orientations (extrinsic, intrinsic, internalized). Recall that the scale is introduced to the children as a questionnaire asking them about the reasons for doing their school work. An item assessing internalized motivation ("I do my schoolwork because I've learned for myself that it's important for me to do it") can be contrasted with an intrinsic reason ("I do my schoolwork because what we learn is really interesting") and an extrinsic reason ("I do my schoolwork because my teacher will be pleased with me if I do").

TABLE 5-2 • Behaviors Associated with Intrinsic Motivation

1. Students spontaneously make connections between school learning and activities or interests outside of school.
2. Students ask questions that go beyond the specific task at hand.
3. Students work on tasks whether or not extrinsic reasons (e.g., grades, close teacher supervision) are salient.
4. Students smile and appear to enjoy working on tasks.
5. Students express pride in their achievements.

TABLE 5-3 • An Example of a Teacher-Developed Measure of Intrinsic Motivation on Typical School Tasks

---

Instructions to Students:
Please rate how much you **enjoy** doing the following activities in this class:

	not at all				a lot
Doing problems in arithmetic workbook	1	2	3	4	5
Doing arithmetic word problems on the board	1	2	3	4	5
Reading stories from reading books	1	2	3	4	5
Answering questions at the end of chapters in reading books	1	2	3	4	5
Working on science projects	1	2	3	4	5
Writing stories	1	2	3	4	5
Listening to the teacher read stories	1	2	3	4	5
Working on the class newspaper	1	2	3	4	5

Ryan and Connell (1989) created a scale which assesses *external*, *introjected*, *identified*, and *intrinsic* motivation. Respondents are asked to rate the degree to which various reasons explained their behavior. As can be seen from the sample items shown in Table 5-4, the authors' conceptualization of introjected and identified motivation overlaps with what other researchers have referred to as ego or performance goals and mastery goals, respectively. Thus, engaging in a task to achieve social approval (a performance goal) reflects introjected regulation, and engaging in a task to develop understanding or skills (mastery goals) reflects identified motivation. Research has shown that external regulation measured by this scale is associated with perceptions of low support for autonomy in the classroom, anxiety, and lower enjoyment of schoolwork. Identified and intrinsic motivation are associated with perceptions of high support for autonomy in the classroom, and greater enjoyment.

TABLE 5-4 • Sample Items from Ryan & Connell's Academic Self-Regulation Questionnaire[1]

I do my homework:

External (rule following; avoidance of punishment)
  Because I'll get in trouble if I don't
  Because that's what I'm supposed to do
  So that the teacher won't yell at me
  Because that's the rule
  So others won't get mad at me

Introjection (self- and other-approval; avoidance of disapproval)
  Because I want the teacher to think I'm a good student
  Because I will feel bad about myself if I don't
  Because I'll feel ashamed of myself if I don't
  Because I want the other students to think I'm smart
  Because it bothers me when I don't
  Because I want people to like me

Identification (self-valued goal; personal importance)
  Because I want to understand the subject
  Because I want to learn new things
  To find out if I'm right or wrong
  Because I think it's important to

Intrinsic (enjoyment, fun)
  Because it's fun
  Because I enjoy it

1. Adapted from Ryan and Connell (1989). The full scale is available from Richard Ryan, Department of Psychology, University of Rochester, Rochester, New York 14627.

Age-Related Changes

In addition to individual differences at any one age, there are systematic differences in these dispositions associated with age. Harter found that scores on her subscales measuring preference for challenge, curiosity and interest, and independent mastery all declined from the third to the ninth grade, while scores on the independent judgment and internal criteria subscales increased. With age and experience in school, students apparently tend to become less motivated to engage in academic activities for their own pleasure, but are better able to judge the quality of their performance.

We can only speculate about the reasons for these shifts. Research on the undermining effect of external reinforcement on intrinsic motivation suggests that children's interest in engaging in tasks for the sake of developing mastery may be replaced by an interest in obtaining external rewards, such as high grades. A second explanation concerns another consistent finding in the achievement motivation literature— that children's self-confidence in mastering tasks encountered in school declines with age and experience in school (Stipek, 1984a, b), and that low perceived competence dampens intrinsic motivation (Boggiano et al., 1988; Gottfried, 1990; Harter, 1981a; Harter and Connell, 1984; Mac Iver et al., 1991).

A third explanation is that the achievement context changes as a function of grade. For example, evaluation may be emphasized more in higher grades and failure may be tolerated less. Eccles, Midgley, and Adler (1984) suggest that school becomes more formal, more evaluative, and more competitive and that the focus shifts from the process of learning to an evaluation of the products. These and other changes in educational practices may contribute to the age-related declines observed on three of Harter's subscales of intrinsic motivation.

The increased reliance on personal criteria and judgment to assess mastery is, no doubt, related to the socialization process discussed above. Over the elementary school years children internalize the standards of parents and teachers. This process enables them eventually to impose their own internalized standards.

INTRINSIC MOTIVATION AND CLASSROOM LEARNING

The competence motive described by White and Piaget can be activated in any situation that provides opportunities for developing new competencies. Tasks that have qualities of surprise, incongruity, and complexity can be naturally appealing whether they are encountered in or out of a classroom. Tasks that students are allowed to choose will enhance intrinsic motivation wherever the tasks are encountered. Intrinsic motivation can, therefore, play an important role in students' classroom learning.

Nevertheless, students usually do not attempt school tasks unless there is some extrinsic reason for attempting them, even if the tasks have the potential for being intrinsically motivating. The absence of intrinsic motivation in the classroom may be explained, in part, by the nature of the skills that need to be learned in school. The skills that older children must learn are cultural inventions; they concern knowledge that was developed and passed from one generation to another.

Presumably, children are not naturally (i.e., biologically) inclined to learn the capitals of the states, or how to dissect a frog, or how to solve a geometry proof in the way that infants and toddlers seem compelled to develop skills that have a strong biological imperative, such as walking and talking. Teachers cannot, therefore, rely on intrinsic motivation to engage students' initial interest in most school tasks.

Once students attempt a task, however, they may become intrinsically motivated to continue working on it if certain conditions are met. I will give two personal examples of how a student's motivation can be shifted from an extrinsic to an intrinsic orientation. I once had compelling external reasons for enrolling in an evening course in home repair at a local high school. I had bought a house that needed a lot of work and I could not afford to have it done professionally. In spite of my external reasons for enrolling, soon after beginning the course I found that I was highly motivated to practice my newly developing skills without any encouragement or external reinforcement. As long as I experienced increased mastery, no matter how far my products were from being useable, I enjoyed the activity. My second example of initially extrinsically motivated tasks becoming intrinsically motivating concerns my students. Some of them have avoided learning how to use a computer until it became essential to their work. Although they approached the task reluctantly, most became "hooked," and continued to develop skills far beyond what was required.

The challenge to the teacher, therefore, is to create tasks and learning contexts that shift students from extrinsic to intrinsic motivation. Ways to achieve this shift are discussed in the next chapter.

ADVANTAGES OF INTRINSIC MOTIVATION

Sustaining Desirable Behavior

Most achievement motivation theorists consider intrinsically motivated achievement behavior more desirable than externally motivated behavior primarily because external reinforcement is not always available. It is Safe Sally's dependency on external rewards, for example, that keeps her from engaging in learning activities outside of school, where grades and other forms of recognition are less available. If learning is perceived as an activity that one does only to obtain rewards and avoid punishment, there is no reason to do it when no rewards are available and punishment is not likely.

Effects on Conceptual Understanding and Creativity

Research suggests further that the conditions that produce interest and enjoyment (i.e., that foster intrinsic motivation) facilitate conceptual learning, and conditions that engender an external locus of causality (such as an emphasis on evaluation) undermine conceptual learning. Ryan, Connell, and Plant (1990), for example, found that college students who reported relatively more enjoyment while reading a text had relatively greater comprehension.

Benware and Deci (1984) compared subjects who were told that they would simply be tested on material they were asked to learn to subjects who were told that they were learning material to teach to other students. The latter subjects claimed that they found the material more interesting and scored better on the conceptual part of an exam, but not on rote learning. Grolnick and Ryan (1987) also found that children who were given controlling directions in a reading task (told that they would be tested on the material) had poorer conceptual, but not poorer rote recall of the material.

Studies have found that conditions supporting intrinsic motivation foster greater creativity (Amabile, 1983) and cognitive flexibility (McGraw and McCullers, 1979). For example, in one study reported by Amabile (1983), the art work of female college students who expected to be graded was judged to be less creative than the work of those who did not expect to be evaluated. In the McGraw and McCullers' study, college students who were promised monetary rewards for solving a series of problems had more difficulty "breaking set" (solving a problem that had a different solution from the previous problems) than students who did not expect a monetary reward.

Butler and Nisan (1986) found that when evaluative feedback was given in the form of grades, children's performance on a quantitative task subsequently increased and their performance on a task assessing divergent (creative) thinking declined; written comments, in contrast, resulted in improved performance on both tasks.

In all of the studies summarized above, conditions associated with extrinsic motivation had negative effects on conceptual and creative thinking. The reason for the effect is not clear, although Amabile (1983) suggests that extrinsic contingencies can create an instrumental focus that narrows attention and orients individuals to take the quickest and easiest solution. It is also possible that students are used to being evaluated on rote learning more than on conceptual understanding; as a consequence, those who expected to be evaluated in the studies described above focused their attention primarily on facts that could be memorized.

Task-Orientation

Nicholls (1979b, 1983, 1984) discusses another advantage of intrinsic motivation. He claims that students' attention is more focused on a task when they are intrinsically motivated than when they are extrinsically motivated. His point is related to the distinction made in Chapter 2 between mastery or learning goals and performance goals. When students are intrinsically motivated they are task-oriented—learning is experienced as an end in itself, and mastery of the task or skill is the goal. The student's attention is focused on the process of completing the task or making sense of and mastering the material.

Meece, Blumenfeld, and Hoyle (1988) demonstrate the relationship between intrinsic motivation and a task (or learning, or mastery) orientation. They found that fifth- and sixth-graders' scores on Harter's measure of intrinsic motivation were strongly associated with scores on a measure of task-orientation and negatively associated with scores on a measure of ego-orientation when working on science tasks. Thus intrinsic motivation has all the benefits of a task-orientation—more active problem-solving strategies, greater persistence, moderate risk-taking—that are described in Chapter 2.

Pleasure

Intrinsic motivation and a mastery orientation are also associated with greater pleasure and greater emotional involvement than extrinsic motivation or a performance orientation. For example, in the Ames and Archer (1988) study mentioned in Chapter 2, the more students perceived their classroom as supporting mastery goals, the more they liked the class. Elliott and Dweck (1988) report that many of the children in their experimentally induced performance-orientation condition who had low perceptions of ability spontaneously expressed negative feelings about the task with comments like, "After this [problem], then I get to go?" "This is boring," "My stomach hurts" (p. 10). Children who were task-oriented rarely made such comments, whether or not they believed they were competent at the task.

Given these advantages, it is important to optimize intrinsic motivation in the classroom setting. We turn now to suggestions for accomplishing this goal.

TABLE 5-5 • Summary of Terms

Term	Definition
Intrinsic motivation	Motivation to engage in an activity in the absence of any extrinsic reward or purpose
Competence motivation	Natural disposition to engage in tasks and activities which contribute to learning and development
Internal locus of causality	Perception of engaging in an activity by personal preference
External locus of causality	Perception of engaging in an activity for some external reward or for some reason other than personal preference
Discounting principle	Discounting a reason for engaging in an activity because another reason is more salient
Task-contingent rewards	Rewards based on engaging in an activity or completing a task
Performance-contingent rewards	Rewards based on achieving a specified level of performance
Internalized motivation	Motivation that was originally based on external figures that becomes self-regulation
Extrinsic regulation	Behavior is controlled by external consequences
Self-Regulation	Controlling one's own behavior without external rewards or constraints
Introjected Regulation	Behaving as the result of emotions (e.g., pride, guilt) associated with previously experienced parental responses (e.g., reward and punishment)
Identification	Caretakers' values are fully internalized

6

MAXIMIZING INTRINSIC MOTIVATION IN THE CLASSROOM

Being able to read, solve math problems or write a good essay should engender the same feelings of competence in a student that being able to walk, take off a shoe, or complete a puzzle engenders for the young child. But few children show the same determination and persistence on school tasks that they demonstrate in infancy and early childhood. Why does this intrinsic motivational system, which has such a powerful effect on children's behavior before school, seem not to be a major factor in most students' behavior in school? Does intrinsic motivation diminish with age? Does the school environment inhibit its expression?

Clearly, intrinsic motivation does not disappear altogether. Even adults occasionally experience the desire to complete some task purely for the feeling of competence it gives. I have known adults who became as obsessed about completing crossword puzzles as one-year-olds are about taking a few steps. I have known adolescents who, like Satisfied Sam, spent virtually all of their free time working on computers. Computer programming is more cognitively demanding than many of the tasks adolescents encounter in school. Nevertheless, the same adolescents who stay up all night working out complicated computer programs may never finish their algebra homework. What is the difference between these two activities?

This chapter discusses how the nature of tasks and the context of learning affect the degree to which individuals are intrinsically motivated to complete tasks. Specifically, the chapter explores how characteristics of the tasks themselves, as well as other aspects of instruction, including external evaluation, assistance, use of rewards, student autonomy, and the social context affect intrinsic motivation. Some of these contextual variables explain why students are often less motivated to work on school tasks than on equally difficult activities out of school.

Although our goal is to create an environment that supports students' intrinsic interest in developing competencies, it is unrealistic to expect children to exert effort voluntarily and enthusiastically on every school task. There is only so much a teacher can do to make learning the multiplication tables or the names of the states intrinsically interesting. Some extrinsic support for learning is essential. The practical issues are, therefore, how to create a context in which intrinsic motivation flourishes and in which extrinsic rewards for learning do not undermine intrinsic motivation and a sense of personal causality and responsibility.

TASKS

Difficulty Level

Easy tasks that will not give students who complete them a feeling of developing competence will not activate the competence motivation drive. This principle is obvious in the behavior of young children. As mentioned earlier, once a new skill (e.g., turning door knobs) has been mastered, and engaging in the activity no longer results in feelings of increasing competence, the activity ceases to be intrinsically motivating. Henceforth, it is done only for instrumental purposes—as a means to some other goal.

The practical importance of this principle is demonstrated in a study by McMullin and Steffen (1982) in which college students played a calculator game with either a constant or an accelerating standard for success. Students who had an accelerated standard spent more time playing the game in a subsequent free-choice situation than students with a constant standard, suggesting greater intrinsic interest in the task.

School tasks that are too difficult are, likewise, not intrinsically motivating. If repeated efforts do not lead to mastery, the student will not experience developing competence, and therefore will not be motivated to continue to engage in the task. This is why low-achieving students typically claim to be less intrinsically interested in schoolwork than high-achieving students (Harter, in press).

It is easier to demonstrate the importance of challenging tasks than it is to put this principle into practice in a group of 20–30 or more students with varying skill levels. The teacher's job is complicated by the need to pace the introduction of new material as well as its difficulty. It is especially difficult to provide an appropriately challenging educational program for children who are far behind most of the other students. Some students, like Hopeless Hannah, need tasks and instruction that are completely different from what the other students receive. Occasionally teachers give up on these students; they make the understandable judgment that it would be unfair to the other children to devote the considerable time required to give such students appropriate tasks and instruction. As a consequence, the student who is far behind and cannot even begin to complete regular class assignments may spend his or her time wandering around the room, gazing out the window, or disrupting other students.

At the other end of the continuum are students, like Safe Sally, who quickly master the curriculum and are not challenged by class assignments. They typically finish assignments in less than the allotted time and with few mistakes. Because tasks that can be completed with no errors are not challenging enough to be intrinsically motivating, students who master the curriculum easily often focus on external reinforcements as the reason for their effort. Thus, the 100 percent at the top of the paper, public display on the bulletin board, or the teacher's praise become the primary motivators.

Some very bright children get so used to 100 percent on their papers that they become upset when they receive anything but the top grade. Like Safe Sally, they try to prevent less-than-perfect performance by being cautious in learning situations. When given a choice they select the assignment or the course that assures them a good grade. This is unfortunate for the student who could benefit from greater academic challenge. It is undoubtedly one explanation why many highly competent individuals (especially females) avoid math and science (Fennema and Peterson, 1985).

Other students who are not challenged by class assignments work halfheartedly because school bores them. A few become disruptive. Others, like Satisfied Sam, engage in activities that interest them but are not necessarily related to the school curriculum.

There are institutional constraints that make it difficult to provide instruction and tasks at the appropriate difficulty level for very high-achieving and very low-achieving students. Schools rarely provide sufficient support services for students who are doing very poorly or who are unusually bright. Some schools have a policy against placing students more than a year behind or above their age-mates. A fifth-grade teacher may be forced to reckon with a twelve-year-old who is working at a third-grade level because he is "too tall" for the third or fourth grade. Teachers in the upper grades sometimes put pressure on teachers in the lower grades to restrain students from moving too far ahead in the curriculum. If a third-grader completes the next year's curriculum, the fourth-grade teacher has to contend with a child who has already mastered the teacher's instructional program.

Ideally, these kinds of problems should be dealt with at the institutional level. Schools should be organized to facilitate individualization of tasks. This can be done by grouping children in a broader age span than one year and by using team teaching. In a group of children from eight to ten years old, for example, a slow ten-year-old may receive reading instruction with mostly eight-year-olds, but he could receive instruction with older students in other areas that do not require high-level reading skills, such as art or science. The bright eight-year-old could be given the same tasks as most of the ten-year-olds.

Teachers are often reluctant to combine different-age children for instruction because they are concerned that the ten-year-old will feel self-conscious about reading with mostly younger children, and that this will damage his self-concept. My own view is that most ten-year-olds know how well they are doing compared to other children in their class, regardless of how they are grouped. The advantage of the broader age range and of team teaching is that children who are behind their age-mates in achievement can more easily be given tasks that are appropriate for their skill level—ones they can complete successfully. If instructional groupings are loose and variable, so the older child is not always grouped with younger children, the older child will suffer less humiliation than he or she would when spending all day as the only ten-year-old in a third-grade classroom or as a fifth-grader who fails to complete assignments day after day.

But most teachers do not work in this kind of organizational structure. How can teachers in self-contained, age-graded classrooms provide challenging tasks to children with a broad range of skill levels? There are a variety of ways to individualize tasks so that they are equally challenging to students who are at the bottom and the top end of the achievement continuum. Dividing students into instructional groups is the most common method, but this does not deal with the considerable variation in skills that is usually found within groups, and care needs to be taken to avoid other problems, such as rigid and erroneous teacher expectations associated with ability grouping (see Chapter 11). Mastery-based programs, described in Chapter 10, in which students advance through the curriculum at their own pace, have also been shown to be an effective way to individualize tasks.

Good and Brophy (1986), and many other education specialists, recommend learning centers to give teachers time to work with children individually or in small groups. Learning centers involve special places in the room where students can work on activities (which could involve computers) that require minimal supervision. Students can rotate through learning centers in pairs or small groups over the course of the day or when they have completed their daily seatwork. Learning centers are more common in kindergarten and the early elementary grades, but they could be used more to help upper elementary grade teachers individualize tasks. Indeed, older children are usually better able to sustain interest in an activity without adult supervision than are young children.

Additional personnel, such as classroom aides, can also make it easier to provide instruction and tasks that are adjusted to each student's skill level, but they are not always available. In schools that do not provide aides or tutors, volunteers might help. Parents can sometimes be enlisted to tutor their own child, if the child is behind classmates, or to assist in the classroom. Goldenberg (1987) argues that parents may be the most underutilized educational support available. He has involved Hispanic parents in the instruction of their children with extraordinary success. Senior citizens and older children can also serve as tutors. In one year-round school I observed, some of the fifth- and sixth-grade students who were "off track" spent several hours a day at the school providing individualized tutoring to younger children. Some of the tutees were behind their classmates and some were ahead. Research indicates that both tutors and tutees benefit from peer tutoring (Chandler, 1980).

Even whole-class instruction can involve some individualization. Stigler and Stevenson (1991) observed in a large-scale comparison of mathematics instruction in Taiwan, Beijing (China), Sendai (Japan), and Minneapolis, that most math instruction in Asian classrooms is done in a whole-class format, even though variation in student skill levels is no less than is found, on average, in American classrooms. Teachers accommodate to individual differences in skill levels by continuously changing their mode of presentation and type of representation. Asian teachers often stop in the middle of whole-class instructional periods and give students one or a few problems to do at their seats, individually or in small groups. Teachers engage all students in the learning process by encouraging different solution strategies, which are discussed by the class when students have completed the brief set of problems. Incorrect solutions, which the researchers found were typically dismissed by American teachers, become, in Asian classrooms, topics for discussion from which all children can learn.

A study by Meece, Blumenfeld, and Puro (1989) also demonstrates the potential for individualizing instruction in a whole-class format. Interactions with students during whole-class instruction was one of the ways in which an American science teacher who was unusually successful in fostering interest in science was most different from a teacher whose students were much less interested in science. Rather than turn to another student when one student failed to provide a satisfactory answer to a question, the "highly motivating" teacher reworded or prompted students who responded incorrectly, and often asked them to explain or justify their responses. These minidialogues with individual students in the context of whole-class instruction allow teachers to adapt to different levels of understanding as well as to provide other students an opportunity to learn by listening.

Chinese teachers have developed a way to make sure that all students in a class are challenged by written tasks without individualizing assignments. In China assignments and tests always include some very easy problems—that every student in the class can solve—and some very difficult problems—that no student in the class can solve (Stevenson and Stigler, 1992). All students, therefore, begin an assignment or test expecting to solve some but not all of the problems. This is a clever method of challenging the fast learners and encouraging them to strive for a higher level of understanding without discouraging the slower learners from trying. It is certainly a more efficient way of dealing with individual differences in skill level than constructing many different assignments and tests.

It is usually easier to provide challenging tasks for high-achieving than for low-achieving students without added resources because high achievers tend to be more self-confident and work more independently. For example, high-achieving students who are not challenged by class math assignments could be encouraged to go ahead in their math book, correcting their own problems by using the teacher's manual or exchanging papers with classmates. Students who are ahead of the class on reading and writing can be encouraged to write their own stories, write and put on a play, keep a diary, edit a class newspaper, or engage in any number of other enriching activities that will allow them to refine their critical thinking and language skills.

The importance of matching tasks to each child's skill level cannot be overemphasized. It is necessary for both intrinsic motivation and optimal learning. As difficult a principle as this is to implement, it is the most important one for motivation and learning.

Complexity, Novelty, and Surprise

Recall that one theoretical perspective on intrinsic motivation stresses novelty, incongruity, complexity, and surprise. Children are likely to be engaged by tasks that involve fantasy or simulation (including role-playing), incorporate game-like features, or involve elements of uncertainty about the outcome, such as suspense or hidden information.

Variety in tasks is always desirable. Many teachers use predictable, unvarying formats. A common practice for elementary level math instruction, for example, is to begin with 15–20 minutes of whole-class instruction, during which students occasionally do a few problems on the board, and then to give 25–30 minutes at their desks to complete an assignment, typically a page out of a workbook. Brophy (1986) suggests that such "... a steady diet of routine and predictable lessons followed by routine and predictable assignments soon becomes 'the daily grind'" (p. 34; Brophy, 1987b).

Often the same skills can be promoted with alternative formats—such as integrating whole-class instruction and seatwork, as Japanese teachers do, or breaking students into small groups or dyads to work on problems. Because research has indicated that no single format for instruction and learning is superior to any other, teachers can safely vary tasks to maintain students' interest and attention.

Variability in tasks was one of the more salient features of the highly motivating science classroom that Meece et al. (1989) observed, and it can easily be achieved (see also Blumenfeld, Puro, and Mergendoller, in press). Minor changes can sometimes have significant effects. A fifth-grade teacher once complained to me that students worked halfheartedly on their daily reading assignment—answering a series of questions at the end of a story they were asked to read. As the result of our discussion she changed the task one day by asking students to generate questions and to exchange them with a friend in the class. This minor modification in the assignment sparked considerable enthusiasm, which was sustained by other, equally modest, modifications made thereafter.

Teachers can also elicit curiosity and interest can also be achieved by asking questions that reveal discrepancies in students' understanding, by asking students to resolve a paradox, or by inducing suspense. In a fourth-grade class I observed, students had learned that oxygen was necessary for plant and animal life. Later, while they were learning about the solar system, most of the students claimed that there was life on some of the other planets. The teacher pointed out that there was no oxygen on other planets. The children, puzzled by the apparent discrepancy between their knowledge and expectations, asked questions about the atmosphere of the planets being studied. The teacher answered their questions and encouraged them to fantasize about what kinds of beings could survive on planets without oxygen. This clever teacher created cognitive conflict in her students and allowed them to engage in fantasy. As a consequence, she generated considerable interest in the atmosphere of planets—a subject that could easily be presented in a way that would put students (and observers) to sleep.

Suspense and curiosity can also be induced by asking students a question before beginning a lesson—"What is the 'iron curtain'?" "Why is blood blue under your skin and red outside?" It is also useful to ask students to speculate or predict answers to questions or results of activities. "What proportion of the U.S. mainland would Alaska cover?" "Why do people in Mexico speak Spanish?" "What will happen when two chemicals are mixed?"

Tasks that require *higher-order or divergent thinking and active problem solving* are more intrinsically interesting to children than tasks that involve memorizing or applying simple rules or procedures. I observed a compelling demonstration of this principle in a fourth-grade class. The teacher allowed children who finished their math worksheets (usually a set of calculations) to work on a math puzzle—usually a fairly complicated word problem. Students rushed through their worksheets for the *opportunity* to work on this more difficult problem. Seeing this day after day made me wonder what the math competencies of these students would be if their math curriculum included more "puzzles" and fewer sets of repetitive calculations.

Tasks that involve a high degree of *student participation* are also more enjoyable than tasks that put students into a more passive mode. Even if a teacher uses lecture format, students should be encouraged to ask questions, provide answers, offer opinions, or share personal observations and experiences. Small groups are conducive to active participation—which may be one reason why children tend to find cooperative learning groups more enjoyable than working independently (Johnson and Johnson, 1985b). Manipulation of materials also tends to generate more enthusiasm than more passive learning activities, such as listening or reading. Thus, acting out a real debate between loyalists and separatists in the New England colonial period is more fun than reading about the controversy and can result in a deeper understanding of the issues.

Multidimensional tasks that require sustained effort and result in a product are particularly motivating because they provide children an opportunity to experience pride in an accomplishment they can point to. In several classes I have visited, children have published a class newspaper. The newspaper task provides students an opportunity to integrate math (determining how much it will cost to produce and how much they should charge for it), social studies (writing on current political events), art (designing a logo), and other practical skills (e.g., using the computer to do word processing). Other examples of long-term projects that I have seen include a model city, a class book of poems, and a map, drawn to scale, of the school. [See Blumenfeld, Soloway, Marx, Krajcik, Guzdial, and Palincsar (in press) for a discussion of the motivating effect of project-based learning].

A few motivation researchers have suggested making tasks more interesting by embedding them in a *fantasy* context, or by using *embellishments* such as color, noise, other complex stimuli, or surprise outcomes. Positive effects of fantasy or other embellishments on motivation have been shown in the context of computer-assisted instruction (CAI), which allows researchers to systematically vary specific characteristics of tasks (Lepper, 1985; Lepper and Malone, 1987; Malone, 1981a, 1981b; Malone and Lepper, 1987; Parker and Lepper, in press). There is some evidence, however, that girls and boys respond differently to such embellishments. Malone (1981a) found in one study that music increased the intrinsic appeal of a fraction-learning game for girls, but decreased the appeal for boys, whereas fantasy enhanced the appeal of the game for boys but not for girls.

Some theorists, however, believe that embellishments actually interfere with learning (Lepper and Malone, 1987). Thus, at present there is little data to guide teachers' attempts to use such embellishments as color, fantasy, surprise outcomes, and music to increase intrinsic interest in school tasks; there is even some question about the desirability of any of these factors. Teachers need to test the effect of various embellishments on the intrinsic interest of their own students.

Summary

Doyle (1983) distinguishes between four different kinds of tasks: (1) *memory* tasks (e.g., the multiplication tables); (2) routine or *procedural* tasks (e.g., copying the definition of words from a dictionary); (3) *comprehension* tasks which require students to go a step beyond the information provided; and (4) *opinion* tasks. The discussion above clearly indicates that the latter two maximize intrinsic motivation. Despite their value, however, students often resist such tasks because of the ambiguity they generate. Many students prefer the first two because they are unambiguous; they know when their answer is correct or not. Comprehension and opinion tasks involve more risk because the standards for evaluation are difficult to judge and there is greater uncertainty about what constitutes a "good" performance.

Students often try to turn open-ended assignments that have considerable potential for creativity into procedural tasks. When I assign a paper in my graduate courses, students invariably ask many questions to decrease the ambiguity: "How many pages?" "Double-spaced or single-spaced?" "Do we need to use sources outside of class readings?" "How many references should we have?" "Is it all right to use quotations?" I find myself making up answers to relieve students' anxiety, even though my answers end up limiting students' options in ways that I did not intend.

There are other ways teachers can relieve anxiety about open-ended tasks, such as not formally evaluating students' products, or by giving them several opportunities to achieve a positive evaluation (e.g., have them turn in a draft and provide feedback before they complete the final, evaluated version). It is also useful to give students as much information as possible about how such assignments will be evaluated, although care must be taken to avoid giving information about evaluation that will reduce an interesting task to an uninteresting, procedural one.

Personal Meaningfulness of Tasks

Stigler and Stevenson (1991) note that in American classrooms teachers typically teach rules for mathematical operations first, and then, *sometimes*, they point out the real-world applications of the rule. Asian teachers, in contrast, begin a lesson with a real-world problem, which they often ask students to solve, and in doing so, construct for themselves the mathematical rule. They describe, as an example, a lesson in which a teacher began by asking students how many liters of colored water were contained in a large beaker shown to the class. Students then generated the concept of fractions by pouring the water into smaller beakers. The lesson ended with a discussion of rules for writing fractions to represent the parts of a whole. Stigler and Stevenson claim that most mathematics instruction in Asian classrooms begins with meaningful, real-world problems which engage the interest of students.

Academic instruction and assignments can also be adapted to students' *own* interests. This is demonstrated in a study by Anderson, Shirey, Wilson, and Fielding (1987). These researchers found that student interest in reading materials was as important a determinant of their learning and recall of sentences as were reading comprehension scores and 30 times more important than the readability index (the difficulty level of the words). Similarly, Asher and his colleagues (Asher, 1981; Asher, Hymel, and Wigfield, 1978) reported that the interest value of materials they asked subjects to read was an important predictor of their memory for the subject matter. (Garner, Alexander, Gillingham, Kulikowich, and Brown, 1991; Garner, Gillingham, and White, 1989; Shirey and Reynolds, 1988.) Further evidence for the value of personally meaningful tasks comes from Meece's (1991) observation that adapting instruction to the personal interests of students was a distinguishing feature of the classroom in which students reported a high level of motivation to increase their knowledge of science.

Many reading, writing and other tasks can be adapted to students' interests by allowing them some choice in topics. For a social studies unit on Native Americans, for example, some students may prefer to do research and write on agriculture or food, others on dress, and others on religion and ceremonies. Similarly, during silent reading periods a wide range of books can be offered for silent reading periods so that all students may read a book on a topic that interests them.

Students' own interests can be integrated into the instruction in other ways. For instance, when giving examples or applications of concepts being learned, teachers can refer to people (TV characters, rock stars) or events that are likely to catch their students' attention. Abstract concepts or new material can be made meaningful by giving examples or analogies which refer to familiar concepts or events. Brophy (1987a) describes a history lesson on Roman society in which the teacher encouraged students to consider possible parallels between Roman gladiators and modern tolerance for violence in sports.

Whatever the topic, students can be invited to ask questions, express opinions, or respond personally to the content in some other way. Teachers can often take advantage of students' questions and comments to provide additional information or to elaborate on a topic. My daughter's kindergarten teacher was a master at making good use of irrelevant student comments. One day a child announced, in the middle of a lesson on measurement, that he was wearing new shoes. The teacher asked him and other students what size shoe they wore and launched into a lively discussion, with considerable student input, on size as a form of measurement.

Teachers can also design activities to increase the meaningfulness of concepts or information that is distant from students' own experience. Children who are learning about money can play store—taking turns being in the role of the buyer (who has to decide how much to give the seller) and seller (who has to calculate change). To learn about measurement children can measure their fingers, their desks, or the height of a house built with Legos. They can learn about geometry by using the length of one side of the Lego house to predict the other.

Social studies can be made interesting and compelling by role-playing. I once observed third-graders, one by one, stand up on a desk (functioning temporarily as a "soap box") to play the part of abolition-ist Nat Turner speaking out in the town square against slavery. The rest of the class participated in the role of the townspeople, hollering out questions or counter-arguments. Issues related to the Civil War were much more vivid and meaningful to these children than they would have been if the students had read about abolitionists in a text book.

Personal meaningfulness is no less important in the upper grades. Consider, for example, economic principles that might be taught in a high-school course. There are many ways to make economics more meaningful besides having students read texts. Each member of the class might be given $1,000 in play money to buy stocks. Class discus-sions could be devoted to the American economy, balance of trade, world events, and other factors that are influencing students' *own* stock prices. Stocks could also be bought and sold by small groups of stu-dents. This might engender some lively discussion of factors that influ-ence the value of the stocks being proposed.

Considerable enthusiasm can be generated by simply asking stu-dents to express their opinions. I have rarely observed much enthusi-asm for history and politics in classes that were taught in a matter-of-fact and unemotional way, with neither the teacher nor the students expressing opinions. Classes in which students debate controversial subjects openly are much livelier. Rather than avoid controversial issues, teachers in lively, interesting classes typically encouraged stu-dents to express opinions, in order to clarify the issue being discussed and to help students understand its complexity.

Teachers can sometimes increase motivation by linking immediate tasks to students' long-range goals or to another, more appealing activ-ity. For example, building a model city to scale might be linked to mastering certain mathematical principles or measuring skills. For elementary-school-age children these long-range goals need to be in close view. By contrast, many high school students are motivated to engage in activities linked to goals as distant as occupational aspira-tions.

At the very least, students should know why they are doing a par-ticular task and what concepts or skills the assignment is designed to teach. Anderson (1981, 1984) interviewed first-graders about why they were working on assignments. He found that most of the low achievers did not know why or even how to do the assignment; their goal was to finish it, and because the task was too difficult, some simply responded randomly to the problems. High achievers knew how to do the assign-ments, but gave little evidence of understanding the content-related purpose. When asked why they were given a particular assignment to do, they responded with something like, "It's just our work," without reference to the skills being practiced or the content being learned. The children's lack of understanding of the purpose of tasks was not surprising; teachers discussed the purpose or the content being taught for only 1.5 percent of the assignments they gave.

Students are more likely to be motivated to engage in a task if they understand its goals, the skills it will help them develop, and the potential uses of those skills outside of school. A teacher who cannot offer a good explanation for the value of working on a particular task needs to reconsider the value of assigning it.

Presentation of Tasks

What teachers say when they introduce a new task can also affect students' enthusiasm. This was demonstrated in a study by Malone and Lepper (1987) in which children who had a CAI task involving fractions presented to them as a game spent about 50 percent more time working on it than children who had the same task introduced as a drill.

Marshall (1987) describes the "lesson-framing statements" in both a classroom where learning and intrinsic (e.g., enjoyment) reasons for engaging in school tasks were stressed, and a classroom where exogenous reasons (grades, rewards) were stressed. In the learning-oriented classroom, the teacher often commented on the personal relevance of the task and the enjoyment that could be expected, and she often challenged children to think or be creative. In the second classroom nearly all of the teacher's motivational statements referred to accountability, time reminders, rewards, and threats.

Research suggests that the teacher of the learning-oriented classroom was exceptional. Brophy (1983) coded teachers' comments when presenting a new task in six elementary school classrooms, grades four through six. Out of 317 presentations, not one teacher commented that a task would help children develop skills that would bring them pleasure or enjoyment. Only a few (3 percent) expressed personal enthusiasm for the task, or tied the task to the personal lives or interests of the students. Many comments would be expected to undermine students' perceptions of the intrinsic value of working on a task. For example, some teachers indicated that students were not expected to like the task or to do well on it (8 percent), or they reminded students that their work would be checked or that they would be tested on it (6 percent), or that there would be negative consequences for poor performance (4 percent), or that they had a limited amount of time (6 percent).

Brophy, Rohrkemper, Rashid, and Goldberger (1983) assessed the relationship between how teachers introduced tasks in intermediate-grade mathematics classrooms and the level of student engagement.

Most of the teachers' remarks to students concerned procedural demands or evaluation—remarks that would not be expected to foster intrinsic interest. Although negative comments, such as those below [described in Brophy (1987a) p. 204], were less frequent, they were associated with relatively low student engagement on tasks.

"Get your nose in the book, otherwise I'll give out a writing assignment."

"You don't expect me to give you baby work every day, do you?"

"You'll have to work real quietly, otherwise you'll have to do more assignments."

"This test is to see who the really smart ones are."

Contrary to the researchers' predictions, however, students were not observed to be particularly highly engaged on tasks that teachers introduced with positive comments about the interest or practical value of the tasks. Brophy (1987a) suggests that the positive comments they observed did not generate student interest because they were brief, perfunctory, and unconvincing. He gives the following examples (p. 203):

"I think you will like this book. Someone picked it out for me, and it's really good."

"Percent is very important. Banks use it for interest loans, and so on. So it is important that you pay attention."

"You're going to need to know fractions for math next year. You will need fractions in the world to come."

Even more positive remarks than these are not likely to trick students into finding a dull, repetitive task interesting. Also, telling students that an activity is a game does not necessarily arouse interest, especially if the activity is boring or the goal is poorly defined. But if a task is not particularly boring and if it is moderately difficult, the presentation can make some difference in how children perceive it. A teacher who expresses enthusiasm about tasks is undoubtedly more likely to arouse interest than a teacher who stresses the negative aspects of tasks or external reasons for doing them.

In addition to presenting specific tasks in a positive light, teachers can model enthusiasm for learning in general. They can let students know that they value learning for its own sake because it enriches their own lives and helps them understand the world around them.

More Than Fun

It is easy to create activities for students that are fun but do not teach anything and it is easy to create tasks that teach but are boring. Developing tasks that are both fun *and* contribute to knowledge and skills is difficult. I have witnessed many lively events, which although at first glance looked like they would enhance understanding or teach a skill, upon close scrutiny were not likely to teach anything. An example is a fourth-grade classroom in which the teacher had children play a dice game designed to teach the concept of probability. The game involved predicting and recording outcomes of a dice throw. Student enthusiasm for the game was extremely high. Nevertheless, informal interviews with children after the game revealed that they had not extracted any principles related to probability from the activity. This might have been accomplished by some discussion of probability theory before and after the game—to make explicit what the teacher hoped children would induce from their experience. But the game itself was not sufficient, and although children had an extremely good time (which may have benefits in its own right), they did not learn much. Another common example is dramatization designed to increase understanding of historical events. In class plays that I have observed, more attention is given to costume and set than to the political or social understandings that the teacher desires to foster. Again, there are surely benefits (e.g., developing artistic talents, developing skills in cooperation) that are derived from costume and set design. But more efficient productions and simulations might result in a better understanding of social history.

The form provided in Appendix 6–A can be used to help teachers assess the intrinsic motivational value of tasks. Teachers also need to ask themselves what children are likely to learn, whether achievement gains are worth the amount of time and energy that the activity requires, and if not, what can be done to enhance its learning value. Teachers can often increase the learning value of an activity through discussion, both before and afterwards, encouraging children to make explicit the principles or understanding that the teacher wants them to derive.

EVALUATION

When given a choice, preschool-age children, and older children and adults in informal learning contexts, usually select moderately difficult tasks that provide opportunities for increasing mastery and feelings of competence. Research suggests, however, that in school students tend not to select challenging tasks because they are concerned about external evaluation. Harter (1978b), for example, asked elementary school children to solve anagrams at four difficulty levels. Half of the subjects were instructed that the task was a game and half were instructed that it was a school-type task for which they would receive letter grades. Under the game condition, children chose and verbalized their preference for optimally challenging problems. Those children working for grades chose significantly easier anagrams to perform, expressed less pleasure (smiling) when they solved a problem, and verbalized more anxiety. In a follow-up study [described in Harter (in press)], children who were told that they would be graded on their performance chose to do anagrams with one fewer letter than the anagrams they were previously able to solve in a nongraded practice session. Thus, under graded conditions children chose to do tasks that they were certain they could do, even though these tasks were not challenging and therefore would not be intrinsically motivating.

Hughes et al. (1985) report that children who were told that their performance on a difficult task was confidential were more likely to return to the task voluntarily than children who were told that their performance would be evaluated by their teacher. Teacher evaluation did not undermine interest in an easy task. The combination of being given a difficult task and being told that the teacher would evaluate performance had the most negative effects on intrinsic interest.

Task difficulty was also a relevant factor in a study by Maehr and Stallings (1972). They told eighth-grade boys either that the results of a task they were given would be reported to the teacher, or that the task was "just for fun." Students who believed their score would be reported were more likely to be interested in doing another task if the first task had been easy than if the first task had been challenging. Students who were told that the task was for fun were more likely to want to do another task if the first task had been challenging. Similar findings were reported in a study of Iranian fifth-graders (Salili, Maehr, Sorenson, and Fyans, 1976).

Any reward made contingent on success may inhibit students from selecting challenging tasks. Pearlman (1984) found that when a reward (+3 points on the next test) or penalty (-3 points on the next test) was made contingent on whether students' solutions to a problem were correct or incorrect, they selected easier problems than when no reward or penalty was at stake. Other studies provide further evidence that individuals select easier tasks under externally rewarded rather than under unrewarded conditions (Boggiano, Pittman, and Ruble, 1982; Pittman, Emery, and Boggiano, 1982; Shapira, 1976). In the Pittman et al. (1982) study, the preference for a simple version of a task carried over even to a situation in which the original reward contingencies were no longer in effect.

Ames and Ames (1990) provide examples from real classrooms that illustrate the effect evaluation or rewards have on students' motivation.

One teacher they worked with was puzzled that no child ever tried to spell any of the challenge words that she added to the weekly spelling test. Students explained to the researchers that they did not try them because if they got any words wrong they would not have their "football" placed on a public chart with a goalpost. The teacher had inadvertently designed a reward system that served as a disincentive for seeking challenge. In another classroom the researchers observed, children received a certificate for a special treat at a local restaurant for writing four book reports in a month; because quantity rather than quality was rewarded, they chose short, easy, and often uninteresting books rather than longer or more challenging ones.

The studies and observations described above support Doyle's (1983) claim that students look upon most work in classrooms as "an exchange of performance for grades" (p. 181), and they demonstrate that external evaluation can seriously dampen a student's desire to take on challenging tasks. Students select easy tasks to maximize the probability of a positive evaluation, and they focus their attention on performing—sometimes even if it means cheating—rather than learning. As a consequence, students learn less and deny themselves the positive feelings and self-confidence that result from mastery on challenging tasks.

Concern about evaluation explains, at least in part, why Safe Sally refuses to take challenging courses and why the adolescents referred to at the beginning of this chapter put so much energy into developing computer programs and so little energy into their algebra homework. Solving a difficult algebra problem can give an individual a tremendous feeling of competence and satisfaction. But the anxiety created by the external evaluation may inhibit intrinsic interest in the task. If the teacher had begun evaluating these adolescents' computer programs, they might have lost interest in this activity also. I suspect that if teachers began evaluating students' memory of the television programs they watched the previous evening, television viewing would lose some of its intrinsic appeal.

Some motivation theorists have proposed that teachers do away with grades altogether and give students only substantive, corrective feedback. Thus, teachers indicate which arithmetic problems were not correctly solved and give substantive information regarding the strengths and weaknesses of the essays. The goal is to focus students' attention on ways to develop mastery rather than on grades.

At least two studies have compared the effects of substantive evaluation to grades. Butler and Nisan (1986) either made substantive positive and negative comments on sixth-grade students' papers with no grade or they gave numerical (normatively distributed) grades with no comments. Students who received comments claimed to find the tasks more interesting. They were also more likely to attribute their effort on the task to their interest, and their success to their interest and effort, than children who received grades. The students who had received comments also performed better on a task requiring creativity. In a later study by Butler (1988), students who received written comments with substantive suggestions for improvement maintained high interest in a task, whereas grades, with and without comments, undermined both interest and performance.

Most schools require grades, and the best teachers can do is to try to minimize the negative effects of grades on students' motivation. Research provides some clues about how this can be accomplished. A study by Harackiewicz, Abrahams, and Wageman (1987), for example, suggests that whether external evaluation has a positive or negative effect on intrinsic motivation depends partly on the criteria used. In their study, evaluation reduced intrinsic interest in a task when competence assessments were based on social norms; however, when competence assessments were based on achieving a predetermined score, evaluation *increased* interest.

There are other ways to minimize negative effects of external evaluation. For example, students do not need to be reminded repeatedly that they will be graded on their work, or that they will be punished with a bad grade if they don't follow the teacher's instructions. Involving students in discussions about grading criteria also fosters better understanding and acceptance of the criteria. And when students express concern about their grades, teachers can encourage them to focus their attention on mastering the skills that are being taught. Also, to a considerable degree, the effect of evaluation on intrinsic motivation is mediated by its effect on students' perceptions of their competence and their ability to attain positive evaluations. Consequently, any strategy that maintains feelings of competence (see Chapter 10) will also support intrinsic motivation.

HELP

Students should be given assistance when they need it, but unnecessary help can prevent children from taking credit for completing a task. Children who are given a great amount of help will not attribute outcomes to their own efforts and competencies. Consequently, they will not experience the feelings of pride or competence that accompany successful mastery efforts and will not be motivated to pursue future tasks on their own.

The negative effect of "overhelp" on intrinsic motivation has been demonstrated in studies of young children. Farnham-Diggory and Ramsey (1971) examined the effect of help on children's play. They found that five-year-old children who the experimenter had often interrupted to offer help in a play session persisted half as long at a subsequent achievement task as children who had played for the same amount of time, even though this second group had been given defective toys to play with in the play session. The interrupted children also persisted less than children who had been socially reinforced but had not been assisted in their play. Fagot (1973) and Hamilton and Gordon (1978) provide further evidence suggesting that preschool children in classrooms in which teachers are directive and intrusive display relatively low task persistence.

Handicapped children who are mainstreamed into regular classrooms, and other children perceived by teachers to be at academic risk, may be particularly vulnerable to overhelp. Handicapped children need extra assistance and should receive it, but teachers often overcompensate for the child's handicap; they offer more assistance than is needed. In one of my studies we observed teachers interacting with handicapped and nonhandicapped children in two preschools (Stipek and Sanborn, 1985). Teachers offered assistance (without being requested) to the handicapped children about 2 1/2 times more often than to nonhandicapped children. To some degree the extra help was needed, but we were not convinced that it was all necessary.

The urge to help a handicapped child (or any child who is perceived to be disadvantaged in a learning context) is very strong. I experienced this while I was doing observations for the study described above. For example, I observed a child with cerebral palsy wrapping a gift for her mother. In about ten minutes of hard work she had made no progress toward wrapping the paper around the gift and she had covered herself with tape. She was having so much difficulty that I had to sit on my hands to keep from offering help. She persisted, and eventually secured the paper, albeit inelegantly. She beamed with pride and I breathed a sigh of relief that I had not helped. If I had, I would have denied her a personal success experience.

The point is not that children should not be helped, but rather that help needs to be given in a way that enables students to complete tasks on their own. A "poor" product completed on one's own may contribute more to self-confidence and intrinsic motivation to attempt similar tasks in the future than a "good" product for which the student cannot take responsibility. Thus, to increase the self-confidence and motivation of students like Hopeless Hannah, teachers need to encourage independent problem solving as much as possible.

EXTRINSIC REWARDS

Most of the research reviewed in previous chapters focuses on the dangers of extrinsic rewards. Nevertheless, rewards are appropriate, effective, and without known negative effects in many situations. Consider, for example, tasks that are not in the least bit intrinsically interesting. Taking out the garbage and ironing immediately come to my mind. Although one hopes that most school tasks are more interesting than taking out the garbage, rewards are necessary to produce learning on school activities that are not inherently interesting to students, and can be given in ways that do not have detrimental effects on intrinsic motivation.

Studies demonstrating that rewards undermine intrinsic interest have involved tasks that appealed to the subjects. Consequently, the reward was superfluous. In real classrooms rewards are often necessary to prod students into engaging in tasks in which they have little initial interest. Some students may not have been socialized to value a particular skill, may find a particular task itself uninteresting, or may not at first believe that they will be able to master it.

When rewards are used as a means of getting students started on a task, an attempt should be made to shift their attention to the intrinsic value of the task as soon as possible. This, of course, can only work if the task *is* interesting and if students experience success and a feeling of competence soon after attempting the task. If these conditions are met, the teacher may be able to maintain students' interest in completing tasks without continuing to offer external rewards. Thus, just as students can turn their attention to extrinsic reasons for engaging in activities that they were previously intrinsically motivated to do, so they can shift their attention from extrinsic to intrinsic reasons for engaging in an activity. I have observed teachers assign tasks (e.g., difficult math puzzles) which students, at first, did only reluctantly and to avoid punishment (a failing grade), but subsequently were just as reluctant to put aside.

There are also ways to give rewards that will minimize their negative effects. In general, research has found that rewards have the strongest undermining effect when they are expected, salient, and contingent on *engaging* in the task rather than on meeting a performance standard (Deci and Ryan, 1987). Thus, a surprise popcorn party on a Friday afternoon can serve as an enjoyable event that may make school more fun without causing children to focus on external reasons for doing schoolwork. A popcorn party promised as a reward for completing assignments will cause a shift in children's perceptions of the reason for doing schoolwork.

Rewards that are contingent on a particular level of *performance* (as opposed to simply doing the task) have different effects, depending on whether or not they are perceived as controlling (and thus become the reason for engaging in the task). Research identifying the conditions that foster an external locus of causality, described in Chapter 5, has clear practical implications for what not to do. For example, emphasizing that the reward is contingent on students' doing what the *teacher* wants them to do focuses students' attention on the controlling aspect of the reward. Apparently, this happens in very subtle ways, such as by using the word "should." Competition, close monitoring of student performance, emphasis on deadlines, and threats of punishment also make students feel controlled rather than self-determining. Clearly, deadlines need to be given and enforced, and teachers need to monitor students closely to be able to provide assistance when necessary. The point is not that these practices should be eliminated, but that they should be applied no more than necessary.

Even when the informational aspect of rewards is emphasized, teachers have to deal with the problem of negative information. Only positive information about competency sustains or enhances intrinsic motivation; negative information results in decreased motivation.

This creates something of a dilemma. Both challenge and competence feedback (success) support intrinsic interest. But if students are given challenging tasks, they will sometimes fail. The teacher walks a tightrope between boring students with tasks that are too easy and dampening their enthusiasm with tasks that are too hard.

This dilemma is real, but accommodations can be made. When I give my daughter arithmetic problems, I intersperse problems that she is likely to get wrong with problems that I know she can do. I have learned that she needs a success rate of about four to one to sustain her interest. When we read together, I volunteer words she is likely to have difficulty with if she hasn't had several successes in a row. Teachers need to be mindful of the negative effect of failure and *incompetence* feedback, and arrange lessons and assignments so that students experience occasional difficulty (to make the work challenging) but also considerable success (to give feelings of developing competence).

To summarize, rewards should be used only for tasks that have limited intrinsic appeal. If they are made contingent on tasks that students may have done anyway, rewards can undermine the original intrinsic interest so that students will no longer do the task without being rewarded. When rewards are offered, they should be contingent on a level of mastery, so they serve an informational function. The level of mastery on which the reward is contingent should be achievable by all students, and teachers should offer rewards in ways that call attention to the knowledge and skills they reflect. An "A" can be given to provide students with feedback about their skill attainment, but it should not be viewed as something that is valuable in itself. The teacher is better advised to say to a child, "You have had 'As' on your last three arithmetic papers; You have really mastered these concepts," than, "Congratulations, you received the only 'A' in the class." The salience of rewards can also be minimized by incorporating them into the activity itself or by having students reward themselves. Finally, when extrinsic rewards are used initially to prod students into engaging in a task, every effort should be made to shift students' attention away from the extrinsic reward and toward the importance of the task and the feelings of competence that derive from mastery.

Threats and punishment should be avoided because these are typically experienced as very controlling and do not foster feelings of autonomy or personal responsibility. Instead, they generate fear and resentment, which undermine intrinsic interest in learning perhaps more than any other teacher behavior.

AUTONOMY

Corno and colleagues (1989; Corno and Rohrkemper, 1985) point out how important it is for children to become "self-regulating"—to make active attempts to use internal resources to solve problems and engage in deliberate planning and monitoring. Students who are always told what to do, and how and when to do it, do not develop a sense of personal responsibility and strategies for regulating their own behavior. Some autonomy is also an essential ingredient of intrinsic motivation.

The benefits of giving children some, but not too much, discretion in their activities is illustrated in a classic study by Lewin, Lippitt, and White (1939). In an examination of the effect of adult control on children's productivity they compared three organizational climates on the behavior of ten-year-old boys who were members of after-school "hobby clubs." In the three different conditions, the adult either controlled virtually every activity (*autocratic* condition), let the children do as they pleased (*laissez-faire* condition), or took an active role in the group's activities, but encouraged the children to participate in decision making (*democratic* condition). The authoritarian and democratic groups were equally productive, and more productive than the laissez-faire group, when an adult was present. The difference between the two productive groups became apparent when the adult leader left the room. Children in the democratic group were little affected by the absence of the leader. They worked at the same level whether or not an adult was present. In contrast, productivity decreased markedly when the adult was absent from the autocratic group.

Classroom studies have demonstrated the negative effect of teacher control on students' motivation to engage in school tasks. In one study Deci, Nezlek, and Sheinman (1981) asked fourth- through sixth-grade teachers to rate the appropriateness of controlling versus autonomous responses to vignettes of typical problems that arise in school—for example, students not completing their assignments. Students in classrooms in which teachers selected more controlling responses to the vignettes scored lower on Harter's (1981) intrinsic motivation scale by the end of the first six weeks of school (Deci, Schwartz, Sheinman, and Ryan, 1981).

In another study, Matheny and Edwards (1974) assessed the effects of increasing student choice and responsibility for learning in 25 elementary classrooms, grades one through seven. Teachers were trained to (1) give students some flexibility and responsibility for determining when they completed assignments; (2) allow students to score most of their own written work and to use individual conferences to evaluate student progress; (3) contract with students for long-range assignments; and (4) set up independent learning centers. Children's perceptions of their control over academic outcomes increased most in classes in which the above strategies were implemented, and teachers who were most successful in implementing these strategies had the highest number of students who gained at least a month in reading achievement for every month in school.

Student autonomy was another important feature of the motivating science class, referred to earlier, that Meece et al. (1989) observed. In small-group activities, for example, students had some choice in their work partners, the materials they used, and how to complete the activity. Moreover, feedback was inherent in many of the small group tasks, minimizing students' dependence on the teacher. In the science classroom in which students expressed less interest in learning science, the teacher determined the groups and specified all aspects of the materials and procedures.

A modest amount of choice has been shown to enhance intrinsic motivation. Zuckerman, Porac, Lathin, Smith, and Deci (1978) simply gave some of the subjects in their study an opportunity to select which three of six puzzles they worked on during an experiment. Subjects who were given a choice were more intrinsically motivated to engage in puzzle solving subsequent to the 30-minute experimental period than subjects who had worked on the same sets of puzzles but without any choice. In a similar experimental study Swann and Pittman (1977) told some children that they could choose one of three puzzles spread out before them. The experimenters actually controlled which puzzle children worked on by saying, before children had a chance to choose, that as long as they were sitting in front of Activity B, why didn't they begin with it. Even this illusion of choice resulted in greater intrinsic motivation than was shown by subjects who were not told they could choose.

The benefits of greater student autonomy have also been demonstrated at the high-school level. In one study high-school science students who were encouraged to organize their own experiments showed more care and involvement in laboratory work than those who were given detailed instructions and directions (Rainey, 1965). Pascarella, Walberg, Junker, and Haertel (1981) report that in classrooms where students had relatively greater control over learning, the students were more interested in science.

Ryan and Grolnick (1986) point out that students' perceptions of autonomy can vary even within a classroom. They found that in the same classroom, upper-elementary-school-aged students varied considerably in the degree to which they thought their classroom environment was one where they could be "origins" (responsible, instrumental, and having an internal locus of causality), versus "pawns" (reactive, with little sense of personal causation). They found, furthermore, that this variation in children's perceptions of control was significantly associated with their perceptions of competence and global self-worth.

In summary, a highly permissive classroom in which children are often not engaged in any kind of learning activity is clearly not desirable. [Recall that the children in the laissez-faire condition of the Lewin et al. (1939) study were unproductive, even with an adult present]. But there are many ways to provide some student choice without creating chaos in a classroom. And if students are not overly concerned about negative consequences of poor performance, the evidence suggests that they will choose challenging tasks that will promote learning. We turn now to practical suggestions for increasing student autonomy.

Approaches to Fostering Autonomy and Perceptions of Control

First, students can *participate in the design of their academic tasks.* For example, rather than the teacher drawing up a list of vocabulary words to accompany a book they are reading, students can be asked to generate their own list. The two lists are likely to be very similar, but students will feel more responsibility for the latter. In one class I visited, each student contributed a word to a class list and became the "expert" for that word. Other students consulted the expert in addition to the dictionary to master the words. This had the additional advantage of giving relatively low-achieving students an opportunity to be consulted by their peers for their expert knowledge.

Second, choice can also be given in *how tasks are completed.* After reading a story students might choose from among several assignments—to write a summary of the story, to write a sequel to the story, or to write about a similar experience of their own. The teacher's goal—for the student to practice writing—is accomplished regardless of the student's choice, but by being given some freedom, the student feels more responsibility and control.

Students can also be given a choice in the *difficulty level of assignments* or tasks that they work on. This kind of choice has to be implemented cautiously because, as mentioned above, students often select school tasks that assure a positive evaluation rather than tasks that challenge their current skill level.

DeCharms (1976) describes a spelling activity with a built-in incentive for selecting the appropriate difficulty level. The teacher uses a spelling book that presents twenty new words each week to the children. On Monday, children take a pretest on the words. Tuesday and Wednesday are devoted to practice. On Thursday children play a spelling game that involves teams, as in a spelling bee. Each child is asked whether he or she wants to try an easy word (worth 1 point for the team), a moderately hard word (worth 2 points), or a hard word (worth 3 points). The difficulty level of the words is individualized as a function of each student's performance on the pretest. An easy word is a word the student previously spelled correctly, a moderately hard word was spelled incorrectly, but the student had two days to study it. A hard word is from a new list tailored to the student's ability. When deCharms tested this game, he found that the number of moderately hard words children chose increased over a five-week period, indicating that students learned to set realistic but challenging goals for themselves. This technique could be adapted to many different kinds of tasks.

Third, students can be given some discretion about *when they complete particular tasks.* Some people like to get the most difficult or least appealing tasks out of the way first. Others prefer to do a few easier or more pleasant tasks to give them a feeling of accomplishment before they tackle the hard ones. Giving students the opportunity to order assignments according to their own preferences will give them a greater feeling of control and responsibility.

A fourth approach to fostering autonomy is to allow students *to correct some of their own assignments.* Students might check their solutions to math problems and their spelling words with an answer sheet.

Ultimately, their mastery would have to be checked by the teacher. But on a day-to-day basis, they could learn to evaluate some of their own work.

Personal goal setting, as described in Chapter 4, has also been used to enhance feelings of autonomy and to teach students self-management skills. Goals should be near (proximal), specific, and challenging. Students can, for example, set such goals as the number of spelling words they will get right on the next spelling test, or the number of arithmetic problems they will solve each day, and record whether or not they meet their goal.

Feelings of autonomy can also be fostered by *involving students in the development of classroom rules*. In one third-grade classroom I observed, the teacher called a "meeting" at the beginning of the year. The students proposed classroom rules, discussed them, and voted upon them. The teacher then appointed a committee of children to write the rules on a large sheet of cardboard that was displayed on the wall to remind students of the rules they had created. The students' rules were more stringent than the teacher would have imposed himself, but since the students developed the rules, they felt that they controlled their own behavior, rather than that they were being controlled by the teacher.

Variations on these approaches to developing student responsibility and autonomy have been combined in two comprehensive programs that have been tested in many classrooms. These programs are described in some detail because the authors have developed materials to assist teachers in implementing the program on their own.

DeCharms' Personal Causation Approach

DeCharms (1976, 1983, 1984) was the first to distinguish between pawns and origins, referred to above, claiming that learning situations that allow students to feel more like origins than pawns—that foster feelings of personal causation—are more intrinsically motivating and result in greater learning than situations in which students feel like pawns. This is not to say that students should be allowed to do what they please. DeCharms does not advocate laissez-faire or permissive teaching. He does, however, advocate learning situations in which students have some amount of choice and control over their learning and in which students are encouraged to believe they are engaging in activities by their own volition.

DeCharms (1976) developed a program to foster feelings of personal causation in both teachers and students. He argues that if teachers feel like pawns, their students cannot feel like origins. When he implemented his program, teachers of sixth- and seventh-grade students attended a week-long personal-causation training course and met regularly during the year that they were teaching the experimental children. The purpose of the training was to develop origins in the teachers, and to teach them classroom exercises that foster origin-like feelings in their students.

DeCharms encourages teachers to give children more responsibility over their school program, and to give them opportunities to set their own goals and make decisions about how to reach those goals. Children are given some choice in the tasks they do and when they do them. And they are encouraged to take personal responsibility, both for failing to meet goals and for meeting them.

DeCharms (1976, 1984) found in the schools serving primarily poor, black children, in which he tested the program, that students who had been in the nine experimental "origins" classrooms in the sixth- and seventh-grade made greater achievement gains than students in the control group classrooms. The advantage of the origin group persisted through the eighth grade, even though neither group continued training that year. The origin group also had a higher high-school completion rate than the control group.

The Adaptive-Learning Environment Model

Wang developed another program designed to foster personal responsibility and autonomy in students (Wang, 1976, 1980, 1983)—the Adaptive Learning Environment Model (ALEM). A mastery-based learning program is used in which students proceed at their own pace (see Chapter 10). Children are explicitly taught how to select appropriate "exploratory tasks," such as creative writing, creative arts, perceptual skills, music, and sociodramatic play. Students are also sometimes given a choice in selecting tasks related to basic skills—reading, math, science, and social studies. The nature of the exploratory learning tasks is determined by student interest and teacher expertise and is limited only by material and space constraints. Students are taught how to plan tasks and how to carry them out with minimal supervision. Although students are also given assignments by the teacher, they are free to work on assignments in the order they choose, as long as they complete them by a predetermined time or date.

Studies of the effect of ALEM have shown that elementary-school-age students can manage their own learning, and that task completion rates actually improve when students have more control over tasks (Wang, 1983; Wang and Stiles, 1976).

Student Choice and "Open Classrooms"

The strategies described above may sound reminiscent of the open-classroom movement that swept the educational community in the late 1960s and early 1970s. Many of the principles discussed in this chapter are indeed related to the open-classroom philosophy. But, you may ask, didn't open classrooms fail? Why return to an educational approach that didn't work?

The research on achievement gains in open versus conventional classrooms is actually very mixed. In some studies the open approach resulted in the greatest gains, and in other studies a more traditional, teacher-dominated approach had better results (Horwitz, 1979). The implications of the research are difficult to evaluate because "open" classrooms vary considerably, and they are not always described well in the research literature. Some of the classrooms that resulted in relatively poor learning may have been more "laissez-faire" than "democratic"—to use the language of Lewin (1939).

When motivational variables were measured, open-classrooms have generally had more positive effects than traditional, teacher-dominated classrooms. For example, Horwitz (1979) reports that of 57 studies reviewed, 23 found that open-classroom children held more positive attitudes toward school, whereas only two of the studies favored traditional classrooms. Twelve of 33 studies showed greater creativity in open-classrooms than in traditional classrooms; no study showed greater creativity in traditional classrooms. Eighteen of 23 studies reported that children were more independent in open-classrooms; only one favored traditional classrooms. These studies, therefore, provide additional support for allowing greater choice and autonomy for students.

Although it may be obvious, there is one caveat that merits discussion. An educational environment that is good for one child is not necessarily good for another (Hunt, 1975). Many children will not select appropriate, challenging tasks when given a choice. Fyans and Maehr (1979), for example, found that children who lacked self-confidence avoided challenging tasks. Recall also Harter's (1978, in press) findings—when being graded, many children selected tasks that they knew they could complete easily. The need to consider carefully the nature of the choices and the context in which they are offered is evident when our hypothetical children are considered. If the options are not personally interesting, Satisfied Sam will choose the task that can be completed with the least amount of effort. Defensive Dick and Helpless Hannah can be expected to choose only tasks on which success is assured. Thus, student choice cannot be provided indiscriminately.

Student and teacher characteristics and other factors, such as the kind of external evaluation given, must be considered in a decision about the best way to foster autonomy and responsibility.

THE SOCIAL CONTEXT

Deci et al. (in press) argue that a feeling of security and satisfying connections with others are innate human needs, and that social contexts which support these feelings contribute to positive motivation. Wlodkowski (1986) claims, similarly, that children need love and a feeling of belonging, and that these needs will interfere with learning if they are not met.

Teachers cannot ignore these basic needs and expect children to perform well on academic tasks. No child will enjoy learning or take risks in a context in which children are commonly criticized for their mistakes, ridiculed, or embarrassed. A teacher who is patient, encouraging, and makes students feel comfortable and secure is more likely to foster intrinsic motivation and enjoyment.

Rogers (1951) urges parents to provide their children with "unconditional positive regard"—to convey to children that they are accepted unconditionally, rather than conditionally on some behavior or performance. This dictum may apply to teachers as well. Students who believe their value in the teacher's eyes depends on their success on academic tasks feel anxious about performance because they risk rejection and humiliation. Students who believe that the teacher respects and supports them, regardless of their performance, take risks and enjoy school tasks more.

Relationships among children also affect students' enjoyment and ability to concentrate on academic tasks. School is a complex social environment in which social rejection is commonplace; teachers need to be aware of students' feelings and address these along with their students' academic competencies.

My daughter's kindergarten teacher understood the importance of students' peer relationships. She was an astute observer of the friendship networks and conflicts that developed among her students, and she organized instruction and activities to support these positive relationships and to minimize tension among children. When my daughter and two other girls developed a problematic triangle (two girls rejected the third), she engaged the entire class in a discussion about problems resulting from friendship triangles, feelings about them, and possible solutions. Thus, the teacher addressed the problem directly and sensitively, without referring to the particular children involved in the conflict. She showed respect and understanding for students' feelings. As a consequence, she contributed to a supportive classroom climate that fostered feelings of security. Teachers can create a supportive climate by treating children with respect and compassion, by using humor, by sharing their own feelings and values and encouraging children to do the same, by making sure that every student has an opportunity to participate actively in classroom activities, and by expressing acceptance and support when students disclose their ideas and feelings.

Researchers have given little attention to the effect of a supportive social context on motivation. An exception is a longitudinal study conducted by Midgley, Feldlaufer, and Eccles (1989b). Students who moved from elementary school teachers who they perceived to be low in support to junior high teachers who they perceived to be high in support, developed a more positive attitude toward math; in contrast, students who moved from high-support to low-support teachers manifested a sharp decline in perceptions of the intrinsic value, perceived usefulness, and importance of math. This study supports common sense—students who are comfortable and secure in school will enjoy learning more. A supportive environment is not a frill. It is an essential ingredient of a learning context in which students are willing to take risks, and thus to learn as much as they can.

SUMMARY

Students are more intrinsically motivated to complete tasks that are moderately challenging, novel, and relevant to their own lives than they are to complete tasks that are too hard or too easy, repetitive, or perceived to be irrelevant. Students are intrinsically motivated to work when they feel self-determining rather than controlled, when the threat of negative external evaluation is not salient, when their attention is not focused on extrinsic reasons for completing tasks, and when they are working in a positive social context that fosters a feeling of security and self-worth. They will also feel more competent and proud, and thus more intrinsically interested in tasks, if they can take responsibility for their success.

Extrinsic rewards are unavoidable. If used sparingly and carefully, the promise of rewards can induce children to engage in learning activities that they may not otherwise attempt. Implementing the suggestions for effective use of extrinsic reinforcement and other methods for enhancing intrinsic motivation described in this chapter should, however, reduce the need for extrinsic rewards.

Allowing some student choice is essential for intrinsic interest in school tasks, and has the added advantage of teaching self-management skills that are needed for success in higher grades and in the workplace. It is impossible for children to develop a sense of personal responsibility and the ability to regulate their own learning behavior if they are always told what to do, and how, and when to do it.

Giving up some control is difficult for most teachers. They are under considerable pressure to teach specific skills, and they are held accountable for their students' performance. The effect of accountability on teachers' behavior was demonstrated in a study by Deci, Spiegel, Ryan, Koestner, and Kauffman (1982). They asked psychology students to train another student in an experiment. Student trainers who were told that they were responsible for how well the other student performed were much more controlling. They talked more, were more critical of the student, gave more commands, and allowed less choice and autonomy than student teachers who were simply instructed to teach the task. See also Flink, Boggiano, and Barret, in press.

Students themselves are another factor that can interfere with teachers' ability to provide an environment that supports autonomy. Students often appear to need extrinsic rewards to engage in tasks, and they sometimes abuse opportunities for control. Studies have also shown that teachers' *beliefs* about students affect the degree to which they grant autonomy, even if their beliefs are not well-founded. For example, in one study subjects who were falsely led to believe that their student was extrinsically motivated were more controlling than subjects who were told that their student was intrinsically motivated (Pelletier and Vallerand, 1989). The more controlling behavior, moreover, resulted in lowered intrinsic motivation to engage in the task.

Teachers who are held accountable for student learning and have students who seem to lack interest in schoolwork may find it especially difficult to encourage autonomy. And recent trends toward an increased emphasis on testing and accountability are very likely to exacerbate teachers' need to control students' behavior. But the research described in this chapter demonstrates that there are important benefits to some student autonomy, and that it is possible to increase student choice without sacrificing student achievement.

7

FROM REINFORCEMENT
TO COGNITION

In contrast to traditional reinforcement theorists, *cognitive motivation theorists* assume that behavior is determined by an individual's *beliefs* and other cognitions, not simply by whether the individual has been rewarded or punished for a behavior in the past. The cognitive theories discussed in this chapter, unlike the social cognitive theory described in Chapter 4, are either concerned exclusively with achievement behavior, or have been applied to achievement behavior more than to other kinds of behavior.

The theories are similar to each other, as well as to social cognitive theory, in their emphasis on beliefs as mediators of behavior. They differ, however, with regard to the particular beliefs they emphasize. Atkinson's expectancy x value theory focuses on students' expectations for success and their achievement-related values; Weiner's attribution theory is concerned with beliefs about the causes of achievement outcomes; and Rotter's social learning theory emphasizes beliefs about the contingency of rewards. The theories also differ in the degree to which they explicitly consider emotions. While they play a major role in Atkinson's theory and in recent formulations of Weiner's, they play no explicit role in Rotter's. Finally, they differ in their relative emphasis on stable dispositions versus variables in the current environment as causes of behavior. Atkinson emphasizes stable individual differences and Weiner emphasizes the immediate context, while Rotter falls somewhere in between.

ATKINSON'S EXPECTANCY X VALUE THEORY

Atkinson's (1964) primary goal was to predict whether an individual would approach or avoid an achievement task. He conceptualized achievement behavior as a conflict between a tendency to approach tasks and a tendency to avoid tasks. These two opposing tendencies are strengthened or weakened by stable individual differences in values and by expectations about the likelihood of accomplishing a particular goal.

Consider first the stable factor affecting the tendency to approach tasks. Atkinson proposes that an unconscious **motive for success** (M_S), or **need to achieve** (Nach), directs individuals toward achievement tasks. M_S represents a relatively stable or enduring disposition to strive for success, conceptualized in the theory as a "capacity to experience pride in accomplishment" (Atkinson, 1964, p. 214).

The motive for success is usually measured by the Thematic Apperception Test (TAT), a projective test in which individuals are shown ambiguous pictures and asked to describe what is happening. It is assumed that subjects "project" their own achievement values into their interpretations of the pictures. Their responses are scored according to the amount of achievement-striving content in their descriptions (i.e., references to accomplishments, achievement concerns, goals, expressions of achievement-related affect). The use of a projective test reflects a Freudian view that motivation is unconscious and expressed in fantasy (McClelland, 1961).

The **motive to avoid failure** (M_{AF}), conceived of as a capacity to experience shame given failure, is the unconscious, stable factor that directs individuals *away* from achievement tasks. M_{AF} is generally operationalized (measured) as anxiety aroused in testing situations.

Any achievement-related activity is assumed to elicit both positive (hope for success) and negative (fear of failure) affective anticipations. What determines an individual's behavior is the *relative* strength of these two emotional experiences.

According to Atkinson's theory, individual differences in both of the stable motives can be traced to parents' child-rearing behaviors. Children whose parents encourage their achievement efforts and provide opportunities for them to demonstrate competence are relatively high in the motive to achieve success. In contrast, children whose parents punish their achievement efforts develop a strong motive to avoid failure. Thus, emotional associations to achievement situations (e.g., anticipating pride in accomplishment and shame in failure) are assumed to be formed in early childhood and evoked later in achievement contexts.

These proposals have not held up well in empirical tests. Although some studies indicate that early independence training (Winterbottom, 1958) and high expectations (Rosen and D'Andrade, 1959) foster a strong achievement motive in children, taken together, findings have been inconsistent. [See V. J. Crandall (1963); V. C. Crandall (1967); Trudewind (1982) for reviews].

Although Atkinson assumes the motives to strive for success and to avoid failure are unconscious, he also believes that individuals' behavior in achievement situations is influenced by their *conscious* beliefs about that particular situation. These situational variables, like the unconscious motives discussed above, direct individuals toward or away from achievement tasks.

Two variables are believed to direct individuals *toward* achievement tasks—the **perceived probability of success** (P_s) and the expectations to feel proud, or, to use Atkinson's language, the **incentive value of success** (I_s). According to the theory, individuals who expect to succeed (believe that the probability of success is high) on a particular task are more likely to approach the task than individuals who are less certain about their chances for success. The amount of pride anticipated (I_s) is proportional to individuals' expectations for success (P_s). Atkinson argues that greater pride is experienced following success at a difficult task (a task with a low probability of success) than following success at a task with a high probability of success. Thus an "A" in a difficult course has a higher incentive value than an "A" in an easy course. Because anticipated pride is determined by the perceived probability of success, these two situation variables in the model are reducible to one.

Two situational variables also inhibit achievement efforts—**perceptions of the probability of failure** (P_f) and the anticipation of shame, which Atkinson refers to as the **incentive value of failure** (I_f). Shame is believed to be greatest following failure on very easy tasks, tasks that have a high probability of success, and least following failure on very difficult tasks. According to the theory, a "C" in physics might be experienced as less humiliating than a "C" in a course that is considered less difficult. Thus, again, because one of these situation variables (I_f) is determined by the other (P_f), they are reducible to one.

In summary, the tendency to approach tasks is determined by an unconscious stable factor (motive for success, or need for achievement) and two conscious situational factors (expectations for success and anticipated pride). The tendency to avoid tasks is determined by an unconscious stable factor (fear of failure) and two conscious situational factors (expectations for failure and anticipated shame). These two motivational tendencies—to approach tasks and to avoid tasks—are represented as opposing forces. The **resultant tendency to approach**

or avoid an achievement activity (T$_A$) is a function of the strength of the tendency to approach minus the strength of the tendency to avoid the task. If the tendency to approach is stronger, the individual will approach the task; if the tendency to avoid is stronger, the individual will avoid it. Atkinson combines these factors in a mathematical equation:

$$T_A = T_S - T_{AF}$$

$$T_A = (M_S \times P_S \times I_S) - (M_{AF} \times P_f \times I_f)$$

The evidence on the effectiveness of the mathematical model in predicting behavior in achievement situations is mixed. There is, however, some evidence suggesting that by measuring the components included in the model, and by combining them according to Atkinson's equations, modestly accurate predictions can sometimes be made regarding individuals' engagement in achievement tasks, the difficulty level of the tasks they will choose, their level of aspiration or willingness to take risks, and their persistence in completing a difficult task. [See Weiner (1980a) for a review of this research].

There are many problems with Atkinson's model, which may explain why it has had only modest success in predicting behavior, even in highly controlled laboratory circumstances. The two major variables in the model, the need for achievement and the motive to avoid failure, are difficult to measure. Also, the incentive values of success and failure are fully determined by the probability of success, regardless of the importance of the task. Consequently, if the probability of success on a puzzle and on a National Merit Test is the same, success on these two tasks is assumed to generate the same amount of pride. Intuitively, it seems that a greater amount of pride would be aroused in the latter than in the former situation, but the model does not differentiate tasks as a function of their importance to the performer.

Despite these and many other problems, Atkinson made a major contribution to achievement motivation theory. His inclusion of expectations and emotions as factors that influence achievement behavior paved the way for future cognitive motivational theorists who have built on some of Atkinson's basic notions. By elaborating upon Atkinson's proposals, more recent cognitive theorists have developed models that have greater relevance to classroom practice.

ROTTER'S SOCIAL LEARNING THEORY

Like Atkinson and the social cognitive learning theorists discussed in Chapter 4, and in contrast to strict reinforcement theorists, Rotter (1966, 1975) believes that thoughts mediate achievement behavior. Recall that reinforcement theorists believe the frequency of a behavior (e.g., paying attention to the teacher, approaching tasks, completing tasks) depends on whether the behavior has been rewarded in the past. Rotter proposed that it is not the reward itself that increases the frequency of a behavior, but an individual's *beliefs* about what brought about the reward. If individuals do not believe that a reward they received was caused by something that they did, they will not expect similar behavior to be followed by a reward in the future. Consequently, the reward will not influence future behavior.

Consider, for example, good grades, which have reinforcement value for most students (Satisfied Sam being the uncommon exception). According to strict reinforcement theory, any behavior (whether it be studying or carrying a rabbit's foot) that preceded a good grade should increase in frequency. Rotter's more cognitive theory would predict increased studying or rabbit foot carrying only under some conditions. For example, a student who usually receives a low grade when she does not study and high grades when she does study is likely to believe that high grades are contingent upon studying. As a consequence of this *belief* (that rewards follow studying), she may study more often in the future. If, however, grades are not consistently associated with studying, the student will not believe that the "A" is the result of studying, and therefore may not study any more after receiving a good grade than after receiving a bad grade. Similarly, if a student knows that everyone in the class received an "A" on a test, he may believe that the teacher gives "As" indiscriminately—regardless of the quality of the product or the amount of effort exerted. He may not study very hard for similar tests in the future because he does not believe that "As" are contingent on his behavior.

Rotter, like Atkinson, assumes that expectancies (both generalized and specific) of reinforcements and the value of reinforcements determine behavior. He conceptualized value, however, more broadly than Atkinson; reinforcement value is linked not just to the probability of success, but also to a person's needs and to associations with other reinforcements. Thus, an "A" in chemistry may have particularly high value for a college student hoping to become a doctor because she has strong needs for recognition and also because the good grade is perceived to be associated with another reinforcement—being accepted to medical school. This student's effort in her chemistry class, therefore, is determined by her expectation that hard work results in valued reinforcement.

Expectancies are based on *subjective* perceptions of the probability that a behavior will be reinforced. Thus a rumor that a teacher is biased against girls or never gives "As," or is unpredictable in her grading can affect students' expectancies, and thus their behavior, even if the rumor is pure invention.

Expectancies in a particular situation are determined not only by beliefs about reinforcement in that situation but also by *generalized* expectancies based on experiences in other, similar situations. Rotter refers to individuals' generalized beliefs regarding the contingency of reinforcement as **locus of control (LOC)**. *Internal locus of control* refers to the belief that events or outcomes are contingent on one's own behavior or on a relatively permanent personal characteristic, such as ability. The belief that events are caused by factors beyond the individual's control (e.g., luck, chance, fate, biased others) has been labeled *external control*. Thus, while Atkinson focused on individuals' *expectations for reward*, Rotter is concerned with their *beliefs* about what causes them to receive or not to receive rewards and the implications that these beliefs have for their expectations.

Some classroom conditions are more likely to result in external LOC than others. For example, students are most likely to develop an external locus of control in situations in which rewards (e.g., grades) are not closely tied to skill mastery. If very lenient or very difficult standards are used, so that different levels of performance result in similar rewards, or if rewards are variably given in conjunction with the same performance (e.g., three errors result in an "A-" one time and a "B" the next), students may perceive rewards to be unrelated to their performance.

Students also bring to each new class their own generalized belief system developed out of past experiences in achievement situations. For example, students who have repeatedly experienced failure regardless of the amount of effort they have exerted often develop the belief that success is not contingent on effort. This generalized belief may override information to the contrary in any specific situation. Thus, students like Hopeless Hannah, who believe that no matter how hard they try they will never get an acceptable grade, are not likely to exert much effort, even in situations in which effort will lead to success.

Once such beliefs are developed they are difficult to change. A few success experiences may not convince a child like Hannah that rewards really are contingent on effort. Firm in her belief that there is nothing that she can do to achieve success, Hannah is likely to interpret any positive outcome as the result of good luck, an easy task, or even the teacher's mistake. She may tenaciously hold to her belief that effort does not lead to success, despite evidence to the contrary. This is why occasional success experiences frequently do not encourage greater effort in students like Hannah.

Rotter's theoretical work has spawned an extensive empirical literature linking students' academic achievement with their locus of control (for reviews, see Lefcourt, 1976; Stipek and Weisz, 1981). Rotter's distinction between the beliefs that rewards are contingent (internal) or not contingent (external) on the subject's characteristics or behavior has important educational implications, but practical classroom application requires certain refinements.

Weisz' Contingency and Competence Model

Recent studies of perceptions of control are based on a more differentiated conceptualization of the locus of control construct in Rotter's theory. Weisz (1986, in press; Weisz and Stipek, 1982) distinguishes between perceptions of *contingency* (beliefs about whether the outcome is causally dependent on variations in the individual's behaviors or characteristics) and perceptions of *competence* (beliefs about one's ability to perform the behavior upon which the desired outcome is contingent). If both of these conditions exist, then control over the outcome is possible. If either condition is absent, then control is not possible.

Skinner, Chapman and Baltes (1988) make a distinction that is similar to Weisz' (see also Chapman, Skinner, and Baltes, 1990; Skinner, 1990). They argue that perceptions of control involve (a) *means-ends beliefs*, the effectiveness of potential means in bringing about positive performance outcomes or avoiding negative ones (e.g., whether high ability causes positive outcomes); and (b) *agency beliefs*, the extent to which a person can access these means (e.g., whether the individual believes he or she has high ability).

Weisz (1986) also points out that, although perceptions of control require both contingency and competence, perceptions of *responsibility* require only contingency. Children sometimes believe that rewards (e.g., grades) are contingent on their behavior (whether they give correct answers), but they also believe that they lack the competence to exhibit the behavior (i.e., giving correct answers) upon which the reward is contingent. Because the competence component is missing, they do not believe they control the outcome. But the perceived lack of competence does not protect them from a feeling of responsibility. Weisz suggests that young children have a tendency to overestimate contingency, a tendency that makes them especially vulnerable to self-blame for events they did not cause (e.g., the death of a loved one, their parents' divorce, a bad grade from an unfair or biased teacher).

Weisz (1986, in press) and his colleagues (Rothbaum et al., 1982; Weisz et al., 1984a, b) make another distinction not made by Rotter—between two processes by which individuals may seek a sense of control. They suggest that individuals can pursue **primary control** (attempt to influence existing realities to bring them into line with personal wishes) or **secondary control** (attempt to accommodate to existing realities in order to effect a more satisfying fit with those realities). The former has implications for actual behavior, the latter for thoughts, such as expectations, goals, and wishes. These theorists suggest that individuals can seek a sense of control through either of these means, and that there may be stable individual differences and possibly cultural differences in the degree to which either approach is used.

The distinction has important classroom implications. Children who do not experience feelings of primary control—who do not believe that anything they do will result in academic success—have the option of secondary control. They can, for example, lower their expectations (I'll be happy as long as I pass), or change their goals (school achievement does not matter; what matters is athletic performance, or popularity). Weisz and his colleagues suggest that this secondary control strategy can provide individuals with an overall feeling of control—if not over objective reality, then at least over their psychological experience. Their analysis is useful for understanding how children like Hopeless Hannah, who experience school failure year after year, and who do not believe that there is anything they can do to bring about success, can tolerate school.

Measuring LOC

According to Rotter, locus of control is a relatively stable trait and can be measured by a questionnaire. He developed the internal-external (I-E) control scale, which, using a forced-choice format, pits an internal belief against an external belief. The items are classified into six subcategories: academic recognition, social recognition, love and affection, dominance, social-political beliefs, and life philosophy (Rotter, 1966). Respondents are asked to select one statement from pairs of statements, such as those below:

1. a. Many of the unhappy things in people's lives are partly due to bad luck. (external response)
   b. People's misfortunes result from the mistakes they make. (internal response)

2. a. The idea that teachers are unfair to students is nonsense. (internal response)
b. Most students don't realize the extent to which grades are influenced by accidental happenings. (external response)

Several scales have been developed to be used with children [see Weisz and Stipek (1982) for a review]. The measure most frequently used to assess children's perceptions of control in achievement situations is the Intellectual Achievement Responsibility (IAR) Scale, developed by Crandall and associates (Crandall, Katkovsky, and Preston, 1965; Crandall, Katkovsky, and Preston, 1962). A few representative items from the IAR are found in Table 7-1. The IAR scale has the advantage of systematically dividing questions between positive and negative outcomes. Children who believe that positive outcomes are contingent on their own behaviors have relatively high internal scores on the success subscale. In contrast, children who believe that negative outcomes are contingent on their own behavior have relatively high scores on the failure subscale.

This distinction made in the IAR between perceptions of control for success and failure is important. Consider Hopeless Hannah, for example; she accepts full responsibility for her failures, believing that they result from her low ability. But she believes that her rare successes are caused by external factors such as luck. Hannah has an internal locus of control with regard to failure and an external locus of control with regard to success. Some students have the opposite pattern of causal beliefs; they accept responsibility for success and assume that some external factor (e.g., a biased or unfair teacher) caused failure.

Connell (1985) has developed a new measure of locus of control which makes even finer distinctions than the IAR. Children respond to questions concerning their perceptions of control with regard to cognitive, social, and physical outcomes. Within each of these domains, subscores provide information on the degree to which children believe they or powerful others (e.g., parents, teachers, popular peers) control outcomes and the degree to which they do not know why certain outcomes occur.

Skinner, Chapman, and Baltes (1988) have developed a measure that reflects their own conceptualization of perceived control. Thus, the measure includes separate subscales for control, agency, and means-ends beliefs regarding school performance. Five types of means to achieve success or avoid failure are included: effort, ability, powerful others, luck, and unknown causes. For each of these five means there are questions pertaining to means-ends beliefs (assumptions about the

---

TABLE 7-1 • Items From the Intellectual Achievement Responsibility Questionnaire[1]

---

1. If a teacher passes you to the next grade, would it probably be

    (a) because she liked you, or
    (b) because of the work you did? *(internal)*

2. When you do well on a test at school, is it more likely to be

    (a) because you studied for it, or *(internal)*
    (b) because the test was especially easy?

3. When you have trouble understanding something in school is it usually

    (a) because the teacher didn't explain it clearly, or
    (b) because you didn't listen carefully? *(internal)*

4. Suppose your parents say you are doing well in school. Is it likely to happen

    (a) because your school work is good, or *(internal)*
    (b) because they are in a good mood?

5. Suppose you don't do as well as usual in a subject in school. Would this probably happen

    (a) because you weren't as careful as usual, or *(internal)*
    (b) because somebody bothered you and kept you from working?

---

1. From Crandall, Katkovsky, and Crandall (1965)

effectiveness of these means in bringing about desirable outcomes) and agency beliefs (perceptions of personal access to the means).

WEINER'S ATTRIBUTION THEORY

In some respects attribution theory is a refinement and elaboration of Rotter's concept of locus of control, yet it also reflects a significant departure from social learning theory. A primary difference is that attribution theorists, unlike social learning theorists, assume that humans are motivated primarily to understand themselves and the world around them—to "... attain a cognitive mastery of the causal structure of [the] environment" (Kelly, 1967, p. 193).

Attribution theorists assume that individuals naturally search for understanding about why events occur, especially when the outcome is important or unexpected. Thus, the student who expects to do well but does poorly on a test will seek information to answer the question: "Why did I fail that test?" Conversely, the student who expected to do poorly but does well might search for an explanation for his or her good performance.

Perceptions of the cause of achievement outcomes are referred to as **causal attributions**. The most common attributions made in achievement situations are *ability* ("I did well because I'm smart"; "I did poorly because I'm dumb"), and *effort* ("I did/did not study"; Weiner, 1986). Other attributions are made—"I was lucky"; "the task was easy"; "the teacher explained things badly"; "my friend or parent helped me prepare"; "I didn't feel well"; "I was tired or hungry," and so on—but these attributions are less common. Some perceived causes are highly idiosyncratic. Indeed, very creative attributions for poor performance are often offered as excuses ("I was distracted by the coughing of the girl in front of me"; "I got hit in the head at football practice and I'm having trouble concentrating").

Weiner (1979, 1985, 1986) claims that the specific causal attributions are less important as determinants of achievement behavior than the underlying dimensions of the attributions. The causal dimensions he describes represent an elaboration and refinement of Rotter's internal-external locus of control dimension. Weiner points out that whether a cause is perceived as "internal" or "external" does not tell the full story, especially if the goal is to predict behavior in achievement situations. He claims, for example, that effort and ability attributions, which are both internal and treated equivalently by Rotter, have different behavioral implications; most individuals see effort as under the control of the individual, whereas most do not see ability as controllable. Ability is also generally perceived as a relatively stable cause, whereas effort can vary from situation to situation. Consequently, Weiner distinguishes between different kinds of internal causes of achievement outcomes with regard to their stability and controllability. The control and stability dimensions that Weiner added to Rotter's original internal-external dimension allow much more specific behavioral predictions from beliefs about the cause of reinforcement (i.e., success).

Thus, Weiner has developed out of Rotter's single internal-external locus of control dimension three separate dimensions: locus, stability, and control. As in Rotter's theory, *locus* refers to the source of the cause, i.e., whether the outcome is contingent on an individual's characteristics or behavior ("internal") or on some "external" variable. The *stability* dimension differentiates causes on the basis of their duration. Ability, for example, is usually considered relatively stable over time, whereas effort, luck, or mood can vary from moment to moment. The *control* dimension concerns the degree of control an individual has over the cause. We control how much effort we exert, whereas presumably we have no control over how lucky we are.

Attribution theorists study how individuals *themselves* interpret a particular cause on a causal dimension; an individual's *own* interpretation, not the attribution theorist's, influences the individual's behavior in an achievement situation. Luck, for example, could be perceived by some as a relatively stable quality (i.e., "I am a lucky or unlucky person"). Similarly, effort could be perceived as a stable characteristic ("He is a lazy or a hardworking person"). Keeping in mind such possible person-to-person or even situation-to-situation variations, the most common placement for a few frequently used attributions on Weiner's causal dimensions is summarized in Table 7-2.

Measurement

Attributions can be measured for a particular achievement outcome by asking open-ended questions (e.g., "Why did you do well/poorly on your spelling test?") or by providing a set of options (e.g., effort, ability, task difficulty) and asking the respondent to rate the importance of each cause listed.

Researchers have also assessed students' *generalized* perceptions of the cause of academic outcomes in several ways. In some studies they ask subjects to rate the causes of an outcome experienced by a hypothetical person described to them in a story. It is assumed that subjects project their own beliefs about the causes of academic outcomes in their ratings. In other studies they ask students to think about their own past academic outcomes. Table 7-3 is an example of how students' beliefs about the causes of outcomes might be measured. The questions could easily be adapted to apply to a particular outcome (e.g., the student's grade on a test) or to outcomes in a particular subject area. [See Weiner (1983) for a discussion of measurement issues].

TABLE 7-2 • Dimensions of Causality[1]				
	Controllable		Uncontrollable	
	Stable	Unstable	Stable	Unstable
Internal Locus	typical effort	immediate effort	aptitude	mood; fatigue
External Locus			task difficulty	luck

1. Adapted from Weiner (1979)

TABLE 7-3 • Measure of Attributions for Performance on Academic Tasks

---

When you do well in school, is it usually because: (rate the importance of each explanation)

	not a reason at all				an important reason
you studied hard?	1	2	3	4	5
you studied the right things?	1	2	3	4	5
you are smart?	1	2	3	4	5
the teacher explained things well?	1	2	3	4	5
you were helped by someone?	1	2	3	4	5
the work was easy?	1	2	3	4	5

When you do poorly in school, is it usually because:

you didn't study much?	1	2	3	4	5
you didn't study the right things?	1	2	3	4	5
you are not smart?	1	2	3	4	5
the teacher didn't explain things well?	1	2	3	4	5
you weren't helped by anyone?	1	2	3	4	5
the work was hard?	1	2	3	4	5

Because some causal attributions are more likely to lead to constructive achievement-related behavior than others, it is important to understand the classroom conditions that foster desirable attributions. Therefore, we turn now to research on the antecedents of attributional judgments.

Antecedents to Attributions

Researchers have identified several factors that affect individuals' perceptions of the cause of achievement outcomes. *Consensus* information (about how well others performed) is associated with the locus dimension of causal attributions. If everyone in a class receives the same high grade, an external attribution (e.g., easy task or easy-grading teacher) is likely to be made. If only one student receives a good grade, that student is likely to make an internal attribution for his or her performance (e.g., high ability, studied hard).

Consistency is associated with the stability dimension. Outcomes that are consistent with previous performance (e.g., "I have always failed in the past, and I failed again this time") are likely to be attributed to stable causes, such as ability. Conversely, outcomes that are inconsistent with previous outcomes are most likely to be attributed to unstable causes, such as effort, luck, or an unusually hard or easy task.

Note that some of the antecedents of attributions discussed above are inherent in the task situation itself. Weiner's focus on situational factors affecting students' attributional judgments is one of the major differences between his and Rotter's analysis of achievement-related cognitions. Rotter emphasizes generalized beliefs that develop with experience in achievement settings and are assumed to hold regardless of situational factors. Weiner admits that relatively stable individual differences in perceptions of the cause of achievement outcomes exist, but he claims that individuals make attributional judgments primarily on the basis of information in the *current* achievement situation. Past experience in similar achievement contexts is still relevant, but it is only one of many factors that the student considers. Weiner's view is optimistic because it suggests that we should be able to change students' causal attributions—whatever their previous experiences in achievement contexts—by manipulating variables in the current classroom environment.

Attribution Dispositions

Although Weiner has focused primarily on situational cues used to judge the cause of outcomes, other researchers have studied relatively stable individual differences in children's tendencies to attribute achievement outcomes to one cause versus another [Fincham, Hokoda, and Sanders, (1989); see Graham (1991) for a discussion]. These researchers conceptualize attributions, as Rotter conceptualized LOC, to some degree as a generalized set of relatively stable beliefs that evolve from previous experiences and socialization. They have studied several factors contributing to children's attributional dispositions—including past performance, culture, gender, and teachers' attitudes and behaviors.

Studies have shown that children who have a *history of poor performance*, like Hopeless Hannah, are more likely to attribute success to external causes and failure to a lack of ability than children who have a history of good performance (Butkowsky and Willows, 1980; Greene, 1985; Marsh, 1984a; Stipek and Hoffman, 1980). Consistent with this research are findings that retarded children, who presumably experience frequent failure, are more likely to blame themselves for their failure than are nonretarded children (Chan and Keogh, 1974; MacMillan and Keogh, 1971), and they are more likely to manifest helpless behavior in task situations (Weisz, 1979).

Past performance also affects attributional dispositions indirectly, through the perceptions of competence that children develop. Thus, children who, as a result of repeated failures, develop a perception of themselves as academically *incompetent*, interpret achievement outcomes consistent with this view. Failure is attributed to their lack of ability and success is attributed to some external cause (e.g., an easy task; Ames, 1978; Marsh, Cairns, Relich, Barnes, and Debus, 1984).

There is also evidence for *cultural differences* in beliefs about the causes of achievement outcomes. The Japanese have been found to attribute outcomes more to effort and less to ability than Americans (Holloway, 1988; Holloway, Kashiwagi, Hess, and Azuma, 1986; Lee, Ichikawa, and Stevenson, 1987; Stevenson et al., 1986). Likewise, observers of Chinese culture suggest that the Chinese also emphasize effort as a cause of performance more than Americans (Chen and Uttal, 1988). This emphasis is consistent with traditional Chinese philosophy that assumes malleability in humans and stresses the importance of striving for improvement. Cultural differences in beliefs about the causes of achievement outcomes suggest that these perceptions are, to some degree, socialized. Parents and teachers within our culture, therefore, may influence children's perceptions of the cause of achievement outcomes.

Gender differences are also commonly found in attribution research. Many studies have found that females were less likely than males to attribute success to their own high ability and more likely to attribute failure to low ability [Dweck and Reppucci (1973); Eccles (1983); Nicholls (1975, 1979a, 1980); Parsons, Meece, Adler, and Kaczala (1982); Stipek (1984c); see Sohn (1982) for a metaanalysis]. Gender differences are more prominent in domains such as math and science, which are often sex-stereotyped as "male," than in other domains. In a study of fifth- and sixth-graders, I found that in math, girls were more likely to attribute failure to their lack of ability and less likely to attribute success to their ability than were boys; in contrast, there were no differences in boys' and girls' perception of the cause of achievement outcomes in spelling (Stipek, 1984c; Gitelson, Petersen, and Tobin-Richards, 1982; Ryckman and Peckham, 1987; Stipek and Gralinski, 1991).

Many researchers have suggested explanations for the observed sex differences in attributional patterns. For example, girls' attributional biases have been linked to low confidence in ability (Frieze, 1975) and to low expectations for success (Deaux, 1976). These perceptions are not easy to explain, given girls' relatively good performance.

Dweck and her colleagues examined an intriguing explanation for girls' greater tendency to attribute failure to lack of ability (Dweck, Davidson, Nelson, and Enna, 1978). In the fourth- and fifth-grade classrooms they observed, boys were criticized more than girls, but most of the criticism the boys received concerned conduct or failure to follow directions, whereas most of the small amount of criticism the girls received concerned the quality of their academic performance. The authors suggest that boys may not view negative feedback as relevant to their intellectual abilities. Because a much larger proportion of the negative feedback girls received concerned their academic performance, they may have been less able to disregard the relevance of the feedback to their intellectual abilities.

Consequences of Attributions

The consequences of attributions are what make them relevant to a discussion of motivation in the classroom. Different dimensions are associated with different kinds of consequences.

Expectations

Performance expectations usually rise following success and fall after failure. Motivation theorists refer to these expectancy changes as "typical shifts." Attribution theorists have shown that typical shifts occur only when a stable attribution for past performance is made (see Weiner, 1980a). This is because past outcomes attributed to unstable causes do not have clear implications for future performance. The stability dimension is, therefore, associated with performance expectations.

It is generally assumed that effort attributions are the more productive than most other attributions for learning, in part because of the implications of effort attributions for expectations about future performance. Effort, unlike ability or luck, is under the student's control. Thus, students who attribute past failure to low effort can hope for success in the future (assuming that they are willing to exert greater effort). Students who attribute failure to lack of ability, on the other hand, are not as likely to exert effort on future tasks because without the prerequisite ability they cannot expect success. This was demonstrated in an early study by Meyer [(1970) described in Weiner (1980a)]. He found that when failure to complete a digit-symbol substitution task was attributed to effort (unstable causes), subjects worked more intensely on the task. When it was attributed to ability or task difficulty (stable causes) the intensity of subjects' efforts declined.

An effort attribution is also desirable when success occurs. The perception that effort was an important cause of success implies that the student possesses the required ability, but acknowledges that success is not achieved without some effort. In contrast, attributing success solely to ability can have negative effects on behavior in achievement situations. When students succeed without trying very hard, they may come to believe that effort is not needed for success. Therefore, they do not try very hard on future tasks and, as a result they perform at a level below their true capability.

Learned Helplessness

Attributing failure to causes that the individual does not control can lead to maladaptive behavior referred to as **learned helplessness**. Learned helplessness was first investigated in animals by Seligman and Maier (1967). Dogs were placed in a situation in which nothing they did prevented them from receiving a mild shock. The dogs soon became passive in the "helpless" situation, making no attempt to avoid being shocked, even when they were later placed in a situation in which they could avoid it. Other dogs who were previously able to prevent shock by their own behavior quickly learned the avoidance strategy. The authors claim that the animals in the helpless situation became passive because they perceived the environment to be unresponsive to (or not contingent upon) their own behavior.

Learned helplessness in achievement situations occurs when students—usually ones who have experienced a great deal of failure, like Hopeless Hannah—believe that there is nothing that they can do to avoid failure. When they do fail, helpless children typically attribute the failure to their low ability, which they believe they have no control over (Dweck and Goetz, 1978). These students exert little effort on school tasks and give up easily when they encounter difficulty. They are unresponsive to teachers' exhortations to try and generally seem disengaged from classroom activities. (See Appendix 7–A for additional behaviors associated with learned helplessness).

Much of the research on learned helplessness in achievement settings has been done by Dweck and her colleagues. In an early study, Dweck and Reppucci (1973) assessed connections between children's beliefs about the cause of achievement outcomes and their reactions to failure. Children who indicated on a questionnaire that they believed that controllable factors, such as effort, determine achievement outcomes tended to persist at an experimental task even after experiencing failure. The performance of children who indicated on the questionnaire that they tended to blame their failures on uncontrollable, external factors, such as the difficulty of the task, or on uncontrollable internal factors, such as their lack of ability, deteriorated under failure conditions; these children gave up quickly when they encountered difficulty on the experimental task.

In a later study (Diener and Dweck, 1978), helpless children's behavior in failure situations was examined more closely. Children were given an opportunity to master a discrimination learning task. They were then given four insolvable problems, and their problem-solving strategy was monitored. The children who indicated on a questionnaire that they tended to attribute failure to uncontrollable factors used less mature problem-solving strategies than they had used before failure occurred; by the second trial, nearly half of these children had already abandoned strategies that could lead to a solution. By the fourth trial, two-thirds failed to show any sign of a useful strategy. In comparison, children who stressed effort as a cause of achievement outcomes continued to search for appropriate strategies to solve the problem. About one-fourth of them actually began using more effective strategies after failure occurred. Similarly, Licht and Dweck (1984) found, in a more naturalistic setting, that the performance of children who minimized the role of effort in achievement outcomes ("helpless" children), unlike children who emphasized effort, deteriorated when they encountered a confusing paragraph inserted into a text. Thus, in both studies the two groups of children behaved very differently in the same achievement situation, and their behavior was directly related to their perceptions of the cause of achievement outcomes.

Diener and Dweck (1980) demonstrated that beliefs about the cause of achievement outcomes also affect children's reactions to success. They found that children who tended to attribute success to uncontrollable causes underestimated the number of successes they experienced, overestimated the number of failures, tended not to view their successes as indicative of ability, and tended not to expect success in the future. These studies illustrate how generalized beliefs can supersede situational variables.

Although learned helplessness is more common among low-achieving children, it can be seen even in children who perform relatively well in school. For some children, like Safe Sally, a "B+" means unmitigated failure. If these children define success as achieving an "A," and believe that they do not have the aptitude to achieve an "A," they may become as discouraged with "Bs" as other children are with not making passing grades. Beliefs about the cause of achievement outcomes are therefore just as relevant to the optimal achievement of high-performing children as they are to low-performing children.

The evidence on sex differences in attributional patterns, reviewed above, suggests that girls may be more vulnerable to learned helplessness than boys, despite their tendency to perform better than boys in all subject areas, at least through elementary school. Miller (1986) demonstrated, for example, that the performance of seventh-grade girls was more impaired by failure experiences when a task was described as very difficult than when it was described as moderately difficult. This behavior is consistent with a learned helplessness explanation—that girls interpreted failure as evidence of a lack of ability, and thus did not believe that their efforts on a difficult task would lead to success. The performance of boys, in contrast, was more impaired by failure when the task was described as moderately difficult. Miller (1986) suggests that boys quit trying in this condition to avoid the perception of being low in competence. Trying while doing a "very difficult" task was not as threatening because failure on a difficult task does not necessarily indicate low ability. Thus, whereas boys appeared to be striving to maintain a perception of competence, girls, perhaps because they had lower perceptions of their ability and less hope of being able to demonstrate ability, gave up.

Licht and Dweck (1984) suggest that high-achieving girls may be particularly vulnerable to learned helplessness. They found, in the study described above, that the higher boys rated their intelligence, the less debilitated they were by the confusing paragraph. In contrast, girls' ratings of their intelligence tended to correlate *negatively* with their performance in the confusing condition. That is, the girls who considered themselves bright (and by objective evidence were relatively bright) were most debilitated by the confusing paragraph. The authors propose that attribution tendencies may contribute to girls' lower participation in higher level mathematics because in math, more than in most other subject areas, students encounter tasks that may, at first, be difficult or confusing. These are the conditions that are most likely to elicit helpless behavior.

Even children identified as gifted are not immune from feelings of helplessness. Indeed, gifted children may be especially vulnerable because parents, usually proud of their child's special academic talents, sometimes express exceptionally high expectations that the child feels incapable of fulfilling. Children who regard any performance that is below parents' expectations as failure, and who do not believe that they can meet those expectations, may give up trying altogether. Gifted children can also develop learned helplessness as a result of being moved to a special class for gifted children. A child who is accustomed to being the highest achiever in a regular class does not always adjust easily to performing at a comparatively lower level among other gifted children. A lower standing in the gifted class can cause feelings of failure and a belief that no amount of effort will assure success (which they define as being one of the best in the class). This belief presumably explains why Safe Sally dropped out of her calculus class after getting a "B-" on the first quiz.

Clearly, it is best to prevent children from developing an attributional pattern that results in helpless behaviors. As we saw with Hannah, such an attributional pattern is difficult to reverse. Children can fall into a self-perpetuating cycle in which they attribute failure to causes over which they have no control, do nothing to avoid failure in subsequent situations, and consequently fail again, thus confirming their perception of themselves as low in competence. And so the cycle continues. In Chapter 10 we will discuss strategies for preventing attributions associated with helpless behavior and for altering maladaptive attribution patterns when they occur.

Emotions

Weiner and his colleagues have examined the effect of different causal attributions on individuals' emotional reactions in achievement situations (Weiner, 1980b, 1985, 1986). In a series of studies with adult subjects, Weiner, Russell and Lerman (1978, 1979) found that some emotions occur strictly as a function of outcome, regardless of an individual's perception of the cause of the outcome. Thus, students feel happy when they succeed and sad when they fail, regardless of their attribution for the cause of their success or failure. Other emotions are tied to specific attributions. Students claim to feel surprised when they attribute success or failure to luck, grateful when they attribute their success to someone else's help, and guilty when they attribute their failure to a lack of effort. Pride and shame occur only when the outcome is attributed to some internal cause. For example, a student who attributes success to his or her own hard work and ability is more likely to feel proud than a student who attributes success to help received from another individual. Failure attributed to internal causes such as lack of effort or ability is, similarly, more likely to result in feelings of shame than failure blamed on external causes (e.g., an unfair teacher, interfering noise while taking a test).

Consider, for example, a situation in which a student receives the only "A" in the class versus a situation in which everyone in the class receives an "A." In the former case the student is likely to attribute the successful outcome to his or her own behavior or disposition; in the latter case the student is likely to attribute the successful outcome to an indiscriminate teacher or an easy test. The student who makes the internal attribution should feel more pride than the student who makes an external attribution. Consider next the student who knows before he begins a multiple choice test that he did not study for the test and has not mastered the material. He nevertheless does fairly well on the exam by guessing and he attributes his successful performance to good luck. Because an external attribution is made, he is more likely to experience relief and happiness than pride.

These emotional consequences of attributions have important practical implications. The anticipation of feeling proud can sustain a student's effort on a difficult task, just as the anticipation of feeling ashamed can inhibit a student from approaching an achievement task (Atkinson, 1964; Weiner, 1980b, 1985, 1986). Support for some of the proposed effects of emotions on achievement behavior comes from a study by Covington and Omelich (1984b), in which college students' guilt about their performance on one midterm was associated with enhanced effort and performance on the next midterm, and humiliation for previous performance was associated with subsequent decreased effort and performance. Since students' perceptions of the cause of their achievement outcomes have important implications for their emotional experiences and, consequently, for their behavior in achievement settings, every effort should be made to encourage students to make attributions that maximize positive emotions.

Links between attributions and emotions also have implications for how children interpret others' behavior. Consider for example, two children who do poorly on a test. The teacher responds with mild anger toward one child and with sympathy toward the other. Studies have shown that children as young as six years understand that people experience anger when they attribute an outcome to a controllable cause, such as low effort, and pity when they attribute an outcome to an uncontrollable cause (e.g., a disability or lack of intelligence; Graham, Doubleday, and Guarino, 1984; Weiner, Graham, Stern, and Lawson, 1982). Children's own judgments about the cause of their performance may, therefore, be affected by the teacher's or their parents' emotional reactions; an angry teacher response to low performance may foster a belief that the outcome was caused by low effort (a controllable cause), and a sympathetic response may foster a belief that the outcome was caused by low ability (an uncontrollable cause; Graham, 1984a, 1990). (See Chapter 11 for a more extended discussion of ways in which teachers convey their perceptions of the cause of students' performance through their emotional expressions.)

SUMMARY

Atkinson's, Rotter's, and Weiner's theories all represent a significant departure from strict reinforcement theory. Reinforcement theory is "mechanistic" in that it does not incorporate beliefs, values, expectations, emotions, or anything else that is not directly observable. Cognitive theorists, such as those reviewed in this chapter, consider unobservable thoughts and feelings to be important factors in understanding achievement behavior. Reinforcement theory focuses on the individual's environment, specifically the contingencies of reinforcement. Cognitive theorists focus on the individual's *interpretation* of the environment.

Atkinson's expectancy x value model is, in some respects, the least cognitive of the three theories discussed above. Two of the three factors considered in his mathematical model of achievement behavior—the motive to succeed and the motive to avoid failure—are assumed to be, at least in part, unconscious. Indeed, the motive to succeed is assessed with a projective measure specifically designed to tap the unconscious. The only factor that is fully conscious is the perceived probability of success (or failure)—a judgment made in the specific task situation.

In contrast to Atkinson's theory, all cognitions in Rotter's theory of locus of control and Weiner's attribution theory are conscious. But Rotter's model differs from Weiner's in several important respects. Rotter assumes that individuals bring to task situations *generalized* expectancies regarding whether outcomes are contingent upon the individual's own characteristics or behavior, and that they interpret each situation according to these expectancies. The expectancies are based on their previous experiences in task situations. Thus, Rotter developed a measure of locus of control that is designed to assess relatively stable beliefs that individuals carry into different achievement contexts.

In contrast to Rotter, Weiner focuses on judgments individuals make in specific task situations. While he acknowledges that past experiences might bias individuals to interpret a situation in a particular way, he emphasizes the situational determinants of the individual's interpretation such as how well others performed on the task and how the individual's current performance compares with past performance on similar tasks.

Despite these differences, in comparison to reinforcement theory these three theories are more alike than different because they include thoughts and feelings as mediators of achievement behavior. The next chapter focuses on individuals' beliefs about their competence. This particular judgment underlies, to some degree, the cognitions (e.g., expectations for success, perceptions of control, and perceptions of the cause of outcomes) emphasized in the achievement motivation models discussed above.

TABLE 7-4 • Summary of Terms	
Term	*Definition*
Expectancy x Value Theory	
Motive for success (M_s) Need to achieve (Nach)	Unconscious disposition to strive for success
Motive to avoid failure (M_{AF})	Unconscious disposition which directs individuals away from achievement tasks
Perceived probability of success (P_s) /failure (P_f)	Individual's expectations regarding the probability of success/failure on a task
Incentive value of success (I_s)	Amount of pride anticipated, inversely related to the perceived probability of success
Incentive value of failure (I_f)	Amount of shame anticipated, inversely related to the perceived probability of failure
Resultant tendency to approach or avoid an achievement activity (T_A)	The strength of the tendency to approach minus the strength of the tendency to avoid a task
Locus of Control Theory	
Locus of Control (LOC)	Beliefs about whether reinforcement is contingent upon one's behavior or characteristics
Primary control	Attempting to influence existing external realities to bring them into line with personal wishes
Secondary control	Attempting to accommodate to existing realities in order to effect a more satisfying fit between the self and those realities
Attribution Theory	
Causal attributions	Perceptions of the cause of outcomes
Learned helplessness	Not trying as a consequence of a belief that rewards are not contingent upon one's behavior

8

PERCEPTIONS OF ABILITY

Perceptions of ability play an important role in all cognitive theories of achievement motivation. In Atkinson's theory, individuals who believe they are competent at a task perceive their probability of success as high and, consequently, are more likely to approach the task than individuals who believe they lack the necessary competencies. In Rotter's locus of control theory, individuals who believe they are academically competent are more likely to believe they control academic outcomes. And in Weiner's attribution theory, individuals who believe they are competent at a task will probably attribute success to their ability and failure to some other cause; in contrast, those who believe they are incompetent will attribute failure to their lack of ability and will search for an external explanation for success. Perceptions of competence are also relevant to White's (1959) intrinsic competence motive. Mastery attempts that lead to feelings of competence sustain the competence motive while mastery attempts that result in feelings of *incompetence* inhibit it. Consistent with these theoretical analyses, many studies have shown that perceptions of ability influence information seeking, task choice, intended effort, persistence, thoughts and feelings while working on tasks, and evaluations and attributions about one's performance (Meyer, 1987).

Two achievement motivation theorists have focused on perceptions of ability. Bandura refers to these perceptions as **self-efficacy**, which he believes has important implications for behavior. Covington addresses the issue of perceived ability in the context of his self-worth theory. He claims that individuals need to perceive themselves—and be perceived by others—as competent, a need that explains much of what would otherwise appear to be illogical behavior in achievement contexts.

Perceived competence is defined by Bandura and Covington in slightly different ways. Before discussing their theories in detail, however, we turn to the issue of how ability is defined.

"ABILITY" AS SKILL VERSUS TRAIT

Dweck and Elliott (1983) claim that adults use two different concepts of ability (see also, Cain and Dweck, 1989; Dweck and Bempechat, 1983; Dweck and Leggett, 1988). According to an **entity** concept, ability is a stable trait. If two individuals exert the same amount of effort, the one with more ability will perform better. An entity theory, like the notion of an intelligence quotient (IQ), is also associated with the assumptions that ability is distributed unevenly among individuals (some have more of "it" than others) and that it is a general trait that affects learning and performance in a variety of areas.

According to an **instrumental-incremental** concept, ability consists of "... an ever-expanding repertoire of skills and knowledge ... that is increased through one's own instrumental behavior" (Dweck and Bempechat, 1983, p. 144). Ability, using this definition, is more task specific and is based primarily on study or practice. One's ability in one area is not necessarily relevant to one's ability in another area.

Most adults use both conceptions, sometimes with regard to the same skill area. For example, occasionally when I play tennis and I feel especially discouraged after a poor performance, I believe that I am constitutionally uncoordinated and unable to learn to play tennis (or anything else that requires physical ability). I am convinced that no amount of practice will result in any significant improvement. But when I am feeling more optimistic, perhaps encouraged by an unusually patient partner, I believe that if I just practice, my game will improve. The former view is an example of an entity theory of tennis ability; the latter illustrates an instrumental-incremental theory.

Dweck and her colleagues argue that children's concepts of intellectual ability have important implications for their behavior in achievement contexts. The goal of children who have an entity concept is to "look smart," regardless of how much is learned. Thus, these children are more likely to have performance or ego goals, as described in Chapter 2. Those who are relatively confident about their ability, like

Safe Sally, seek opportunities to demonstrate it, but they tend to select tasks in which there is no risk of failure, so the limits of their ability are never revealed. In contrast, children who have an entity concept of ability but lack confidence in their ability avoid achievement situations, especially those in which their lack of ability would become public. If they are given a choice in tasks, they may select very easy or very difficult tasks so that failure is not necessarily attributable to low ability. These children who lack self-confidence, like Hopeless Hannah, often develop learned helplessness. They avoid achievement tasks whenever possible because they are convinced that they lack the ability to succeed, and that this lack cannot be remedied by any amount of practice or effort.

The goal of children who have an instrumental-incremental concept of ability is not to "look smart," but to increase their skill level. Thus, these children have learning or mastery goals, also described in Chapter 2. If they fail, they assume that practice and effort will increase their chances of future success. They should select moderately difficult tasks because moderately difficult tasks are more likely to produce learning than very easy tasks, which require little effort, or very difficult tasks, which may be impossible to complete. They evidence mastery-oriented behaviors, as opposed to helplessness, thus intensifying their effort, using effective strategies, and persisting when they encounter difficulty.

Research on teachers suggests that teachers, like students, differ in the degree to which they see intellectual ability as stable or as malleable and expanding. Midgley, Feldlaufer, and Eccles (1988) found, moreover, that teachers who believed that math ability was fixed perceived themselves to be less efficacious and had a stronger need to control student behavior than teachers who believed that math ability was amenable to change. This study demonstrated the importance of teachers monitoring their own beliefs and the effects their beliefs have on their instructional strategies.

Relationship Between Effort and Ability

Nicholls and his colleagues studied children's understanding of ability, distinct from effort, as explanations of performance in particular situations (Miller, 1985; Nicholls, 1978, 1983; Nicholls and Miller, 1984a, 1984b, 1984c; Nicholls, 1989, 1990; Nicholls, Jagacinski, and Miller, 1986). They found that children below about the age of six do not differentiate between ability and effort; young children assume that people who try hard are smart and people who are smart try hard. They also do not distinguish effort and ability from outcome. If a person succeeds, then he must have tried hard and he must be able. If he fails, he must not have tried and he must not be smart.

Between the ages of about seven and nine, children see effort as the primary cause of performance outcomes—equal effort, therefore, should lead to equal outcomes. Nicholls and Miller (1984b) describe a study in which children were shown a videotape of two actors, one who obviously did not try and the other who tried hard. Both actors were shown to receive the same high score. Many of the younger children simply refused to believe that one of the actors succeeded without working hard. Some claimed that this actor must have started earlier or "must have been thinking while fiddling" (p. 195).

Not until about the age of 11 or 12 do children fully differentiate performance, effort, and ability—what Nicholls refers to as a differentiated, or "mature" concept of ability. Only the adolescents in the study described above claimed that the actor in the videotape who worked very hard was less smart than the actor who did not work hard but achieved the same level of performance. Thus, they had a concept of ability as capacity which influenced the effectiveness of effort on performance.

Thus, Nicholls (1984a) distinguishes between an undifferentiated and a differentiated concept of ability. An **undifferentiated** concept of ability is based on perceptions of mastery or learning; the more individuals believe they have learned, the more competent they feel. When the more **differentiated** concept is used, ability is judged in relation to others. High ability means *above average*. According to Nicholls (1984), ego-involvement (described in Chapter 2) occurs when individuals seek to demonstrate ability in the differentiated sense.

The development of a mature concept of ability has important implications for children's perceptions of the value of effort. Although young children understand that effort does not always produce success, they assume that mastery following high effort always indicates high ability. By early adolescence, children understand that when two children obtain the same outcome, the one exerting the higher effort is judged to have lower ability. For adolescents, therefore, whether mastery following high effort indicates high or low ability depends on others' as well as one's own effort and performance, and under some circumstances, high effort can be used as evidence for low ability.

Consistent with this analysis, research suggests that young children emphasize effort more than older children as a cause of achievement outcomes. In one study I asked children how they assessed both their own and their peers' ability in school (Stipek, 1981). Many of the kindergarteners and first-graders cited their work habits, including effort. A few of the children referred to competence or ability in their explanations of a peer's poor performance (e.g., "He's not very smart in reading"), but they often hastened to add, "If he practices he'll be smarter." One second-grader in a study by Harari and Covington (1981) succinctly expressed his version of the incremental theory of ability: "If you study, it helps the brain and you get smarter" (p. 25). Clearly, young children emphasize the importance of effort for achieving successful performance in particular situations and for developing competencies over time. By early adolescence, in contrast, effort takes on a potentially negative meaning in relation to judgments of ability.

The distinctions that Dweck and Nicholls make in definitions of ability are relevant to the two theories of self-perceptions of ability mentioned above. Implicit in Bandura's self-efficacy theory is an incremental definition of ability. Bandura and his colleagues are concerned with individuals' perceptions of their ability in an undifferentiated sense—their judgment about whether they can complete a particular task or achieve a particular goal. An entity definition, on the other hand, is implicit in Covington's theory; his work concerns students' perceptions of intellectual ability relative to others (i.e., in a differentiated sense).

SELF-EFFICACY IN BANDURA'S SOCIAL COGNITIVE THEORY

Bandura (1986) proposed that the ability to reflect upon experiences is uniquely human, and that among the types of thoughts that affect action, none is more central than people's judgments of their capabilities to achieve certain goals. Self-efficacy pertains to students' personal judgments of their performance capabilities on a particular type of task —that is, whether they're capable of succeeding (Bandura, 1977a, b, 1982a, 1982b, 1986; Schunk, 1989a, b). Efficacy, in Bandura's theory, is, therefore, related to Weisz' concept of competence as well as the concept of agency beliefs, as defined by Skinner et al. (1988; Chapter 7). Self-efficacy, however, refers to specific judgments in specific situations, not to global perceptions that apply to many situations.

Sources of Self-Efficacy Judgments

There are four principal sources of information for self-efficacy judgments in academic situations—actual experience, vicarious experience, verbal persuasion, and physiological arousal.

Actual experience—especially past successes and failures—is an important source. Typically, successes raise efficacy appraisals and failures lower them. There is not, however, a simple relationship between objective experience and self-efficacy judgments. Self-efficacy judgments involve inferences, which are influenced by prior beliefs, expectations, difficulty of the task, amount of effort expended, amount of external help, and other factors. For example, success will not contribute to perceptions of efficacy if the individual perceives the task to be easy or if the individual did not feel that much effort had been put forth. Perceptions of the cause of outcomes also affect subsequent self-efficacy judgments. A person convinced of his incompetency may attribute success to some external factor, such as a great deal of help from another, or good luck. The success, consequently, does not engender feelings of efficacy.

Second, *vicarious experiences* affect self-perceptions of efficacy. For example, children sometimes become persuaded that they are able to perform a task after watching another child the same age complete the task. I observed this when I taught swimming lessons. Private lessons were often not as effective as group lessons for young children because seeing an age-mate execute a behavior (e.g., swim across the deep end, dive off the diving board) often convinced children that they could do the same, a conviction not as readily engendered by my modeling the same behaviors. Bandura (1986) points out that vicarious experiences are most influential in situations in which individuals have little personal experience with the task.

Schunk and Hanson (1985) demonstrate the value of having children observe other children successfully complete a task. Children who were having difficulty doing subtraction observed either a same sex peer or a teacher demonstrate mastery. Observing a peer led to higher self-efficacy for learning the procedure, as well as to better mastery following a subsequent training intervention than observing a teacher did.

Verbal persuasion constitutes the third factor that influences, albeit more modestly, self-efficacy judgments. Thus, a teacher or parent can sometimes persuade children that they are able to achieve some goal. Verbal persuasion is not likely to be effective unless it is realistic and reinforced by real experience. But in some circumstances, encouragement (e.g., "try it, I know you can do it") can be effective in bolstering a child's self-confidence for a new task, especially when given by a credible person.

The final factor affecting self-efficacy judgments is *physiological arousal*. Consider, for example, a student taking a test who becomes aware that his palms are sweaty and his heart is beating rapidly. If a high state of anxiety has negatively affected his performance in the past, he may lose confidence in his ability to perform in this instance;

the lowered perceptions of efficacy can, in turn, increase anxiety, and become seriously debilitating.

Consequences of Self-Efficacy

Perceived efficacy can affect how individuals behave and their thoughts and emotional reactions in achievement settings. People tend to avoid tasks and situations they believe exceed their capabilities, and they seek out activities they judge themselves capable of handling (Bandura, 1977a, 1986). The novice skier who falls repeatedly and makes slow progress toward the bottom of the hill may be reluctant to charge back to the top; the student who is unable to solve any of the algebra problems and judges himself incompetent is not likely to attack a new set of problems eagerly.

Self-efficacy beliefs also affect students' thoughts and behaviors while they work on tasks. Students who are not confident that they can complete a task and who do not believe that practice and effort will lead to success often become anxious and preoccupied with feelings of incompetence, especially when they are being evaluated. To use the term introduced in Chapter 2, they become ego-oriented. In contrast, students who are convinced of their competence are task-oriented— they can concentrate on problem-solving strategies (Bandura, 1981, 1986).

Judgments of self-efficacy while solving a problem or completing a task are associated with positive emotional experiences, which in turn foster future mastery attempts. Consider the novice skier who finally makes a successful run to the bottom of a hill. He is likely to want to go right back up the hill, or possibly even a steeper hill, as a consequence of this success and the positive feelings it engendered. School tasks, like solving a difficult algebra problem, can also engender feelings of efficacy. The student who solves a difficult problem should feel efficacious and be eager to attempt more.

The feelings of self-efficacy Bandura refers to have much in common with those White (1959) and other intrinsic motivation theorists propose. In contrast to White, however, Bandura does not assume a competence *motive*, and he claims that judgments of efficacy can be derived from sources other than personal experience. Bandura also assumes that the emotional experience is mediated entirely by cognitive judgments, which is not necessarily the case in White's formulation.

These consequences of high self-efficacy—willingness to approach and persist on tasks, a focus on problem-solving strategies, reduced fear and anxiety, and positive emotional experiences—affect achievement outcomes. Researchers have demonstrated the effect of self-efficacy beliefs on achievement behavior. Collins (1982), for example, identified students who were low, average, and high in mathematical ability on the basis of scores on standardized tests. Within each ability group students with higher self-efficacy solved more problems correctly and chose to rework more problems that they had missed than students low in self-efficacy. Self-efficacy thus predicted achievement behavior over and above actual ability level in all three groups. Pintrich and De Groot (1990) report a study in which self-efficacy is strongly associated with constructive cognitive strategies and self-regulated learning (e.g., a student's attempts to make connections between textbook and classroom instruction; rereading material; making outlines), independent of prior achievement (Locke, Frederick, Lee, and Bobko, 1984). These studies clearly point to the importance of fostering self-efficacy in learning situations.

COVINGTON'S SELF-WORTH THEORY

Self-worth concerns people's appraisal of their own value. It is similar to such concepts as self-esteem and self-respect. A fundamental assumption of Covington's self-worth theory is that human beings naturally strive to protect their sense of self-worth when it is threatened, such as in the case of public failure (Covington and Beery, 1976; Covington, 1984, 1985). Consistent with this assumption, research indicates that individuals often take more responsibility for their successes than for their failures (Miller and Ross, 1975). And, as we shall see later, students employ creative strategies to maintain a sense of worthiness when they face failure in school.

Covington and his colleagues believe that individuals' emotional reactions in achievement situations are strongly influenced by the implications outcomes have for their own and other's perceptions of their ability—that is, whether outcomes make them look competent or incompetent [using Dweck's entity definition of ability; see Covington and Omelich (1981)]. Thus, failure engenders shame and distress most when the failure appears to reflect low ability, and least when the failure can be attributed to some other cause.

As we saw with Defensive Dick, the desire to avoid being perceived as low in ability can have negative effects on behavior in achievement situations. Recall that by the age of 11 children understand the inverse relationship between effort and ability—that given equal performance, the student who exerts the least effort is judged the most able (see Chapter 7). Unfortunately, this means that negative feelings can be minimized, in some circumstances, by *not* exerting effort, or at least by appearing not to exert effort.

This understanding leaves children who anticipate failure in a real bind. If they try but fail, their failure will clearly be attributable to low ability. If they don't try, they have an alternative explanation for their failure, but effort is also valued and rewarded in this culture, and students who do not try risk disapproval and punishment. Many studies have shown that effort is a significant factor in teacher rewards (Blumenfeld, Hamilton, Bossert, Wessels, and Meece, 1983; Eswara, 1972; Rest, Nierenberg, Weiner, and Heckhausen, 1973). In these studies students who are perceived as having tried are rewarded more for success and punished less for failure than those who did not try. Thus, failure with high effort engenders more shame or humiliation for the students, but failure with low effort elicits the most disapproval from teachers. This is why Covington and Omelich (1979a) refer to effort as a "double-edged sword." And it is why teachers' and students' goals sometimes conflict with one another. Teachers want to maximize student effort and students want to maximize perceptions of their ability, which sometimes means the students do not try. [1]

A study by Covington and Omelich (1979a) exposes this dilemma. They asked college students to rate the ability, feelings of dissatisfaction and shame, and the appropriate teacher punishment for hypothetical students who failed and did or did not try hard. High effort resulted in lower punishment, but also in *lower* ratings of competence and *higher* ratings of dissatisfaction and shame. Apparently the subjects in this study preferred to risk punishment because they claimed that if they failed a test they would prefer to be perceived as high in ability and having not tried; they preferred this even to being perceived as high in ability and having tried, presumably because effort in the context of failure might cast some doubt on their ability. [See also Nicholls (1976a) and Sohn (1977) for evidence that individuals would rather be seen as competent than as hard working]. In another study, these investigators demonstrated that high effort did not lower ratings of competence when success was achieved, as it did for failure, indicating that high effort does not involve a risk for students who expect to succeed (Covington and Omelich, 1979b).

Self-worth theory is relevant to school because in most educational settings academic performance is the dominant criterion for evaluation. Ability in the sense of a stable trait is often perceived to be a critical ingredient for academic success, and academic ability is generally valued in this culture. Indeed, in one study a good report card contributed more to students' self-esteem than any other variable (Rosenberg, 1965).

The strong link between self-perceptions of ability and of self-worth is problematic for students who receive negative evaluations of their ability. Covington points out that a competitive educational setting precludes success for some students. Because everyone cannot be a relatively high performer, some students' self-worth is inevitably threatened. When the number of rewards and other indicators of ability (e.g., high grades) are restricted by reliance on a normal curve, then one person's success is achieved at the expense of another's. Even if grading is not done on a normal curve, a competitive atmosphere leads students to weigh classmates' performance in their evaluations of their own performance.

According to Covington, many characteristics of typical American classrooms threaten students' self-worth. For example, in most school settings goals are determined by the teacher and are not individualized. Because some students face goals that are too difficult for them, failure is guaranteed. Even if the teacher attempts to individualize goals, students attend to their classmates' accomplishments and often strive to keep up with them—whether or not their classmates' achievements represent realistic goals for themselves.

The emphasis on ability as an important attribute in this culture, the impossibility of all students' succeeding in most American classrooms, and the value placed on correct responses force some students, like Defensive Dick, to develop defensive strategies to protect themselves from the negative implications that failure usually has for one's ability. Most of these strategies, vividly described in Covington and Beery (1976), are self-defeating. A few of the more common strategies are described below.

Avoiding the Negative Implications of Failure for Ability

Students can avoid school failure, to some degree, by *minimizing participation*. Absenteeism is, of course, the most extreme method. Not volunteering answers to questions in class is less drastic. But students in most classrooms cannot escape some level of participation. They therefore have to resort to more subtle methods to avoid failure, or in those cases in which failure is unavoidable, to sidestep a low ability attribution. The student's task is to shift causal attributions for failure to external factors beyond his or her control, to factors that do not have negative implications for ability.

For example, many students, like Defensive Dick, simply do not try. Performance with no effort provides no information regarding students' ability because it cannot be determined what they would have accomplished had they exerted more effort. This common strategy is seen in elementary grades as well as in college classrooms. Some students publicize their refusal to work and downgrade the importance of studying. In extreme cases students come to take a perverse pride in failure as a mark of nonconformity (Bricklin and Bricklin, 1967). Teachers are often frustrated and puzzled by such behavior, but obstinate refusal to exert any effort has its own logic. It achieves the short-term goal of avoiding a low ability attribution for the failure.

There are risks, of course, when such strategies are employed. As mentioned above, teachers expect students to try and they reward and punish students accordingly. Students must therefore balance their need for avoiding the implications of failure with their desire to avoid punishment. They must simultaneously deal with the knowledge that failing with high effort suggests low ability, and that not trying often results in punishment and has its own negative implications for self-worth. Students who anticipate failure are in a no-win situation. If they try hard and fail, they look stupid; if they do not try, they get into trouble with the teacher. The evidence is clear, however, that some students who have to choose between the teacher's wrath for not trying and the feelings of humiliation and incompetency associated with trying and failing will choose the former (Covington, Spratt, and Omelich, 1980), or at least may try to give the impression that they did not try (Jagacinski and Nicholls, 1990).

Some students are clever enough to find some middle ground to avoid punishment for not trying. They try just enough to stay out of trouble, but not so hard that failure unambiguously implies lack of ability. They know that to maximize the desired image of a hard worker it is best to look eager, and then pray that the teacher calls on someone else. Extreme attention to note-taking with head bowed so as not to catch the teacher's eye is a technique I used as a college student. Sitting in the back of the room, positioned out of view of the teacher, is another useful technique.

Covington gives examples of similar strategies that he refers to as *"false effort"*—feigning attention during a class discussion, asking a question even though the answer is already known, or giving the outer appearance of thinking by adopting a pensive quizzical expression. These behaviors do not reflect a real attempt to learn. Rather, they are designed to make the student look smart and attentive and to allow him or her to stay out of trouble.

There are other ploys used to maintain a perception of ability while avoiding censure for not trying. Excuses are probably the most typical strategy used to avoid the negative sanctions associated with low effort, although clearly, to be effective, excuses must be used sparingly.

In my experience college students are exasperated by a refusal to listen to their excuses. My leniency in allowing a student to retake an examination or rewrite a paper seems to be less important to them than my hearing out the nonability-related reasons for their previous poor performance. An opportunity for success on the second round, apparently, is less effective in preserving a perception of competence and self-worth than the opportunity to publicly attribute previous failure to external causes (e.g., "I was ill and unable to study").

Procrastination is another common strategy used to avoid the negative implications of failure. Creating a personal handicap by studying at the very last minute provides the student with a ready, nonability-related explanation for subsequent failure. Successful students occasionally use this technique to enhance their image as highly competent. They are careful to announce before a test that they did not begin studying until midnight the night before and are concerned about their performance. Then, their good performance can be attributed to extremely high ability, since effort has been ruled out as an explanation. This technique is also a useful safeguard for students who are uncertain about their performance; if they do poorly they have a ready excuse that has ambiguous implications for their ability.

There are other strategies used by students to avoid the implications of failure for ability. One paradoxical strategy is to *set unattainable performance goals*. Failure is assured, but failure at an extremely difficult task does not necessarily imply low ability, whereas failure at a task that is considered to be very easy inescapably results in a judgment of low ability. Sears (1940) found that while children who had a history of success in school set their academic goals at a realistic level, students who had experienced considerable failure often overestimated, sometimes by extreme degrees, how well they would perform on various arithmetic and reading tasks. For some of the failure-prone students, the poorer their performance, the higher they set their aspirations. Sears suggests that the unrealistic goal setting might result from the poor-performing students' unfulfilled desire for approval; the mere statement of a worthy goal, not its attainment, becomes the source of gratification.

If an individual is uncertain about his or her ability and wants to preserve an image as an able person, then tasks that provide the least information on ability should be attempted. Selecting either very easy or very difficult tasks allows individuals who are uncertain about their abilities to avoid evidence suggesting incompetence. If they choose a very easy task, they will probably succeed. Although success will not suggest a high level of competence, it will not provide any evidence of incompetence; similarly, even though failure may be assured on the difficult task, the failure provides little information on the individual's competency.

There is evidence that simply describing a task as highly difficult can improve the performance of those who chronically worry about failure (Feather, 1961, 1963; Karabenick and Youssef, 1968; Sarason, 1961). Presumably, their performance is less debilitated by anxiety because if they fail, they can attribute the failure to the extreme difficulty of the task rather than to their own incompetence.

Miller (1985) provides a compelling demonstration of how describing a task as difficult can alleviate students' anxiety and enhance effort. He gave sixth-grade children a series of matching tasks that were constructed in such a way as to assure failure. Following this failure experience, children were given an anagram task to work on and their behavior was carefully observed. Children who were told that the subsequent task was moderately difficult completed fewer anagrams than children who were told that the anagram task was very difficult. Thus, the concerns about competence that were created by the failure experience on the matching tasks, and the performance deficits associated with such concerns, were alleviated by simply telling children that the next task was very difficult. Presumably this message allowed children to try hard without risking demonstrating low competence on yet another task (see also Miller and Hom, 1990). The effect was especially prominent for boys, suggesting that boys may be more concerned about their public image than girls.

Success Without Learning

Another approach to maintaining an image of ability is to *assure success*. Perhaps the most common method of assuring success without learning is cheating. Another method is to attempt only very easy tasks. Success is assured, but little learning results. This was Safe Sally's technique. She avoided challenging tasks and, therefore, preserved her image as an able person. A related strategy is to have very low aspirations. A student may announce to friends before a test that he or she would be delighted just to be able to pass the test. Anything above a passing grade, therefore, can be construed as a success. In any new skill situation, it is useful to announce beforehand that "I'm not very good at this." This lowers the expectations of observers. Then, even mediocre performance is perceived as evidence that the person is "actually pretty good." (I do this every time I play tennis.)

A strategy to assure success in a group question-and-answer period is to rehearse answers to the problem that one is likely to receive. I will use an example of my own to illustrate. A few years ago I took a

Spanish class in an adult evening program. The teacher frequently gave us a printed set of questions and proceeded around the table in order, asking students to answer the questions. I expertly avoided the public humiliation of giving a wrong answer by counting around the table to figure out which question I would be asked. I concentrated all my efforts on figuring out how to answer that question before the teacher reached me. This classic technique effectively achieved my immediate goal—to be successful and therefore to avoid looking stupid; but the positive consequences were short-lived. By not attending to questions that other students answered, I minimized the amount I learned and assured my position as the worst student in the class. My strategy temporarily allowed me to preserve an image of competence, but I still can't speak Spanish.

Related to these kinds of success-assuring (but not necessarily learning-assuring) tactics is what Covington and Beery (1976) refer to as *"overstriving."* The overstriver is driven by an intense desire to succeed, but more importantly, to avoid failure. Again, Safe Sally is a good example. Her school work is characterized by overpreparedness and excessive attention to detail. Because of the tremendous effort exerted, successes are naturally attributed to effort. Thus, she continues to harbor some doubts about her real abilities. Covington and Beery point out that overstrivers' uncertainty about their abilities make them extremely vulnerable in the event of failure. As a consequence, they develop a "loathing of failure far out of proportion to its importance" (p. 57).

These strategies can reduce anxiety or humiliation in the short run. But all of them inhibit real learning and, in the long run, make real success impossible. Evidence suggesting incompetence will mount, despite all efforts to avoid such a conclusion, and plausible self-serving explanations become more and more difficult to provide. Children who are uncertain about their competence and, as a result, expend their energies on avoiding "looking dumb" rather than on learning, eventually become convinced of their incompetence and give up the game. Thus, the child is transformed from a failure-avoiding student to a failure-accepting student. This difference is illustrated in Dick and Hannah. Defensive Dick's approach in achievement settings was hardly conducive to learning, but it did preserve some semblance of competence. Hopeless Hannah had given up altogether and instead of making an effort to give the impression that she knew what she was doing, she became resigned to her incompetence. Rather than search for some external explanation for her failures, Hannah took responsibility for them. Thus, while Dick is able to maintain some, albeit fragile, sense of self-worth, at least for the time being, Hannah must either exclude academic ability as a factor related to self-worth, which is not easy in most schooling environments, or she must devalue her own worth, which is a tragedy.

AGE-RELATED CHANGES IN PERCEPTIONS OF ABILITY

Hopeless Hannahs and Defensive Dicks are more common in higher grades than in the first few grades of school. This is because children's concepts of ability change, as discussed above, and because their judgments of their own ability decline, on average, with age.

When asked about their academic ability, most kindergarten-age children claim to be the smartest in their class. In many studies of self-perceptions of academic ability, children's ratings are near the top of the scale through the early elementary grades and decline, on average, thereafter (Stipek and Mac Iver, 1989). As they decline, self-perceptions of ability become more accurate in the sense that they correlate more strongly with external indices (e.g., teacher's ratings), (Eshel and Klein, 1981; Newman, 1984; Nicholls, 1978, 1979a.)

The typically strong positive bias in young children and the ensuing decline in perceived competence can be explained, in part, by changes in children's conceptions of academic competence (referred to above) and the criteria they use to assess competence. Children in preschool (and to some degree in the first year or two of elementary school) have a broadly defined concept of ability that includes social behavior, conduct, work habits, and effort (Blumenfeld, Pintrich, Meece, and Wessels, 1982; Stipek and Daniels, 1990; Stipek and Tannatt, 1984; Yussen and Kane, 1985). Over the elementary years children's definitions of academic ability become narrower and more differentiated by subject matter (Marsh, Barnes, Cairns, and Tidman, 1984). And, as discussed earlier, not until early adolescence do children have a concept of ability, in the sense of capacity, that is fully differentiated from their concept of effort.

Systematic age differences have also been found in the type of information regarding competence that children attend to most, in how they process different types of information, and in their propensity to make judgments based on *intra*-individual versus *inter*-individual comparisons. Interview studies suggest that preschool-age children and children in the first few grades of elementary school focus on *effort expended* (Harter and Pike, 1984), *personal mastery* (Blumenfeld, Pintrich, and Hamilton, 1986; Stipek 1981), and *social reinforcement* (Lewis, Wall, and Aronfreed, 1963; Spear and Armstrong, 1978) in their ability assessments. Emphasis on these sources of information declines with age, and the way children interpret this kind of information changes.

Consider effort, for example. Harter and Pike (1984) report that about a third of the preschool through second-graders they interviewed explained high self-perceptions of cognitive competence by citing habitual engagement in activities that foster skill development (e.g., "I practice a lot"). But other studies have shown that older children, who presumably understand the inverse relationship between effort and ability given equal outcomes, consider high effort, in some circumstances, as evidence of relatively *low* ability (Nicholls and Miller, 1984a).

Young children cite mastery as evidence of their competence, but unlike older children, they tend not to accept *non*mastery as evidence of *in*competence. Repeatedly failing to demonstrate mastery on a task does not undermine perceptions of competence for preschool-age children as much as it does for older children (Stipek, 1984a).

While effort, mastery, and social feedback decline in importance as indicators of academic competence and change in their implications, children pay increasing attention to grades (Blumenfeld et al. 1986; Nicholls, 1978, 1979a), and they become more sensitive to differential treatment by teachers (see below). However, the most important developmental changes in the ability-assessment process concern the use of social comparative information.

Children as young as preschool age make social comparisons and competitive, "besting" verbal statements (Mosatche and Bragonier, 1981). By the age of $3^{1}/_{2}$, children also react differently to winning and losing a competition (Heckhausen, 1984). The evidence suggests, however, that although preschool-age children may make simple comparisons with one other individually, they do not use group normative information (i.e., their own performance compared to the performance of a group of age-mates) to assess their competence until later (Aboud, 1985; Boggiano and Ruble, 1979; Nicholls, 1978; Ruble, Boggiano, Feldman, and Loeb, 1980; Ruble, Parsons, and Ross, 1976).

A study by Ruble et al. (1980) is illustrative. First- and second-grade children were given tasks in groups of four. The outcome of the task was ambiguous, so that the experimenter could give children predetermined but believable information about their own and the other three children's performance. Subjects were either told that they had succeeded or that they had failed; in each of the success and failure conditions children were either given no information about the other children's performance, were told that all of the other children had succeeded, or were told that all of the other children had failed. The first-graders' subsequent ratings of their ability on the task were affected by whether they succeeded or failed, but not by the information about the other children's performance. Second-graders' ratings were influenced both by their own outcome and the normative information.

The evidence on whether children use normative information to evaluate their competence in the first few grades in school is inconsistent (Levine, Snyder, and Mendez-Caratini, 1982; Morris and Nemcek, 1982; Ruble et al., 1980; Ruble and Frey, 1991). It is clear, however, that dramatic changes occur between kindergarten and about the second or third grade (Butler, 1989; Ruble, Feldman, and Boggiano, 1976; Ruble et al., 1980; Stipek and Tannatt, 1984). By the third or fourth grade, children's ability judgments are consistently affected by normative information, and they begin to explain their self-perceptions of ability in social-comparative terms. Older children are also more skilled than younger children at interpreting social comparative information (Aboud, 1985; Ruble, 1983). For example, in one study, fifth-graders took differences in the amount of time they and a peer were given to work on a test into consideration when judging their performance relative to the peer, while second graders did not (Aboud, 1985).

Students' attention to social comparison information increases even more upon entry into junior high (Feldlaufer, Midgley, and Eccles, 1988). Furthermore, during the junior and senior high school years students place their achievement into an increasingly broader social context. Elementary school children compare themselves primarily with classmates. In junior high children begin to pay attention to grade point averages, which can be compared school-wide. By the final years of high school, outcomes of scholarship competitions, college admissions, and other indicators of achievement relative to national norms figure into some students' judgments of their competence. Analogous changes are likely to apply to athletic and other spheres of performance. While younger children most likely compare their performance to teammates, as they get older children presumably begin to assess their own competence in comparison to children on other teams, and eventually for some, to national records.

The shift toward using normative criteria to judge ability is undoubtedly a major factor in the average decline from early grades to high school observed in children's ratings of their ability. Children's own competencies, in an absolute sense, are constantly improving. Focusing on mastery and accepting praise at face value assures most young children of positive judgments of their competence. In contrast, social comparison inevitably leads to some negative judgments because half of the children in a class must, by definition, perform *below average*.

Classroom Practice Effects

Age-related changes in children's definitions of competence, self-ratings of ability, and predictions for success are to some degree a consequence of systematic shifts in the organizational, instructional, and evaluation practices that children are exposed to in school (Stipek and Mac Iver, 1989). Evidence for some of these changes is discussed below.

Preschool teachers usually accept a child's product as satisfactory as long as the child has worked on it for a reasonable amount of time, and most children end up receiving positive feedback on tasks they complete (Apple and King, 1978; Blumenfeld et al., 1982). Tasks are typically done individually or in small groups, and comparative information about classmates' performance is not readily available. Under these circumstances, it is not surprising that preschool-age children rarely compare their performance with peers and are able to maintain positive perceptions of their competence.

But children are not protected for very long from the potentially harsh effects of academic competition. The nature of tasks, competence feedback, and student-teacher relationships all change gradually over the early elementary school years, and sometimes dramatically when children enter junior high.

Several changes in school tasks and evaluation practices presumably contribute to a more differentiated concept of ability. Throughout the early elementary grades, teachers tend to emphasize effort and work habits, even in report card grades (Blumenfeld, et al., 1983; Brophy and Evertson, 1978). However, effort figures less prominently in report card grades as children move through elementary school (Entwisle and Hayduk, 1978), and by junior high, grades tend to be based more narrowly on test performance (Gullickson, 1985). Tasks, too, become more focused on intellectual skills as children advance in grade, and in junior high school teacher-student relationships become much more formal and centered on school performance (Midgley, Feldlaufer, and Eccles, 1988, 1989b). Accordingly, children's concept of ability shifts from a poorly differentiated construct that includes effort, work habits, and social skills to a more narrowly defined construct that focuses more exclusively on performance on academic tasks.

Many changes in the nature of instruction and evaluation also foster student interest in social comparison. Over the elementary school years children are increasingly given tasks that involve a single right answer (Eccles, Midgely, and Adler, 1984; Higgins and Parsons, 1983). They also encounter ability grouping (Hallinan and Sorensen, 1983) and other public evidence (e.g., star charts) of their own and classmates' skills (Higgins and Parson, 1983). Assignments become more uniform among children and over time (Eccles and Midgley, 1989), and older children experience more whole-group and less individualized and small-group instruction than younger children (Brophy and Evertson, 1978).

Social comparison is more salient as a result of these changes because uniform task structures reduce intra-individual variation in performance across time and make it easier to compare inequalities in performance across students. When tasks do not vary much from day to day, children perform more consistently than when the format and nature of tasks vary. When all students do the same task at the same time, performance is more comparable, more salient, and more public than when tasks vary or are individualized (Blumenfeld et al., 1982; Marshall and Weinstein, 1984; Rosenholtz and Simpson, 1984b).

The amount of positive social reinforcement also declines as children advance in school (Pintrich and Blumenfeld, 1985) and grades are given more frequently. Partly because grades are increasingly based on relative performance (i.e., a normal curve)—a criterion which requires some children to do poorly—grades decline, on average (Blumenfeld et al., 1983; Gullickson, 1985; Hill and Wigfield, 1984; Nottlemann, 1987). Because grades are easily comparable, these changes in evaluation practices no doubt contribute to children's interest in social comparative information, as well as to the decline in average self-ratings.

In summary, the nature and diversity of tasks, evaluation practices, and relations with teachers change as children progress through school in ways that increasingly emphasize individual differences in performance on academic tasks. These changes make it difficult for average and below-average students to maintain positive perceptions of competence. Changes in instructional and evaluation practices occur, however, in conjunction with changes in children's information processing abilities. We do not know, therefore, to what degree an increased emphasis on social comparison and declines in ability and expectancy judgments are an inevitable consequence of cognitive development, or primarily caused by changes in school experiences.

FRAME OF REFERENCE

Several researchers have studied systematically the frame of reference children use to judge their competence. Marsh (1984b) found in one study that students' ratings of their academic competencies were relatively low in schools that enrolled relatively high-ability students (Meyer, 1970; Marsh and Parker, 1984; Bachman and O'Malley, 1986). Marsh (1987) claims, therefore, that students primarily use their immediate social context for a standard—which he refers to as the "big-fish—little-pond-effect." Thus high-ability students should have *lower* perceptions of their academic competence in a high-ability group, track, or school (because they compare themselves to high-ability peers) than they would if they were heterogeneously grouped (giving them low- as well as high-ability peers to compare themselves to); conversely, low-ability students should have *higher* perceptions of their competence in a low group, track, or school than in a heterogeneous group.

The above analysis suggests that ability grouping should, on average, have a positive effect on relatively low-performing students' and a negative effect on relatively high-performing students' perceptions of competence. Research indicating that self-ratings of ability are also based on group membership, however, suggests the opposite (Felson and Reed, 1986). To the degree that students base their perceptions of their ability on group membership, students placed in relatively high groups should rate their academic ability higher than students placed in relatively low groups, regardless of their performance *within* the group.

Eder (1983) provides ethnographic evidence that both frames of reference—one's own performance compared to members of the immediate group and the relative standing of one's group—are used by children as early as in the first grade. The effect of grouping or tracking, therefore, should vary according to how salient performance differences are within and between groups. To the degree that differences among students in the immediate social context are salient, students' performance relative to other students in their group should affect their perceptions of their own ability. To the degree that differences among groups in a classroom or in a school are salient, students' group placement, relative to other groups, should affect their perceptions of competence. Variations across studies related to these variables may explain why research on the effects of ability group placement on students' perceptions of their competence is not consistent (Goldberg, Passow, and Justman, 1966; Weinstein, 1976).

That children do not necessarily choose a frame of reference that will result in the most positive judgment was demonstrated in a study by Renick and Harter (1989). They found that most of the mainstream learning disabled students they studied *spontaneously* compared their academic performance to the "normal" children in their regular classroom. This was found even though they rated themselves higher when they were specifically asked to rate their competence relative to students in the learning disabled class they attended for part of the day. Their global self-worth ratings were also better predicted by their perceptions of their competence relative to their "normal" classmates than by their perceptions of their competence relative to their learning disabled peers.

In addition to comparing their performance to classmates, students use a personal frame of reference to judge their competence; that is, they compare their own performance in different subject areas. Although the evidence is not entirely consistent (Skaalvik and Rankin, 1990), some studies suggest that judgments about competence in one domain are based partly on a person's perception of his or her performance in that domain relative to other domains (Marsh, 1986; Marsh, Byrne, and Shavelson, 1988). Thus, to some degree, a student who is particularly good in math may rate himself lower in English than would be expected on the basis of his performance in English relative to classmates. A common (and annoying) example of the use of a personal frame of reference to judge competence is the straight "A" student who claims to be *terrible* in a subject in which he or she once received a grade of "B."

MEASURING PERCEPTIONS OF ABILITY

Researchers have measured perceived academic competence both at a general level and for specific subject areas. Harter (1982) developed a commonly used measure for children above the second grade. The format is similar to her intrinsic motivation measure, described in Chapter 5; children are asked to identify which of two statements applies most to them (e.g., "Some kids often forget what they learn" versus "Other kids can remember things easily"), and then to indicate whether the selected statement is "really true for me" or "sort of true for me." The 36-item measure includes three subscales that measure self-perceptions of cognitive, social, and physical competence, and a fourth general self-worth subscale. Harter and Pike (1984) developed another version of the measure for children in preschool through the second grade which includes pictures and has four subscales: cognitive competence, physical competence, peer acceptance, and maternal acceptance.

Marsh and his colleagues (Marsh et al., 1984; Marsh and Gouvernet, 1989; Marsh and Holmes, 1990; Marsh, Smith, and Barnes, 1983) developed a measure of perceived competence that differentiates between subject areas. The 66-item Self-Description Questionnaire (SDQ) includes subscales for perceived competence in reading, mathematics, and all school subjects, as well as subscales in four nonacademic areas: physical abilities, appearance, relations with peers, and relations with parents. The measure is appropriate for children in the upper elementary grades through junior high school.

Many researchers have asked a smaller set of questions to assess children's perceptions of their academic competence in school in general or in particular subjects. Eccles (1980) and her colleagues ask just a few questions, usually using 7-point Likert scales, such as the following (descriptions for the endpoints of the scale are indicated in parentheses):

How good are you at math? (not at all good/very good)

If you were to rank all the students in your math class from the worst to the best, where would you put yourself? (the worst/the best)

Compared to most of your other school subjects, how good are you at math? (much worse/much better)

These and similar questions have been used to assess perceived competence in various academic subjects and for schoolwork in general (also Stipek and Gralinski, 1991).

Self-efficacy needs to be measured in regard to a specific task. Schunk asks children to rate how certain they are (from "not sure" to "really sure") of completing problems which they are shown long enough to appreciate their difficulty level but too briefly to solve (Schunk and Hanson, 1985).

Teachers as well as researchers can use these measures to identify children who have low perceptions of their ability. Teachers are often surprised to find that some high-achieving students are less confident about their abilities than the teacher would expect from their objective performance. Students' answers to questions about their perceptions of their ability to succeed on school tasks can help explain maladaptive (e.g., not trying, giving up easily) behavior, and can help teachers to structure the curriculum and assignments in ways that maximize children's self-confidence. Thus, it is useful to ask students how difficult they find tasks or whether they believe they are able to complete tasks. If students are reluctant to admit low self-confidence in their abilities, anonymous questionnaires can be used to inform teachers of general problems with their students' perceptions of their abilities vis-à-vis classroom tasks.

SUMMARY

No child or adult enjoys confronting tasks that engender only feelings of incompetence. It is not surprising that individuals use a variety of tactics to avoid failure, or if failure is inevitable, to avoid looking stupid.

TABLE 8-1 • Summary of Terms	
Term	Definition
Entity concept of ability	Ability is a stable trait which individuals have a fixed amount of and which is only moderately affected by practice and effort
Instrumental-incremental concept ability	Ability, like a skill, can be increased through practice and effort
Undifferentiated concept of ability	Concept of ability is based on mastery or learning; high effort produces high ability
Differentiated concept of ability	Ability is judged in reference to others; relatively high effort suggests relatively low ability given equal outcomes
Self-efficacy	Personal judgment of one's performance capabilities on a particular type of task
Self-worth	People's appraisal of their own value

The common tactics described by Covington and Beery (1976) may achieve the short-term goal of avoiding the implications of failure, but in the long-term they undermine learning and performance. Yet this is the situation that many students face day after day in school.

Positive perceptions of ability and self-confidence in being able to succeed is an essential ingredient for effective learning. Without these, students will not engage in productive learning behaviors. In Chapter 10 instructional strategies designed to maintain self-confidence in students are discussed.

ENDNOTE

1. There has been some dispute among motivation researchers regarding the relative emotion-generating power of ability versus effort attributions (Brown and Weiner, 1984; Covington and Omelich, 1984a; Sohn, 1977; Weiner, 1977; Weiner and Brown, 1984). Attribution theorists have emphasized the importance of effort, arguing that reward and punishment are based primarily on effort; in contrast, self-worth theorists have emphasized the importance of ability attributions, arguing that self-worth in this culture is based largely on perceptions of competence. Weiner and Brown (1984) conclude from a series of studies designed by researchers representing both schools of thought that these two attributions give rise to distinct affective experiences. Thus, failure

attributed to lack of effort is associated with guilt whereas failure attributed to lack of ability is associated with feelings of humiliation. Pride, they argue, is elicited by success whether one attributes success to effort or ability. They conclude, furthermore, that attributions suggesting high ability are most valued (and therefore generate the most affect) in situations in which outcomes have implications for future success, presumably because ability is assumed to be stable, and past successes attributed to ability seem to promise future successes.

9

ACHIEVEMENT ANXIETY

Low perceptions of competence often create feelings of anxiety in evaluation situations. Anxiety is not all bad; a small amount of anxiety can facilitate performance, especially if the task is not very difficult (Sieber, O'Neil, and Tobias, 1977). But for some students anxiety debilitates performance in achievement settings by interfering with learning and with retrieving previously learned material. In this chapter we will examine the measurement, the effects, and the origins of achievement anxiety. Specific recommendations will be made for minimizing the negative effects of anxiety on learning and academic performance.

Anxiety is believed to be aroused in situations threatening an individual's self-esteem. In the early work on test anxiety, Sarason, Davidson, Lighthall, Waite, and Ruebush (1960) described the test-anxious child as one who has "self-depreciatory attitudes, anticipates failure in the test situation in the sense that he will not meet the standards of performance of others or himself, and experiences the situation as unpleasant" (p. 20). Hill (1972, 1980, 1984; Hill and Wigfield, 1984) claims that high-anxious children are fearful of failure; they therefore avoid highly evaluative situations and choose easy tasks on which success is fairly certain. When they must perform in evaluative situations, they are overly concerned about parents' and teachers' evaluations of their performance, and these concerns interfere with their performance on the task.

Some researchers believe that the strong association between anxiety and low perceptions of competence and expectations for failure call into question the need to measure them separately (Nicholls, 1976b). I believe that anxiety needs to be considered and measured separately because the level of the arousal is affected by factors other than perceptions of competence and performance expectations. For example, the value or importance students place on academic success may affect their tendency to become anxious in achievement contexts. Thus, although self-confidence is strongly related to anxiety, other factors are also important.

A distinction is usually made between **trait anxiety**, a relatively stable personality characteristic, and **state anxiety**, a temporary emotional state (Spielberger, 1972). Most questionnaire measures of anxiety assess trait anxiety. Individuals who are generally more prone than others to experiencing a state of anxiety in achievement situations score high on these assessment tools. But they are not necessarily experiencing anxiety all of the time. Trait anxiety is believed to interfere with learning and performance only when the achievement conditions create a *state* of anxiety. Accordingly, under some educational conditions, debilitating anxiety can be minimized even for students who are prone to feeling anxious.

Anxiety in achievement contexts is usually referred to as "test anxiety." However, "test" is used broadly in this literature and the research is usually applicable to all situations in which a student's intellectual abilities are being evaluated. Evaluation may occur in a formal testing situation or simply when the teacher asks a student a question.

There are two components to test anxiety, a cognitive component (worry), and an emotional component (Liebert and Morris, 1967). The emotional component refers to the autonomic (physiological) reactions that are evoked by evaluative stress, such as sweating and an accelerated heart rate (Holroyd and Appel, 1980). The cognitive, worry component of test anxiety (negative expectations for success, concerns about one's performance) is believed to interfere most directly with learning and task performance (Deffenbacher, 1980; Morris, Davis, and Hutchings, 1981).

How serious a problem is achievement anxiety? In most classrooms, evaluation is always present, and many children develop considerable, sometimes paralyzing, anxiety about how their intellectual competencies will be evaluated by their teacher, parents, and peers (Hill and Wigfield, 1984).

MEASURING ANXIETY

Several self-report instruments have been developed to measure students' propensity to experience anxiety in evaluative situations. The original instrument given to children, the Test Anxiety Scale for Children (TASC), was developed by Sarason et al. (1960). Students respond to questions, such as "Do you feel nervous while you are taking a test?" or "Do you think you worry more about school than other children?" Because some children (especially boys) seem unwilling to report anxiety, the authors developed a defensive measure—the Lie Scale for Children (LSC)—with questions such as, "Do you ever worry?" This supplementary scale assesses the child's reluctance to admit feelings of anxiety.

A positively worded revision of the TASC (called the TASC-Rx), was developed by Feld and Lewis (1969). An example of a question is "Do you feel relaxed while you are taking a test?" The authors found, using factor analysis, that students' responses to the questionnaire fell into four categories: (1) specific worry about tests; (2) physiological reactions to evaluative pressure; (3) negative self-evaluation, and (4) worry about school while at home.[1] Children with a high score on the fourth factor fantasize about possible school failure even when they are at home. Children who were high on one factor or category were not necessarily high on other categories. Thus, anxiety seems to be experienced by children in different ways and in different situations.

The results of this factor analytic study have potential implications for the classroom. Remedies for high anxiety may be different, depending on which "kind" of anxiety a child experiences. For example, the child who has unpleasant physiological reactions in test situations may need a different kind of intervention than a child who has a negative view of his or her ability to succeed. The first child may need instructions on test-taking strategies or simply more experience taking tests. The second child may need success experiences and other interventions designed to build self-confidence.

Harnisch, Hill, and Fyans (1980) selected seven items from the TASC-Rx, primarily from the test-worry category, to create the Test Comfort Index (TCI). This scale, as well as the others, has been used extensively in classrooms for diagnostic and research purposes. Hill (1984) reports that school personnel like the TCI because it is quick and easy to administer and is worded positively. These seven questions are reproduced below. The student responds "yes" or "no" to each item.

1. When the teacher says that she is going to give the class a test, do you feel relaxed and comfortable?

2. Do you feel relaxed before you take a test?
3. Do you feel relaxed while you are taking a test?
4. Do you feel relaxed when the teacher says that she is going to ask you questions to find out how much you know?
5. When the teacher says that she is going to give the class a test, do you usually feel that you will do good work?
6. While you are taking a test, do you usually think you are doing good work?
7. Do you like tests in school?

According to research by Hill and his colleagues, it is highly likely that the test performance of students who respond "no" to these items does not provide an accurate assessment of their true competence. Their anxiety probably interferes with their performance in ways that are described below.

ANXIETY AND ACHIEVEMENT

Considerable evidence indicates that children who report high anxiety in achievement situations perform poorly compared to children who report relatively low anxiety. The association is stronger for older than for younger children. Hill and Sarason (1966), for example, found in a five-year longitudinal study of about 700 elementary school children that the negative relationship between test anxiety (TASC) scores and achievement test scores increased steadily from first to sixth grade. Hill (1979) reports an even stronger association between achievement test scores and the TCI among junior high and high school students.

Demonstrating a link between achievement and anxiety, however, does not establish the causal direction of the association. Do students who have not mastered the material become anxious when they are being evaluated? Do anxious students have difficulty learning new material? Or do anxious students have difficulty demonstrating what they know in evaluative situations?

Research suggests that the association between anxiety and achievement is extremely complex (Covington and Omelich, 1988), but certainly, all of the above are true. Anxiety interferes with learning and with demonstrating understanding, and students who are poorly prepared and who expect to fail are more likely to experience anxiety than students who are well prepared and self-confident. Anxiety is, therefore, a cause as well as a consequence of poor preparation.

Tobias (1977, 1980, 1986) suggests that anxiety interferes with learning and performance at three levels. First, anxiety inhibits the efficient *preprocessing* of new information, that is, of registering and internally representing the instructional input. For example, the student may have difficulty attending to and organizing the material presented. Second, anxiety interferes with *processing*—applying new understanding to generate a solution to a problem. The student understands the new material, but when asked to apply the new knowledge to a specific problem, he or she is unable to remember what has been learned or use effective problem-solving strategies. Third, Tobias suggests that anxiety interferes with the *output* of a response. The correct answer may be grasped and then lost before the student verbalizes or records it. Or the student may be able to demonstrate understanding immediately after the material is learned, but has difficulty reproducing it on a summative test given later. When we claim that our mind "went blank," or that we are "blocking on a name," we are referring to the output level of a response.

Preprocessing and Processing

There is considerable evidence for the effect of anxiety on these three levels of learning and performance. Consider first the preprocessing and processing levels. Several researchers have found that high-anxious students have less effective study skills than students lower in anxiety (Culler and Holahan, 1980; Desiderato and Koskinen, 1969; Mitchell and Ng, 1972; Naveh-Benjamin, McKeachie, and Lin, 1987; Wittmaier, 1972); for these students, interventions involving training in study skills have been successful in reducing anxiety (Tryon, 1980). In a study by Benjamin, McKeachie, Lin, and Holinger (1981), high-anxious college students reported spending more time studying for an exam than low-anxious students reported, but the high-anxious students had more problems in learning the material. High-anxious students also did more poorly on a take-home exam, which presumably tested the students' ability to analyze and organize information that was in front of them rather than to retrieve previously learned material.

Research evidence also suggests that high-anxious children are easily distracted when they are learning new material (Dusek, 1980; Dusek, Mergler, and Kermis, 1976), and can therefore be assisted by instructions that enhance their attention (Dusek, Kermis, and Mergler, 1975). In the Dusek et al. (1976) study, for example, children were asked to memorize the position of animal drawings in a stimulus array; the performance of high-anxious, but not of low-anxious, children was improved considerably when they were asked to label the drawings as they were placed in the stimulus array. Presumably, the labeling helped the high-anxious children focus their attention on the central stimuli.

Output

Anxiety is believed to interfere in several ways with students' ability to demonstrate their knowledge. Wine (1980) claims that attention in testing situations is divided between task-relevant and task-irrelevant thoughts. Individuals with a high level of anxiety devote a significant amount of attention to task-irrelevant thoughts, leaving only small amounts of attention for task-relevant responses.

Task-irrelevant responses may take several forms. Some test-anxiety theorists claim that students high in anxiety are self-conscious in evaluative situations and that this interferes with their performance. The interference is both cognitive and autonomic. Cognitive interference is in the form of self-depreciating thoughts (e.g., "I'm too stupid to get these right"; "I must be the slowest person in the class to finish these problems"). Autonomic interference is in the form of physiological reactions (e.g., trembling).

An example of interfering self-preoccupation was described in Chapter 2 with regard to Peterson and Swing's (1982) study. When one child, Melissa, was asked what she was thinking about while working on a probability task, she commented that she was mostly thinking about how well she was doing compared to a classmate and how concerned she was about looking foolish. Jani, on the other hand, responded to the same question by giving a detailed account of the strategies she used to solve the problems. Melissa's concerns about avoiding demonstrating incompetence are what Nicholls (1983) refers to as "ego-involvement," which, as is described in Chapters 2 and 5, can negatively affect learning.

Other studies have also shown that high-test-anxious individuals report having had more task-irrelevant thoughts—preoccupation with how they were doing, how other people were doing, and what the examiner thought about them—while they worked on a task than low-test-anxious individuals (Sarason, 1984). These thoughts may also interfere with performance by distracting a student's attention from the task. For example, when Nottelmann and Hill (1977) asked students to make as many words as they could out of the word "operable," high-anxious children glanced more at the experimenter, a task the experimenter was working on, and in other directions, and made fewer words than did low-anxious children.

When children are highly anxious, they may become obsessed with unimportant aspects of the task, such as their handwriting. Or in severe cases, they may attend to entirely irrelevant aspects of the task. I once observed a child who was supposed to be answering a set of questions based on a paragraph. Rather than reading the paragraph, he busily counted and recounted the number of words it contained. This activity seemed to offer some relief; at least he was doing something. And by giving the teacher the impression that he was engaged in the task at hand, it delayed the inevitable negative teacher reaction to not completing the assignment.

Test-anxious children have also been found to display several forms of interfering, dependency-related behavior, such as disruptive attention-getting and dependence on the teacher for guidance (Phillips, Martin, and Meyers, 1972). The high-anxious child who spends his or her time soliciting the attention of the teacher rather than working on the task at hand is not likely to perform very well.

Deficiencies in test-taking skills are also believed to account for poor performance (Bruch, Juster, and Kaflowitz, 1983). Students who are anxious in test situations seem to lack such abilities as accurately interpreting instructions, appropriate pacing, and other strategies (e.g., doing the easy questions first).

Summary

The research on anxiety and achievement provides strong evidence that anxiety interferes with both learning and performance. Thus, students who are highly anxious in achievement contexts have difficulty learning new material and demonstrating what they have learned. Before discussing possible ways to minimize the debilitating effects of anxiety on learning and performance, we will consider some explanations that have been offered for the development of high achievement anxiety in some children.

ORIGINS OF ACHIEVEMENT ANXIETY

It has already been suggested that low confidence can cause anxiety in evaluative situations. Nevertheless, some individuals who usually perform well on tests do experience severe anxiety, while some individuals who generally do poorly show little evidence of it. Why do some high-performing children experience so much anxiety, and why do some low-performing children appear relatively relaxed in achievement situations?

The original developers of the TASC believed that anxiety has its roots in parent-child relationships (Sarason et al., 1960). They maintained that parents of a highly anxious child hold unrealistically high expectations and are overly critical. The child internalizes the parents' negative evaluations and consequently feels inadequate in evaluative situations regardless of his or her performance. The unconscious hostility toward the parent for being so critical is internalized in the form of anxiety, rather than externalized in overt aggressiveness. This explanation of the cause of achievement anxiety has considerable plausibility, but little evidence has been presented to support it.

Early school experiences may also affect anxiety. The amount of success versus failure is undoubtedly important. Phillips (1967), for example, found that children's mastery of reading in the first grade predicted their test anxiety in the fourth grade. This association between poor reading mastery and high anxiety was especially strong for girls. Hill (1972) also reports that although not all students who consistently fail become highly anxious, students with high achievement anxiety are more likely to have a history of failure than students low in anxiety. It is possible that early school failures have a powerful effect on later performance in part because students who fail develop a propensity to experience anxiety in evaluative situations, anxiety that interferes with their future learning and performance. Test anxiety scores do not stabilize until the latter part of the elementary school years perhaps because several years of failure in school are needed for high anxiety to develop (Dusek, 1980).

If low perceptions of competence and low expectations for success are major factors in performance anxiety, then anxiety should increase with age. Recall that children's perceptions of their academic ability decline with age, and an understanding of ability as capacity is not fully developed until early adolescence (see Chapter 8). Consequently, older children high in test anxiety have had both more failure experiences than younger children and differing interpretations of the meaning of failure. That is, they understand failure to have implications for their ability, which they may not be able to change.

The origins of anxiety may therefore be different for low- and high-achieving students. Wigfield and Eccles (1989) suggest that low-achieving students develop anxiety as a result of repeated failures and low expectations for success. In contrast, relatively high-performing students may become anxious because of unrealistic parental, peer, or self-imposed expectations that they should excel in all academic areas.

Classroom climate and other school-related factors may also be important. It is likely that frequent or harsh teacher criticism and a strong emphasis on performance outcomes (as opposed to the process of learning) foster anxiety. Consistent with this proposal is a study by Zatz and Chassin (1985), in which high-anxious children performed more poorly on tests than low- or middle-anxious students only in classes in which students perceived the threat of evaluation to be high. Wigfield and Eccles (1989) suggest that the transition to junior high may engender anxiety because the uncertainty of a new school context, including a larger school and many teachers, is compounded with stricter grading, less autonomy, and more formal relationships with teachers. Standardized testing is another feature of school environments that can engender anxiety, especially if over-emphasized. In high school, standardized tests, such as the Scholastic Aptitude Test (SAT), play a major role in students' long-term educational and occupational options, and are no doubt a major source of anxiety for some students.

Sex differences are also commonly found in studies of test anxiety (Hembree, 1988). Girls are often found to have higher scores on the TASC than boys, and the difference increases with increased time at school and age (Hill and Sarason, 1966). Sarason et al. (1960) suggest that boys may score lower than girls on measures of test anxiety because they are more reluctant to admit anxiety, not because they actually experience it less. Relatively higher anxiety among girls could also result from their lower perceptions of their ability (see Chapter 5).

Sarason et al. (1960) find that when asked to rate student anxiety, teachers often underestimate the anxiety of high-performing students. They suggest that anxiety in bright, high-performing students is the most likely to be overlooked by teachers because these children are usually not as obvious as hostile children who act out, or extremely shy, withdrawn children. They point out that although anxiety is a painful experience for all children, its overt manifestations (except in extreme cases) are frequently difficult to recognize.

MATH ANXIETY

Anxious Amy is in good company. Math anxiety, or "mathophobia" is widespread (Lazarus, 1975). Suinn (1970) reported that over a third of the college students applying for a behavior therapy program to reduce test anxiety indicated that their primary difficulty was related to mathematics.

Math does not generate as much anxiety in young children as in older children and adults. In Goodlad's (1984) study of over 17,000 young students, math was rated about the same as reading in a list of "liked" subjects (after art and physical education). In the National Assessment of Educational Progress, nine-year-olds ranked math as their best-liked subject; thirteen-year-olds ranked it second best, but in contrast to the younger children, seventeen-year-olds claimed that math was their *least* liked subject (Carpenter et al., 1981). Significant declines in positive attitudes toward math have also been shown over the adolescent years (Brush, 1979; Wigfield, Eccles, Mac Iver, Reuman, and Midgley, 1991). Apparently children are not born with math anxiety. Rather, negative attitudes toward math develop over time, especially during adolescence.

Why does math, in particular, cause so much anxiety in older students and adults? One can only speculate. Lazarus (1975) points out that math anxiety has a ". . . peculiar social acceptability. Persons otherwise proud of their educational attainments shamelessly confess to being 'no good at math'" (p. 281). Math may also appear to be more divorced from real life than other subjects, and, therefore, is not perceived by students as having as much value as other subjects.

The way math is taught may also explain why math anxiety is common. Lazarus (1975) suggests that the cumulative nature of math curricula is one explanation; if you fail to understand one operation, you are often unable to learn anything taught beyond that operation.

From an observational study of math and social studies classes, Stodolsky (1985) proposed that math instruction fostered in students the belief that math is something that is learned from an authority, not figured out on one's own. She found that math classes were characterized by (1) a recitation and seatwork pattern of instruction, (2) a reliance on teacher presentation of new concepts or procedures, (3) textbook-centered instruction, (4) textbooks that lacked developmental or instructional material for concept development, (5) a lack of manipulatives, and (6) a lack of social support or small-group work. The instructional format, the types of behavior expected from students, and the materials used were also more similar from day to day in math than in social studies classes. This lack of variety may contribute to anxiety because students who do not do well in the instructional format used in math are not given opportunities to succeed under alternative formats.

Stodolsky (1985) also suggests that math is an area in which ability, in the sense of a stable trait, is believed to play a dominant role in performance—either one has the ability or one does not. And if one lacks ability in math, nothing can be done about it. By contrast, people generally believe that performance in other subjects, like reading or social studies, can be improved with practice and effort.

As indicated above, there is consistent evidence that females suffer more from math anxiety than males (Hembree, 1990; Richardson and Woolfolk, 1980; Wigfield and Meece, 1988). Recall that in my study of fifth- and sixth-grade children discussed earlier, girls had lower expectations for success in math but not in reading, and were more likely to attribute poor performance in math to low ability (Stipek, 1984c). Some researchers have proposed that math anxiety contributes to observed sex differences in mathematics achievement and course enrollment (e.g., Tobias and Weissbrod, 1980), but the one study assessing anxiety and enrollment plans found no relationship (Meece, Wigfield, and Eccles, 1990).

There is little agreement on the reasons for such sex differences. Ability differences, socialization differences, and the number of math courses taken, have all been proposed as explanations (Parsons, Adler, and Kaczala, 1982). Whatever the reasons for the frequency and intensity of math anxiety, particularly among women, it is a problem that warrants special attention by educational researchers and practitioners.

MINIMIZING THE NEGATIVE EFFECTS OF ANXIETY

Individuals high on trait anxiety do not always experience a state of anxiety in achievement contexts, and their performance in educational settings is not always debilitated by anxiety. Aspects of the educational environment that can be manipulated to minimize the negative effects of anxiety are discussed below. They cannot, however, be implemented indiscriminately. The recommendations made for highly anxious students are not necessarily good for students who are low in anxiety. Indeed, occasionally conditions that maximize performance for highly anxious students undermine performance for students who are low in anxiety. This is because, for some students, a mild amount of anxiety actually facilitates performance.

Different interventions are also appropriate for different problems related to anxiety. Benjamin, McKeachie, and Lin (1987) distinguish between anxious students who have good study habits but cannot handle evaluative pressure (whose anxiety interferes with performance in the production phase) and students who do not master the material presented to them (whose anxiety interferes in the preprocessing and processing phases). More relaxed testing conditions and training in test-taking strategies would be appropriate for the former students, while study skill training would be more appropriate for the latter.

Preprocessing

There are several ways that anxious students' ability to process new information or material can be improved. First, highly anxious students can be helped by having opportunities to reinspect material. If new information is being presented in a lecture, it is important for the teacher to pause frequently for questions, and to review the material. Helmke (1988) demonstrated the value of such teaching techniques. He found a relatively weak association between test anxiety and test performance in classrooms in which teachers spent relatively more time reviewing material. If the material is presented in a film, for example, highly anxious students can be allowed to review the film. If it is presented in written form they can be permitted to reread the material.

Clear, unambiguous instructions and a fair amount of structure also seem to facilitate the processing of new information for anxious students. For instance, teachers can give explicit instructions for strategies for learning material. In one fifth-grade class I visited, the teacher gave children a list of written instructions designed to help them learn spelling words (e.g., "look at the word; say the letters to yourself; close your eyes and picture the word; write the word; check accuracy"; and so on).

A self-paced curriculum is especially helpful to highly anxious students, especially those who are achieving poorly. Having to keep up with the group can create anxiety. Knowing that new material and demands for performance will be regulated according to the student's own mastery should relieve some anxiety.

Processing and Output

As discussed above, some anxious students also have difficulty storing new information, bringing their knowledge to bear on new problems, and demonstrating their knowledge in a testing situation. Most of the research on alleviating anxiety in the production phase has involved desensitization and relaxation techniques (Wigfield and Eccles, 1989). Students typically work through a desensitization hierarchy, usually in a group setting. Thus, for example, they begin by imagining the teacher announcing a test, and continue to imagine more threatening situations, such as taking home a test with a poor grade. Although desensitization methods show some promise, their long-term effects have not been assessed.

There are many things that teachers can do to alleviate the effects of anxiety at the processing and output stages that are better integrated into the classroom curriculum than desensitization. One approach is to introduce tasks in a nonthreatening way. Anxiety debilitates performance most when a task is introduced in such a way that poor performance could damage a student's ego. For example, I. Sarason (1973, 1975) reports that task-irrelevant, self-deprecatory thinking among

high test-anxious individuals is especially likely when tasks are introduced as a test of ability, or when attention is oriented to the evaluative
aspect of a task. In one study he gave a group of college students who
were high and low in test anxiety a serial learning task of meaningless
words (I. Sarason, 1961). Some students were simply given instructions
necessary to respond to the task. Other students were told that the task
was a measure of intelligence. High-anxious students who were told
that the task measured intelligence performed significantly more poorly
than high-anxious students who were given neutral instructions. The
instructions had no effect on the low-anxious students' performance.

I. Sarason (1958) demonstrated in another study that instructions
designed to allay concerns about ability can enhance the performance
of high-anxious students. He eliminated performance differences
between high- and low-anxious students by simply suggesting to the
high-anxious students that they should relax even if they do not learn
the task immediately because it is a very difficult task. The low-anxious
students actually performed better without the reassuring introduction,
presumably because their own motivation was heightened when they
assumed that their performance provided information about their
ability.

This study illustrates how the same instructions can have different
effects on different students, depending on the level of anxiety they
bring to the task. In general, Sarason and others have found that when
preliminary instructions have an evaluative or achievement-orienting
flavor, high-test-anxious subjects tend to perform at a relatively low
level, whereas a modest evaluation or achievement orientation seems
to have a positive effect on the performance of low-test-anxious
individuals.

Giving students opportunities to correct errors can also alleviate
anxiety. Situations in which students have only one opportunity to give
an answer and the answer is either right or wrong should be avoided.
When the student corrects an error there should be no remaining evidence of there ever having been an error. Students can be allowed to
correct their own papers in some situations, and to redo incorrectly
solved problems before their responses are turned in to the teacher.
Permitting students to improve written products, such as themes, before
a final grade is given will also alleviate anxiety. Self-correction for
writing assignments will no doubt be facilitated by the introduction of
more computers and word processing programs into classrooms.

Several techniques have also been developed to alleviate the debilitating effects of anxiety in testing situations. Tests should be presented
as a means of assessing current understanding to help the student and
teacher determine whether, and what kind of, additional instruction

and practice is needed. They should not be presented as the final assessment of the student's competence. Thus, when a test is introduced the teacher might say, "This is to let each of you find what you understand and what you do not understand, so you know what you will need to study," rather than, "This is to test how well each of you is doing."

Having to rely entirely on memory in a testing situation can create unnecessary anxiety. Memory supports have been shown to be helpful in alleviating anxiety (Gross and Mastenbrook, 1980; Sieber et al., 1977). Thus, a highly anxious student might perform better on a math task if she is allowed to refer to a sample problem; she might do better on a set of questions related to a reading assignment if she is allowed to review the text on which the questions are based. Even when questions are constructed in such a way that having books and notes available is not very helpful, students often feel more secure just knowing that they have access to them.

Providing an opportunity to retake a test can enhance motivation and improve test scores, in part because it relieves anxiety. Covington and Omelich (1984c) found that undergraduate psychology students who were allowed to retake their midterm after several days of study were more self-confident and ultimately received significantly higher scores than students who were not given this option.

Hill and his colleagues have done many studies on the effect of the conditions of testing on the performance of anxious children (Hill, 1980, 1984). In all of his studies the high-anxious students' performance was considerably improved by optimal testing conditions. Three features of testing have consistently been shown to affect the performance of high-anxious students: (1) time limits; (2) difficulty of the test material; and (3) test instructions, question-and-answer formats, and other mechanics (e.g., computerized responses).

Hill and Eaton (1977) investigated the effects of *time pressure* on the performance of upper elementary grade students on an arithmetic computation test. When students were pressured for time, the high-anxious students took twice as long to do the problems and made three times as many errors as the low-anxious children. When there was no time pressure, high-anxious students worked almost as fast as low-anxious students and made only a few more errors. Several subsequent studies provide further evidence that relaxing time pressure improves the performance of high-anxious students (Plass and Hill, 1986; see Hill, 1984, for a review).

Since anxiety interferes with learning only on relatively *difficult subject matter*, it can be alleviated by making the task slightly easier. One study found that students prone to anxiety performed better on tasks that began with easy problems that became progressively more difficult than on tasks in which some difficult problems were placed early in the test [Lund, (1953), cited in Phillips, Pitcher, Worsham, and Miller, 1980]. Zigler and his colleagues (Zigler and Harter, 1969) found that children's IQ test performance could be improved by simply adjusting the order of questions so that an easy question followed several consecutive incorrect responses.

Finally, *test instructions and the test format* can affect the performance of highly anxious students. Unfamiliar question formats, computerized answer sheets, and other unfamiliar aspects of standardized achievement tests can be especially intimidating to children who are prone to anxiety. Hill's research (reviewed in Hill, 1984) suggests that many students perform below their capacity on standardized tests because they do not understand instructions or do not know how to use the answer sheets.

Hill has developed a curriculum to train high-anxious students in standardized test-taking skills. Optimal student performance on standardized tests is particularly important now that basic skills are being emphasized by policy makers, and teachers are being held accountable for student learning—which is typically assessed by standardized tests. Hill's eight-session curriculum has been implemented in many schools throughout the states of Illinois and Florida and has led to significant gains in achievement test performance (Hill and Horton, 1985).[2]

SUMMARY

Not all anxiety is debilitating. For some children, a modest amount of anxiety can motivate optimal performance. But anxiety can also interfere with learning and performance. One of the teacher's many tasks is to minimize the debilitating effects of anxiety. A general principle is to remove, as much as possible, the threat failure can have for the student's ego.

TABLE 9-1 • Summary of Terms	
Term	*Definition*
Trait anxiety	A relatively stable personality characteristic; Proneness to a state of anxiety in evaluative contexts
State anxiety	A temporal state of anxiety in a particular evaluative context

ENDNOTES

1. Factor analysis is a statistical technique that groups responses as a function of their level of association. If, for example, respondents who give a high rating to question number 1 also give a high ratings to questions number 5, 9, and 11, those four questions will be grouped in the same "factor."

2. Additional information on Hill's test anxiety reduction program can be obtained by writing to Dr. Kennedy Hill, 149 Children's Research Center, University of Illinois, 51 Gerty Drive, Champaign, IL 61820.

10

MAINTAINING POSITIVE ACHIEVEMENT-RELATED BELIEFS

Students' *beliefs* are important determinants of their behavior, whether or not the beliefs are based on any objective reality. Research discussed in the two previous chapters reveals that students who lack self-confidence in their academic ability and expect to fail avoid achievement situations when they can. When they are required to do a task, they often exert more effort to avoid looking stupid than developing skills, and they attend more to their concerns about being negatively evaluated than to problem-solving strategies. When students who perceive themselves to be low in competence encounter difficulty, they give up easily; when they succeed, they attribute their success to some external cause, such as an easy task, and are consequently unable to take pride in their achievement. In contrast, students who believe that rewards are based on good performance and who are confident that they are able to perform well are likely to approach academic tasks eagerly, to exert effort in order to increase mastery, to focus their attention on strategies to solve the problem at hand, to persist on tasks when they do not immediately succeed, and to experience positive emotions in task situations.

This chapter discusses ways to foster the positive beliefs that lead to productive learning behaviors and to minimize the negative beliefs that inhibit learning. The goal is not to dupe all students into thinking that they are the smartest in the class. Not only would it be impossible to convince all children that they are "smart" in a normative sense, it would serve no useful purpose. By definition, half the children in a class are below average. Regardless of what the teacher does, students will eventually become aware of differences between their own and their classmates' performances, and some students will perceive themselves as inferior to others in particular skills. Moreover, children need to know their strengths and weaknesses to make wise decisions about where to invest effort and about feasible long-term educational and professional plans.

But teachers have some control over the salience and meaning of these individual differences. A realistic goal, therefore, is for all students to feel efficacious—to believe that they have the competence to learn and to complete their school tasks. A second, related goal is for all students to feel relaxed in achievement contexts and to experience a sense of personal responsibility and pride in their accomplishments. A third goal, necessary for achieving the first two, is to foster an incremental concept of ability and a task orientation. Students learn best when they focus on the work at hand and how to master it rather than on how they are performing relative to others. Results of research reported by Nicholls, Cheung, Lauer, and Patashnick (1989) suggest that this focus can be fostered even among children who believe that their academic ability is low relative to their classmates.

These goals are not always achieved easily, however. After the first few grades in school students develop a powerful set of beliefs about their abilities to perform in educational settings, and most students judge their ability in comparison to their peers. Some students develop negative beliefs about their competencies, and without some significant intervention they maintain these beliefs from grade to grade. Mason and I documented this stability in achievement-related beliefs in a study of upper elementary-school-age children. Students' perceptions of their competence in math and reading, their perceptions of the cause of success and failure in these subjects, and their emotional experiences while engaged in math and reading tasks were fairly stable over a two-year period, even though all of the students changed classrooms and teachers (Mason and Stipek, 1989).

Although it can be frustrating for a teacher to try to convince students who lack confidence that they have the ability to learn, negative beliefs and expectations can change. I have observed dramatic improvements in students' expectations and behavior over a short period of time. These changes can occur when a student enters a new classroom with a new teacher, or as the result of changes initiated by the same teacher in the same classroom with the same set of peers. The variability in students' beliefs related to different subjects also reveals the potential impact of the current classroom context. I have known junior high school students whose self-confidence and other achievement-related beliefs varied considerably with regard to different classes taken at the same time and requiring similar skills (e.g., English and social studies or math and science). Presumably, the environment of one class fostered positive beliefs and the environment of the other class did not.

It is important for teachers to understand each student's beginning set of beliefs about his or her own ability. But teachers must not be discouraged by what they find. An individual teacher can have an enormous impact on students' beliefs and, consequently, on their behavior and learning. We turn now to a discussion of classroom conditions that enhance positive achievement-related beliefs.

DIFFICULTY LEVEL OF TASKS

As discussed in Chapter 6, challenging but achievable tasks maximize intrinsic motivation. This same principle applies to beliefs about competence. Very easy tasks do not produce feelings of competence because no improvement in skill level or understanding is required to achieve success. Very difficult tasks generally do not produce feelings of competence either because attempts to complete the task usually do not result in success, or when they do, the amount of effort required diminishes the value of the accomplishment. Tasks of intermediate difficulty—ones that allow students to observe their skills improving and to experience some success—are the most effective in enhancing feelings of competence.

Note intermediate difficulty, or challenge, is defined relative to a child's own skill level. Thus, a task that one student finds easy may be moderately difficult for another. Although students who are behind their classmates may feel badly about having to work on tasks that are too easy for most of their peers, the alternative is worse—continually failing at tasks that are appropriate for their classmates but too difficult for them. Completing assignments and being able to take personal responsibility and pride in success are far more likely to encourage future effort than repeatedly failing to do the more difficult tasks that classmates are given, especially if the teacher creates a classroom climate in which effort and success is valued for all students.

To experience a feeling of developing competence students need clear information that they are improving their skill level or acquiring knowledge. Initial failures in developing a skill are inevitable. But a long series of failures prior to any success may inhibit feelings of competency. Therefore, problems and assignments ordered by difficulty level to provide students with a sense of increasing mastery are the most likely to enhance perceptions of competence and self-efficacy.

Proximal Goals

Difficult tasks can be broken down into subunits to make sure that students receive competence feedback before they become discouraged. Also, students themselves can be encouraged to set achievable short-term or **proximal goals**. Proximal goals can enhance perceptions of competence by giving continual feedback that conveys a sense of mastery (Bandura, 1981; Schunk, 1984a, 1990, 1991). Progress toward a long-term or **distal goal** is, in contrast, sometimes difficult for students to gauge. Younger children especially have greater difficulty assessing progress and keeping a long-term goal in mind.

A study by Bandura and Schunk (1981) demonstrates the advantage of proximal goals. They gave elementary-school-age children seven sets of subtraction problems to work on over seven sessions. Children were told either to complete one set each session (proximal goal), to complete all seven sets by the end of the seventh session (distal goal), or simply to work on the problems with no mention of goals. The proximal goal situation produced the highest level of motivation and led to the highest self-efficacy and subtraction skill. Students in the distal goal condition performed no better than students who were given no specific goal. (Schunk, 1983b, 1986; Schunk and Rice, 1989).

In a study of first and second graders, Gaa (1973) demonstrated that encouraging children to set proximal goals can also help them develop skills in setting appropriate goals for themselves—ones that are challenging but likely to be achieved. Children who met weekly with an experimenter to set goals for the next week and discuss achievements relative to the previous week's goals attained a higher level of reading achievement, and also set fewer and more appropriate goals at the end of the intervention than children who had not had experience setting and reviewing personal goals. (Gaa, 1979; Tollefson, Tracy, Johnsen, Farmer, and Buenning, 1984; Schunk, in press.) Involving children in the goal-setting process has also been shown to raise self-efficacy (Schunk, 1985), and enhance performance (Hom and Murphy, 1985) more than goals imposed by others.

Locke, Shaw, Saari, and Latham (1981) concluded from a review of research that goal-setting has the best effects on performance when goals are challenging and specific (quantifiable or framed in terms of specific action as opposed to general, such as "do my best"), and when feedback provides information on performance relative to the goal.

Wlodkowski and Jaynes (1990) recommend that teachers discuss with children the following criteria when setting goals:

1. *Achievability* — Is there enough time to reach the goal? Does the student have the prerequisite skills?
2. *Believability*—Is the child confident in his or her ability to achieve the goal?
3. *Measurability*—How will the student be able to gauge his or her progress?
4. *Desirability*—Is the goal something the student *wants* to do?
5. *Focusing*—How will the student be reminded of the goal?
6. *Motivating*—Is the process of reaching the goal stimulating, competence building, and reinforcing?
7. *Commitment*—Has the child made an informal or formal gesture to pledge his or her effort and responsibility?

Reactions to Help-Seeking

When students work on challenging tasks they will inevitably encounter difficulties and will need help. Children vary considerably in their help-seeking behavior; some can be reluctant to ask for help even when it is needed, and others can be dependent and unwilling to do much without assistance. Research reviewed by R. Ames (1983) suggests that students who have low perceptions of their ability are more reluctant to seek help when they are ego-oriented than when they are task-oriented, presumably because help-seeking is threatening only when a child is concerned about avoiding a perception of incompetence. Researchers have shown also that the students who need help the most are typically the least likely to ask for it (Karabenick and Knapp, 1988; Newman, 1991). Good, Slavings, Harel, and Emerson (1987) report a decline in low-achieving students' question-asking with age. They found that low-achieving students were fairly active participants in the classroom until the end of the third grade, but subsequently became relatively passive. The decline is most likely explained by an age-related increase in children's concerns about how well they perform compared to classmates (Ruble, 1983).

Children should feel free to seek help when they need it to complete tasks. Some kinds of help, however, are more likely to foster feelings of mastery and competence than others. Nelson-Le Gall (1981, 1990, in press) makes a useful distinction between "instrumental" or mastery-oriented help-seeking, which enables the child to complete the task on his or her own, and "excessive" or dependency-oriented help-seeking, which is done to make someone else solve the problems that the child has not earnestly attempted to solve independently. Mastery-oriented allows students to take responsibility for their achievements and thus can contribute to students' perceptions of competence.

Teachers' reactions to requests for help also have implications for the degree to which students are able to take responsibility for their achievements and thus for their perceptions of competence. Clearly children should be helped when they need it. But teachers should recognize the difference between a real need for help and a failure to try, and when help is given, it should be minimal. The more children can accomplish on their own the better, both in terms of their learning and their perceptions of mastery.

Summary

To experience feelings of competence students need clear feedback indicating mastery. But the task must be sufficiently difficult for them to perceive their skills as improving. Success on an easy task does not convey a sense of mastery, nor does failure on a difficult task. Consequently, teachers need to vary assignments to some degree so that all students are given tasks that are moderately difficult for them. Proximal goal-setting is a useful strategy for giving students frequent mastery feedback. When it is used, goals should be specific and challenging, and children should participate in determining the goal. Help should be given only as it is needed.

TEACHER STATEMENTS

What teachers say to students influences students' conceptions of their ability and their beliefs about their competence. The way teachers introduce a test, for example, can affect a student's concept of ability. Emphasizing relative performance (e.g., "Remember, I'm only giving 'As' to the top five scores") will reinforce a differentiated (relative) concept of ability and foster an ego-orientation, whereas emphasizing other purposes of the test (e.g., "I'd like to know what people understand and what they do not to determine what needs more attention") fosters an undifferentiated concept of ability and a task-orientation. Experimental studies have shown that simply stating that a task measures something important (e.g., intelligence) engenders an ego-orientation, whereas instructions which focus students' attention on the task itself engender a task-orientation (Stipek and Kowalski, 1989).

Teachers' explicit comments about students' performance also have important effects. When a student fails, the teacher can explicitly attribute the failure to a lack of effort, e.g., "I don't think you were really concentrating," indicating a belief in the student's ability to succeed. Or the teacher can inadvertently reinforce the student's doubts about his or her ability by saying something like, "You really can't do these problems, can you?" When a student succeeds the teacher can point out that his or her success reflects ability and hard work, i.e., "You're good at these problems and you're really concentrating hard," or the teacher can undermine self-confidence by attributing the success to some other cause, e.g., "You were lucky you solved that one," or, "These problems must be easy, you're getting them all right."

The goal is to get students to believe that they are able to succeed if they try, and that when they fail it is because they need more practice, they were not trying hard enough, or they didn't use an appropriate strategy. Several researchers have demonstrated that students' maladaptive beliefs can be changed into these more adaptive ones by making explicit statements to them about the causes of their successes and failures.

Dweck (1975), for example, has shown that the belief that failure is caused by low ability can be changed into the belief that failure is caused by low effort or insufficient practice. She identified a number of extremely "helpless" elementary-school-age children. These "helpless" children showed the attributional pattern associated with learned helplessness; that is, they took less personal responsibility for outcomes of their behavior and tended to place less emphasis on the role of effort than nonhelpless children do, and their performance following the occurrence of failure was severely impaired. During 25 daily training sessions, half of these children were given a heavy dose of success. The other half of the children received **attribution retraining**; they had considerable success, but several failure trials were programmed each day. When failure occurred, the experimenter explicitly commented to the child that the failure was due to a lack of effort. At the end of the training the children in the attribution retraining condition, but not the children in the success-only condition, attributed outcomes more to effort than they had previous to the training. Attribution-retraining children also showed improvement in their response to failure; they persisted, using appropriate problem-solving strategies, rather than giving up. Children who had been in the success-only treatment, in contrast, showed no improvement in their response to failure. Some of these children even showed a tendency to react somewhat more adversely to failure than they had before the start of the treatment. This study suggests that success experiences may not be sufficient to get a child like Hopeless Hannah to try harder; instead, the teacher needs to change the child's perceptions of the cause of failure.

Teacher modeling can also be used to influence students' attributions. In a study designed to improve learning strategies among learning-disabled students, the teacher purposefully made mistakes while giving instruction and then made explicit attribution statements focusing on effort or strategy attributions: e.g., "I need to try and use the strategy" (Borkowski, Weyhing, and Carr, 1988).

Several researchers have encouraged *strategy* attributions (Clifford, 1984, in press). Children who do poorly despite considerable effort can be confused and discouraged if the teacher explains that their poor performance is caused by poor effort. Focusing on the use of strategies provides recognition for their effort, and conveys a positive, and sometimes constructive suggestion that the child needs to try an alternative approach to the problem. Schunk (1989a) points out that encouragement to use strategies can also enhance feelings of self-efficacy by giving students a perception of control over outcomes. The usefulness of strategy attributions is suggested by studies indicating that effective adult tutors are more likely to attribute outcomes to strategy than to effort (Lepper, Aspinwall, Mumme, and Chabay, 1990).

Strategy attributions were specifically encouraged in a study by Reid and Borkowski (1987) that was designed to increase self-control and effective learning strategies in hyperactive children. They combined cognitive behavior modification techniques (described in Chapter 4) with attribution retraining. Children were instructed in self-verbalization procedures (i.e., repeating instructions aloud) as well as specific learning strategies, and the instructor encouraged children to attribute outcomes to controllable causes and pointed out repeatedly how the use of the strategies they were taught had helped them succeed. Thus, the attribution training was integrated into the instruction. These and many other studies have shown that improvement in effort and performance can be achieved by explicitly focusing children's attention on effort as causes of their performance (Forsterling, 1985).

When teachers explicitly attribute failure to low effort, a poor strategy, or lack of practice, they imply that they believe the student possesses the ability to succeed with effort and practice. Thus, Schunk (1982, 1984a,b) claims, on the basis of self-efficacy theory, that effort attribution training is effective because it implicitly gives students the message that they have the competency to succeed on the task.

Schunk suggests that teachers can enhance self-confidence just as well by attributing *success* to ability. Moreover, he cautions against making effort attributions when success occurs, because this can actually undermine feelings of competence. This was demonstrated in a study in which third-graders were told while they were working on sub-traction problems either, "You're good at this," or "You've been work-ing hard," or both (Schunk, 1983a). The children who received only the ability attribution judged themselves the most efficacious and solved correctly the highest number of post-test problems. In a later study he found that children who were given ability feedback (e.g., "You're good at this") early in a subtraction training program developed higher per-ceptions of efficacy and developed better subtraction skills than chil-dren who received effort feedback ("You've been working hard"; Schunk, 1984b). Schunk suggests that attributing success to effort reduces children's perceptions of their ability because they believe that success requiring high effort indicates lower ability than success achieved without effort.

Schunk's findings notwithstanding, teachers should not give suc-cessful students the impression that effort is not necessary to achieve success. Optimal motivation on any task occurs when students assume that they possess the ability to achieve success, but that some effort is also required. No learning or increase in skill will result from success that is achieved without effort. Consequently, while teachers need to provide a learning context in which students feel competent, students must not perceive ability alone to be sufficient to achieve success.

CLASSROOM STRUCTURE

In addition to feedback directed toward individual students, there are many aspects of the classroom environment that influence students' conceptions of ability and their evaluations of their own and their classmates' ability. Aspects of classroom structure that might affect stu-dents' judgments of their abilities, discussed below, include the differ-entiation of tasks and whether instruction is delivered in small or large groups.

Task Differentiation

Rosenholtz and Simpson (1984a, 1984b) have demonstrated that the degree to which tasks are differentiated across students and over time affects students' judgments about their own ability relative to class-mates, as well as the way they conceptualize ability (Simpson, 1981; Simpson and Rosenholtz, 1986; Rosenholtz and Rosenholtz, 1981; Rosenholtz and Wilson, 1980). They claim that an **undifferentiated** academic task structure—in which all students work on the same task, using the same materials, requiring the same responses—promotes social comparison and results in students performing consistently at the same relative level over time.

Rosenholtz and her colleagues claim that classrooms using undifferentiated task structures, what they refer to as **"unidimensional" classrooms**, produce stable, stratified (i.e., highly unequal) perceptions of ability. Bossert (1979) points out further that teachers in unidimensional classrooms often face managerial problems with high achievers who finish work earlier than others. Students who know they can finish regular assignments in less than the allotted time also sometimes fool around while they are working on the assignment, causing additional discipline problems.

In a **differentiated task structure**, on any day different students may work on several different kinds of tasks, and from day to day the types of tasks students are given vary. The differentiated task structure, used in **"multidimensional" classrooms**, makes social comparison more difficult and results in less consistency in students' relative performance from task to task and from day to day.

When students' performance varies from task to task, teachers have the opportunity to convey to them the idea that skill development is incremental and domain-specific. They can, for example, point out to students who are having difficulty in one domain that they are doing well in another, and that with effort and persistence they will catch on in this domain as well. A differentiated task structure also allows the teacher to give fast-learning students longer or more difficult tasks, so they are less likely to waste time.

Rosenholtz and Simpson (1984a) explain that task structure influences classroom processes in several mutually reinforcing ways. It influences (1) the distribution of actual performances, (2) the amount of information available to students concerning their own and their classmates' performance, (3) the comparability of information about self and others, and (4) the consistency of information concerning any one type of performance for any one student. These consequences, in turn, affect the process of forming perceptions of ability.

Research findings are generally supportive of their analysis. Pepitone (1972) demonstrated experimentally that uniformity in curricular tasks results in greater social comparison behavior ("I got fewer wrong than you") than differentiation in tasks. Studies also show that both teachers' evaluations of students and students' evaluations of themselves and their peers are more stratified (that is, there is greater dispersion in judgments) in unidimensional than in multidimensional classrooms (Rosenholtz and Rosenholtz, 1981; Rosenholtz and Simpson, 1984b), and children's self-perceptions in unidimensional classrooms correspond more strongly to teacher evaluations (Rosenholtz and

Rosenholtz, 1981; Simpson, 1981). Students also tend to agree with each other on their own and their classmates' relative ability in unidimensional classrooms (Rosenholtz and Simpson, 1984a). In short, compared to multidimensional classrooms, all actors in unidimensional classrooms agree more closely in their ratings of particular students. Thus, students develop a perception of ability as stratified, measurable, and consensual—that is, as something that has an objective reality that can be perceived by others and the self. This concept of ability is similar to IQ, and to what Dweck (1986) refers to as an "entity" theory, discussed in Chapter 8.

There is also evidence that students define school work more narrowly in unidimensional classrooms. In a study of third-graders, Simpson (1981) asked students to rate their ability in "schoolwork" in general and in five specific curriculum areas—arithmetic, reading, social studies, art, and athletics. He found that in unidimensional classrooms students' ratings of ability in schoolwork were determined to a significant degree by their ratings in three areas—arithmetic, reading, and social studies. In multidimensional classrooms, ratings in these three areas were not as strongly associated with students' ratings of ability in schoolwork. Thus, in multidimensional classrooms students could build their self-confidence by performing well in a variety of domains.

Studies by Mac Iver (1987, 1988), however, demonstrate that task structure needs to be considered in the context of other classroom instructional variables. He found, for example, that in multidimensional classrooms in which grades were heavily emphasized, students were highly reliant on adult evaluations in judging their own math ability (Mac Iver, 1987). Apparently the grades provided a standardized, easily comparable criterion and, when given frequently, they overrode the multiple performance dimensions created by a differentiated task structure.

This body of work on task differentiation and the ability-formation process has important practical implications. To minimize the perception that ability is a stable, normatively distributed trait that is demonstrated by performance in a narrow set of skill areas, teachers should vary tasks to some degree so that at any one time students are not all working on the same task, and they should vary the nature and format of tasks from day to day. Variability can be achieved, to some degree, by offering students choices in tasks. Teachers should also give students opportunities to publicly demonstrate competence in many different domains, and they should express positive values for good performance in a variety of areas, including those that are not typically part of school requirements (e.g., playing an instrument, break dancing, athletics).

Whole-Class Instruction

Whole-class instruction can also make relative performance levels very salient. Bossert (1979) points out that in whole-class recitation, right and wrong answers automatically become both public and comparable. It is not unusual for a few self-confident students to dominate large-group instructional periods, while children lacking in self-confidence, and fearful of humiliating themselves, refuse to participate.

Group instruction, whether involving a small group or the whole class, does not need to have negative effects. Sensitive teachers who integrate wrong answers into their instruction can engage the participation of all children and avoid making students feel humiliated or embarrassed for giving wrong answers by giving each child a feeling of having made a constructive contribution. I have observed teachers use many creative strategies to encourage children to participate in group discussions and to protect their self-esteem when they give a wrong answer. I heard one teacher tell a child that his was the "most creative" answer she had heard that day, and that he must have a very good imagination. Another teacher told a student that her answer would have been excellent if the teacher had asked a slightly different question.

A classroom structure in which students' interactions with the teacher are either private or in small groups can also minimize the publicness of performance and evaluative feedback and therefore can have positive effects on children's perceptions of their competence. Whether an individualized, small group, or whole class instructional format is used, teachers need to do everything possible to protect students from the embarrassment that can accompany giving a wrong answer.

Other public evidence of students' relative performance—such as charts displaying students' performance levels or exemplary work prominently placed on bulletin boards, or the names of students requiring extra help or remedial work announced publicly—should also be minimized. Teachers should base recognition for good performance (e.g., papers on the bulletin board) on merit, but recognition must be distributed as evenly as possible across all students. This can be accomplished by recognizing accomplishments in a broad set of domains, and by recognizing effort and improvement, as well as outcome.

EVALUATION

Some form of evaluation is necessary in achievement contexts. Students need specific, detailed feedback to assess their skills and understanding and to identify their strengths and weaknesses. Performance feedback helps students make judgments about where and how to exert effort, and it helps them develop skills in assessing their own work. Specific and informative teacher feedback may be particularly important for low-achieving students, who often have a poor understanding of why they are being negatively evaluated (Connell, 1985).

Letter grades usually provide very little useful information. A writing assignment, for example, that is returned with a "B-" and no other feedback does not help a student determine strengths and weaknesses in writing skills, nor does it provide information that would help the student improve his or her writing skills. Written comments are much more informative. These should be specific, even if positive (e.g., "the paper is well-organized," "the transitions are weak"), rather than global (e.g., "good paper"). It is important to make positive, or at least encouraging, comments in addition to providing constructive criticism. Students need to be told what they are doing right as well as what they are doing wrong, both for purposes of providing useful information and for bolstering self-confidence.

In addition to being useful for skill development, written comments have been shown to enhance intrinsic motivation (see Chapter 6). Mac Iver (1990) claims also, on the basis of his research, that retention and dropout rates can be improved by including handwritten comments on report cards. He suggests that handwritten notes let low-achieving students know that teachers are paying attention to them.

However evaluation is given, it is essential that the information value be stressed. As mentioned in Chapter 6, when teachers stress the controlling function of evaluation (e.g., by continually threatening bad grades or reminding students that if they engage in a particular behavior they will be rewarded with a good grade) students will perceive themselves to be engaging in the behavior only to receive the positive evaluation. When the information value is emphasized, evaluation gives students useful information about their skills, and when it is positive, it gives them a feeling of efficacy and competence, which contribute to intrinsic interest.

I recommend giving global evaluations, such as letter grades, infrequently because students typically focus their attention on the grade even when it is accompanied by more useful information. Global performance feedback also fosters global self-evaluations (e.g., "I'm a 'C' student"), which serve no purpose, whereas students who get specific and informative feedback on assignments should make specific judgments about their strengths and weaknesses and focus their attention on what they need to do to improve.

Criteria for Evaluation

Teachers vary considerably in the criteria they use for evaluating students and allocating rewards. In many classrooms evaluation is based on a competitive standard and rewards are allocated among individuals according to their *relative* performance. Among students of equal ability, competition can increase effort because success becomes largely a function of effort. In typical classrooms, however, students begin the competition with unequal abilities and the outcome is determined only in part by their effort. Evaluation based on a competitive standard inhibits high effort in high-ability students because they can succeed without great effort when competing against students of lower ability, and it can have devastating effects on the achievement behavior of low-ability students because no amount of effort will ever lead to success. Competition is fundamentally flawed as a strategy for increasing student motivation because, by definition, it renders success unavailable to some children.

Ames and her colleagues have studied the motivational effects of competitive versus alternative strategies for evaluation (Ames, 1984, 1986; Ames and Ames, 1984). These researchers have found that the criteria for evaluation affect students' goals (to perform versus to learn), their perceptions of the cause of success and failure, and the kind of information they attend to in evaluating themselves.

Evidence that competition fosters performance goals comes from a study in which children were asked to indicate what they had been thinking while they were working on a task in either a competitive or an individualistic (i.e., challenge yourself) goal structure (Ames, 1986). Competing children were more likely to claim that they were concerned with their ability and less likely to claim that they engaged in self-monitoring and self-instructions related to the task.

With regard to attributions, researchers have shown that in competitive contexts children emphasize ability (and sometimes luck) when interpreting their performance; effort attributions are emphasized in situations in which evaluation is based on group performance, personal improvement, or meeting a pre-established standard (Ames, 1978, 1981; Ames and Ames, 1978, 1981; Ames, Ames, and Felker, 1977; Rhein-berg, 1983).

A study by Ames and Ames (1981) demonstrated that the criteria used for evaluation affects the information children use to evaluate themselves. Children were given an opportunity to establish a personal performance history on a task (success or failure) and then were introduced to either a competitive (with another child) or individualistic (challenge yourself) goal structure. When subsequently asked a series of questions, children's self-reward and feelings of satisfaction in the competitive situation were based on whether they won or lost, and not on the quality of their performance. Children in the individualistic goal structure focused on their personal history with the task (i.e., whether they improved).

There are alternatives to a competitive standard for evaluation. Evaluating students on personal improvement or in terms of a predetermined standard is recommended by many motivation researchers for both relatively high- and low-achieving students. High-achieving students always have a higher standard of excellence to aspire to when the objective is to surpass their own previous level of performance. Low-achieving students benefit because success is attainable and effort should always have some payoff. By fostering the belief that effort leads to success, noncompetitive evaluation also engenders a perception of ability as something that improves with effort; it should increase low-achieving students' expectations for success, and it may also contribute to a perception of fairness.

Some of these benefits were demonstrated in a study by Covington and Omelich (1984c) on college students. They found that undergraduate psychology students who were graded using a mastery standard (i.e., grades were determined by what score the student attained) perceived the grading system to be fairer and more responsive to effort than students who were graded using a competitive, norm-referenced standard (i.e., who were graded on a curve). The students in the mastery condition also aspired to a higher grade and had more self-confidence about being able to achieve a high grade.

Public versus Private Evaluation

Whatever form of evaluation is used, it should not be made public. Wall charts and other public displays of students' performance may enhance the motivation of a very small group of top performers, but they can threaten and discourage other students, especially if evaluative criteria are uniform despite varying skill levels among children. And for all children, these public displays orient attention to *relative* performance rather than personal improvement or mastery. I experienced the negative effects of public displays of performance outcomes during a year in a French university, where it was a standard procedure to hand back papers and exams *in the order of students' scores.* The assumption, I am sure, was that the humiliation of being among the last to receive one's paper would foster greater effort to avoid future humiliation. What I observed in other students and experienced myself was withdrawal and discouragement. My solution, contrary to the instructor's intentions, was to miss class on the day that exams were returned.

If public evaluation is used at all, it must be a "fair contest." All children need to be able to "look good." This can be done by charting progress toward the mastery of goals that are adjusted to be realistically attainable by all children. I observed an example of this in a classroom in which paper boats with students' names on them "raced" across a blue sheet of paper on the bulletin board. The position of each student's boat was determined by how much *progress* that student had made in mastering an increasingly difficult set of spelling words. All children began at the same point on the sheet of blue paper, even though their actual beginning level of mastery varied considerably. Consequently, the student who won the race would not necessarily have attained the highest level of mastery. Rather, the winner would have made the most progress from his or her personal starting point.

A better method than public displays for helping students monitor their progress is to have them keep records, including charts, in their desks. A personal chart, unlike a class chart, focuses children's attention on their own improvement and mastery, rather than on how they compare to classmates.

TABLE 10-1 • Summary of Suggestions for Evaluation

1. Base evaluation, at least to some degree, on personal improvement or mastery rather than on relative performance.

2. Give specific and informative evaluation (such as written comments), that will give students guidance for developing their skills.

3. Minimize global assessments (e.g., grades) that do not provide information that can be used to improve skills.

4. Emphasize the information value of evaluations, not their controlling function.

5. Don't make evaluations of individual students public.

6. If public displays of performance are used, all students should have an equal chance of "looking good."

7. Encourage students to evaluate their own work, rather than to rely entirely on teacher feedback.

Students should be encouraged to evaluate their own work as well as to monitor their progress. This can be achieved in part by giving them opportunities to check their own work. For example, students can check their solutions to math problems against an answer sheet or with a peer. They can be given specific instructions in how to look for problems and errors in their writing. Teachers can also encourage students who ask for feedback (e.g., "Is this right?") to venture a judgment on their own (e.g., "What do you think, does it look right to you?").

Most important, teachers should try to convey to students that evaluative feedback is not a measure of students' worth as human beings, but rather an index of what they know and how far they need to progress to achieve mastery. Evaluation should not be something to fear, but something to help guide students' efforts toward developing academic skills.

Treatment of Errors

Related to evaluation is the issue of how teachers and students view errors. Outside of school errors are considered a natural part of learning a skill. No one would expect to make only perfect serves when learning how to play tennis or to bake a perfect souffle on the first attempt. But in most classrooms errors are viewed negatively—as something to avoid. Red checks next to answers are reason for distress, and 100 percent at the top of a paper is cause for celebration. In school, children learn to devalue errors, even on assignments based on new material.

Many evaluation practices lead to this view of errors. Papers with no errors receive stars, smiling faces, and "As" or they are displayed on the bulletin board. These practices are discouraging to low-achieving students who rarely achieve such recognition for perfect or near-perfect papers, and they lead some high-achieving students, like Safe Sally, to find anything less than 100 percent correct cause for severe disappointment. High-achieving students can become so obsessed with perfect papers that they avoid as much as possible situations in which they expect to make errors and are highly distressed when they do. Thus, treating errors as something to be avoided negatively affects the poorly achieving students who are continually humiliated by errors, and it is harmful to the high-achieving students who become more motivated to complete assignments with no errors than to engage in activities that challenge their current level of competence.

Research has shown that expert tutors rarely label a student's mistake as incorrect or as an error, and they do not offer direct help or suggest answers (Lepper et al., 1990). Instead, they rely on indirect strategies; they direct children's attention to the source of the difficulty, offer hints, and give them a second chance. Thus, errors are never treated directly as errors, but as part of a process that occurs enroute to achieving a correct solution.

Thoughtful teachers have developed many methods to provide evaluative feedback but avoid the negative effects of incorrect responses. Many teachers provide children with multiple opportunities to correct errors, or they allow children to keep working until they have achieved a satisfactory level of mastery or performance. One teacher I interviewed developed the simple but ingenious method of marking incorrect responses on written assignments with a dot. Students continued to work on assignments until all answers were correct. Dots could easily be changed to check marks indicating correctness, without leaving any evidence of the original error. Thus, when a student had completed a workbook, only checks, indicating total mastery, were evident. By using a symbol for incorrectness that could be easily changed into the symbol for correctness, errors were treated as a natural step in mastering new material. Students can also be given opportunities to rewrite papers or redo assignments to achieve a high grade or demonstrate a higher level of mastery.

The information value of errors can also be emphasized. Consider, for example, a child who has many punctuation errors in a writing assignment. The teacher can help the child identify the erroneous rule the child was using (e.g., that commas are placed after prepositional phrases) that resulted in so many errors. In this way the student is shown that errors provide important information that can be used to increase skills.

When corrected papers are returned, children can be encouraged to examine, themselves, the kinds of errors they made, rather than simply to glance at the number of errors indicated at the top of the page. (I would recommend not writing a score at the top of the page.) In one fifth-grade classroom I observed the teacher ask children to try to identify the pattern to the errors they made on math problems, and then to make up and try to solve similar problems. In this way she stressed the information conveyed in errors and their use for increasing skills and understanding.

Children can also be given multiple opportunities to complete tasks—to focus their attention on the *process* of learning rather than the outcome. This is a critical feature of the current popular approaches to teaching writing (Graves, 1983). Children write several drafts of their paper, concentrating on correcting different aspects of the writing (e.g., developing and organizing ideas, syntax, punctuation, spelling) at different points in the process.

In general, I think it is good for students to be required to correct errors before an assignment is put away. This forces them to try to remedy misunderstandings, and is preferable to having students simply take note of *how many* errors they made and move on to another assignment.

Praise and rewards should not be limited to errorless or perfect papers. Children deserve praise for attempting hard tasks, even if their efforts result in more errors than they would have made on an easier task. Safe Sally will not take academic risks until she is rewarded for doing so. Sally would benefit more from teachers who praised difficult tasks with a few or even many errors than from teachers who praised perfect papers.

MASTERY-LEARNING PROGRAMS

In addition to recommending evaluation based on improvement and mastery, educational researchers have developed and tested the effectiveness of programs that can be implemented in most classrooms. Evaluation based on mastery is a central component of the various mastery-based educational programs that have been developed by Bloom (1971, 1974, 1976, 1981) and others. Bloom's model has been used in hundreds of classrooms throughout the United States and in as many as 20 other countries (Block, 1979). Consequently, many variations of the original model exist. The fundamental assumption underlying mastery learning models is that nearly all students can learn the basic school curriculum, but that some take longer than others. By providing slower-learning students with more time to master skills, all students will master the curriculum and all students will receive high grades.

Although mastery learning programs vary, they share several characteristics (Guskey, 1987, 1990). Students are given *regular feedback* on their progress and *corrective feedback* to help them achieve mastery. Most programs also provide *enrichment* activities for students to extend and broaden their learning. Guskey (1990) emphasizes the importance of congruence among the different instructional components—including what students are expected to learn, the instructional activities, feedback on learning progress, corrective activities, and procedures used to evaluate students' learning.

The mastery learning program developed by Bloom, and another program developed by Keller, are briefly described below to illustrate different ways that mastery-based evaluation systems have been implemented in regular classrooms. Although guidelines and commercial materials for these programs are available, it is possible (and usually preferable) for teachers to design their own program and to develop materials that are suited to their own style of teaching and the particular characteristics and needs of their students [see Guskey (1985); Block, Efthim, and Burns, (1989) for practical suggestions].

Introducing the mastery learning model into a classroom does not necessarily affect the mode of instruction. Varying the amount of time students spend on learning concepts or skills and evaluating them on their progress does not preclude, for example, whole-class instruction and lecturing, although more individualized instructional techniques may be easier to use.

Whatever the mode of instruction, however, mastery learning programs require clear instructional objectives. It is necessary to break a course or subject into small discrete units of learning to give students specific skills to work towards and to allow individualized evaluation of increments in mastery. In Bloom's *Learning for Mastery* (LFM) program, the teacher is instructed to develop brief, ungraded, student-scored, diagnostic-progress tests used for formative evaluation of students' levels of understanding (Bloom, Hastings, and Madaus, 1971). These evaluations provide the teacher and student with feedback about the student's progress toward achieving the educational objectives. The student is given additional instructional material ("correctives") based on his or her specific level of mastery. The correctives are used for further instruction and should differ from the teacher's group instruction. Students continue the diagnostic test and corrective instruction cycle until they have achieved mastery. Students are supposed to do the additional studying on their own time, although class time is often set aside for this purpose (Block, 1974).

In the LFM program, grading is noncompetitive in that any student who has mastered the curriculum designated for that length of instructional time is given an "A." Ideally, all but a few students should achieve the predetermined level of mastery.

Keller (1968) developed an instructional model that is compatible with the basic assumptions of Bloom's model, but in practice works quite differently. In Keller's Personalized System of Instruction (PSI) students proceed through a set of written curriculum materials at their own pace. After initially attempting to complete the unit's material, a student takes the unit mastery test, given by a "proctor" (who may be the teacher, a teacher's aide, or a more advanced student or classmate). If the student passes the test, he or she advances to the next unit. Otherwise, the student uses the unit correctives to restudy the unmastered material. The cycle continues until the student demonstrates mastery on one form of the unit's test. Grading is noncompetitive, as it is in LFM programs.

The major difference between LFM and PSI programs is that in LFM classrooms, students are expected to work on their own time to master material so that the entire class can, together, go on to the next unit of study. In PSI classrooms, students continue to work at their own pace throughout the school year. This difference has two important implications. The LFM method theoretically should reduce the variability in achievement levels among students. Students who learn more slowly take more time to achieve mastery, but some of that additional time is their own. The PSI method could actually result in increased variability in mastery because the fast learners are not at all delayed in their progress by the slower learners, as they are to some degree in traditional classrooms using whole-class instructional techniques. An advantage of this is that fast learners can create a highly challenging and highly motivating educational program, and they are spared the boredom that can result from having to go over material they have already mastered.

A second major difference concerns the role of the teacher. In LFM classrooms the teacher may use more traditional large- or small-group teaching methods, whereas PSI converts the teacher from a "dispenser of information to the engineer or contingency manager of all students' learning" (Block, 1974, pp. 18–19). There are many other differences, described in detail by Block (1974) concerning the size and sequence of the instructional unit, the specificity of feedback provided by the formative evaluation instruments, and the mode of correction.

Mastery learning programs such as these two have been implemented in schools throughout the world, and their effects on motivation and learning have been extensively evaluated. Evaluations suggest that mastery learning programs have positive effects on student attitudes and achievement, particularly for weaker students (Guskey and Pigott, 1988; Kulik, Kulik, and Bangert-Drowns, 1990a; Kulik, Kulik, and Cohen, 1979), although whether research has demonstrated positive effects on students' standardized test performance is disputed among reviewers (Anderson and Burns, 1987; Slavin, 1987b, 1990; Kulik, Kulik, and Bangert-Drowns, 1990b).

Although most of the mastery learning programs that have been studied appear to have some positive effects on achievement, they are not entirely effective in achieving some motivation-related goals, such as focusing students' attention on improving their own skills as opposed to competing against classmates. Informal observations of mastery-based programs suggest that it is difficult to eliminate altogether students' interest in comparing their performance with classmates. Crockenberg and Bryant (1978) point out that booklets or units are usually organized hierarchically, and the level is usually indicated by a salient marker, such as color. Learners can easily determine who is more or less advanced in the curriculum, and some observers claim that many children are keenly aware of where they are in comparison to their classmates. Buckholdt and Wodarski (1974) and Levine (1983) have noted children's tendency to create a "race to the end of the curriculum." Even when grading is noncompetitive, children sometimes themselves create a competitive situation. Notwithstanding this limitation, these well-tested programs provide teachers with models, which can be adapted to their own teaching style and student needs, of evaluation that is based on a mastery standard.

COOPERATIVE INCENTIVE STRUCTURES

One way to use competitiveness constructively is to create group competition that pits groups of students of equal ability levels against each other. Educational researchers have developed and tested instructional programs that involve cooperative group learning and team competition.

Johnson and Johnson (1985b, 1989) identify four basic elements that characterize cooperative group learning and distinguish it from traditional group learning. First, there is *positive interdependence among group members*—students need to be concerned about the performance of other students. Second, there is *individual accountability*—every student's mastery of the material is assessed and "counts." Third, there is *face-to-face interaction among students*. Fourth, students learn the *social skills* (such as communication and managing conflict) needed to work collaboratively. (Cohen, 1986; Johnson and Johnson, 1985b; Slavin, Sharan, Kagan, Hertz-Lazarowitz, Webb, and Schmuck, 1985).

Slavin (1983a, 1987a) points out that cooperative learning programs vary in terms of two principal aspects of classroom organization: *task structure* and *reward structure*. All cooperative learning programs use cooperative task structures, in which students work collaboratively with classmates, usually in small groups. Not all programs reward students on the basis of their group (referred to as a **cooperative incentive structure**) as opposed to their individual performance. Slavin's (1983b, 1984) reviews of research on cooperative learning strongly suggest that the cooperative incentive structure results in the highest level of motivation and learning.

The defining feature of a cooperative incentive structure is that a group is rewarded contingent on the performance of all group members. Rewards can be based on a group's achievement of a predetermined level of mastery or on the basis of the group's relative performance. By combining high- and low-performing students in groups and by making rewards contingent upon the group's performance, cooperative incentive structures can equalize opportunities for rewards. A group reward structure can, therefore, relieve motivation problems that many low-ability students have in individual competition situations in which they have no hope of "winning."

Evidence suggests that when rewards are based on the sum of each member of the group's performance, simply being a member of a successful group allows all students some of the advantages of success, such as high self-perceptions of ability, satisfaction, and peer esteem (Ames, 1981; Ames and Felker, 1979). Because cooperative incentive structures give all students an equal chance at being a member of the winning team, they also focus students' attention on effort as a cause of outcomes, rather than on ability (Ames and Ames, 1984).

Johnson and Johnson (1985b) also stress individual accountability, suggesting that positive interdependence can be achieved by dividing up roles, materials, resources, or information among group members in a way that requires all students to contribute. Group size is an important consideration; as the size of the group increases it becomes more difficult to identify individual members' contributions. They suggest groups composed of two to six children. It is also important for all students to realize that their efforts are required in order for the group to succeed.

Cooperative learning approaches have other potential benefits. By rewarding groups as well as individuals for their academic achievement, peer norms favor rather than oppose high achievement (Johnson and Johnson, 1985b; Sharan, 1980). As in sports, where excellence in individual performance is encouraged by peers because it benefits the whole team, team competition in the classroom can result in greater student support of each other's achievements. Studies have found that students in cooperative incentive structures are more likely than students in individual competitive situations to agree with such statements as, "Other children in my class want me to work hard" (Hulton and DeVries, 1976).

Research has also shown that students in cooperative incentive structures are more likely to tutor, help, and encourage classmates than students in individualistic competitive structures (Johnson and Johnson, 1985a, b). Such peer assistance has its own advantages. Students achieve a higher level of understanding in the process of helping other students, and students having difficulties benefit from their peers' assistance (Johnson and Johnson, 1985a). Having average or poor achieving children tutor younger children can also build the older children's self-confidence, as well as help them consolidate skills.

Three programs using cooperative incentive structures stand out for their amount of systematic development and research: Team-Games-Tournaments, Student Teams and Achievement Divisions, and Jigsaw. These cooperative programs (described below) illustrate how cooperative incentive structures can be implemented in the classroom to make productive use of students' competitiveness and to maximize effort and performance.

In *Teams-Games-Tournaments (TGT)* students are assigned to four- or five-member teams. Each team is diverse in terms of its members' level of achievement, race, gender, or other important variables. Teams should be equally matched, especially on initial skill level. Students practice with teammates for game sessions in a tournament which takes place once or twice a week. In the tournament each student is assigned to a tournament table where he or she competes individually against students from other teams. The students at each table are about the same in achievement level. At each three-person game table students answer questions posed on card sets or game sheets to demonstrate mastery of specific skills. At the end of a game session, the top scorer at each table receives six points, the middle scorer four points, and the low scorer two points. Team scores are the sum of the points won by each team member. Team standings, based on the cumulative scores for each team over all of the games in the tournament, are publicized in a weekly classroom newsletter.

In contrast to TGT, *Student Teams and Achievement Divisions (STAD)* programs do not include games and tournaments. Students are assigned to four- or five-member teams which are heterogeneous in terms of past performance levels, sex, and ethnicity. Teammates are usually assigned adjacent seats and encouraged to work together. The function of the team is to prepare its members to take individual quizzes twice a week. Students' scores on the quizzes are compared to the scores of others in their "division"—composed of students who are roughly equal in terms of past performance. The highest ranking score among that group of equals earns the maximum number of points regardless of the relative level of achievement of the division. Rewards are therefore contingent upon performance within a group of children performing at about the same level, rather than upon relative performance in a classroom of students achieving at very different levels. Thus, every child has an equal chance of attaining a high score.

The *Jigsaw* method was originally developed to foster peer cooperation and race relations by creating interdependence among students. A different portion of a learning task is assigned to each of five or six members on a team, and task completion requires contingent and mutual cooperation (Aronson, Stephen, Sikes, Blaney, and Snapp, 1978). Groups are heterogeneous in terms of academic achievement, sex, and ethnicity. The material to be learned is divided into as many parts as there are group members. All groups in the classroom study identical material, subdivided in identical fashion among members. After receiving the task on cards, the jigsaw group disbands and new groups of students with the same task are formed. These new groups help each other learn the material and prepare presentations for the original jigsaw group. Students then return to their original jigsaw group and teach their parts to groupmates. All group members are therefore ultimately responsible for learning all the curriculum material. Teachers move among the groups, offering assistance, encouragement, or direction where it is needed. In the original Jigsaw model, students received individual grades based on their own test scores. In an adaptation, Jigsaw II (Slavin, 1980b), students' grades are based, in part, on their team score.

The three cooperative learning programs reviewed here are representative of a vast number of cooperative learning experiments (by Johnson and Johnson, 1985a; Sharan, 1980; Slavin, 1977, 1980a, 1983a, 1984; Slavin et al., 1985). Practical guides exist to assist teachers in implementing cooperative learning and group evaluation structures (Burns, 1987; Cohen, 1986; Gibbs and Allen, 1978; Johnson et al., 1984; Kagan, undated; Roy, 1982; Slavin, 1988).

Although cooperative learning approaches have the potential for increased motivation and learning, their potential is not always realized. Cohen (1986) argues that children need to be carefully prepared and trained to engage in cooperative learning, and she provides many practical suggestions for such training. Webb (1984, 1985) has conducted many studies that demonstrate important differences in students' interactions (e.g., the nature of help sought and given) and learning as a function of the composition (e.g., gender and ability-level mix) of the group. Issues such as student training and group composition need to be carefully considered before a cooperative learning approach is implemented.

Students' ages must also be taken into consideration when implementing cooperative learning in the classroom. Very young children usually do not have effective strategies for helping peers. I observed a first-grade classroom in which the children were generous with their help, but they had only one strategy—to give the answer. These first-graders were so "helpful," they often wrote the answers into their classmates' workbooks. Such cooperation will not contribute to the learning of the child being helped. If students are encouraged to assist each other, informally or in a special cooperative learning program, they may need to be given explicit instructions in how to assist in a way that will enhance their classmates' understanding.

Although cooperative and mastery learning programs differ considerably in many respects, Guskey (1990) points out that they are not incompatible and share certain characteristics. For example, criterion referenced evaluation is used in both types of programs. That is, students' work is evaluated according to what they have learned, not in terms of their relative standing. He suggests that the benefits of each approach could be enhanced by integrating them. Cooperative teams could, for example, provide a structure in which peers could give corrective feedback to students having difficulty mastering material.

LEARNING TO FAIL

Many motivation theorists emphasize the importance of success in building children's self-confidence (Clifford, 1984). To be sure, success is important. But a steady diet of success does not prepare children to deal with non–success—even in situations in which they encounter new material or new tasks—situations in which some initial failure is to be expected. Many high-achieving students who enter a new academic arena—whether it be moving from the regular to the honors track in high school, from high school to college, or from college to graduate school—are ill-prepared for the challenges that they face. Because they have always succeeded, often without much effort, they are severely debilitated by the initial difficulties they encounter in the more demanding academic context.

Most high-achieving students have not been sufficiently challenged in their academic programs to have experienced initial problems with understanding or performance. As a consequence, they have not learned that obstacles can be overcome. Some harbor doubts about their competencies because they have never really been tested. They know they are good students but they are not confident that in a more challenging context they would continue to perform well.

High-achieving students are also often praised too much for their successes and too little for taking risks or seeking challenge. When performance is emphasized over learning, and success is good and failure is bad, high-achieving students become more invested in performing well (to sustain the positive regard they have become accustomed to) than in learning or mastery (which involves the risk of initial failures).

Children's reluctance to encounter failure is evident in a study by Clifford (1988). She provided students in fourth, fifth, and sixth grades with items varying in difficulty from the Iowa Tests of Basic Skills in mathematics, spelling, and vocabulary. Children were told to select any six problems in each domain. Students in all grade levels chose problems considerably below their ability level and the low-risk-taking tendency increased markedly with each grade level. It is worth noting, however, that when points were linked to the difficulty level of problems (that is, more points were given for more difficult problems), children were more willing to take risks (Clifford, in press). Risk-taking was also enhanced by presenting tasks as a game rather than as a test (Clifford, in press).

Although self-confidence and willingness to take risks can be a problem for high-achieving as well as low-achieving students, strategies for addressing these problems may be somewhat different. Low-achieving students, like Hopeless Hannah, may need a steady diet of success for a while to counteract the steady diet of failure they have experienced; this is necessary to give them some confidence in their ability to learn. But even low-achieving students need to experience *real* success. False praise, as discussed earlier, can actually lower children's perceptions of their competencies, and children know when they are making real progress—when the outcome has been achieved with real effort. High-achieving students, like Safe Sally, may need to encounter some material that they cannot easily master, to find out that the world does not end when they do not initially succeed, and that effort and persistence help them achieve their goal.

SUMMARY

It is important for students to have a realistic understanding of their competencies. Without this they are not likely to select tasks that will foster learning, and they will not develop appropriate aspirations. However, it is equally important for students to feel confident that with some practice and effort they can successfully complete the tasks they encounter in school. It is disheartening for students to be in an environment in which day after day they are assigned tasks that they believe they cannot do at all or will do less well than their classmates, regardless of how hard they try.

Teachers cannot and would not want to eliminate individual differences in students' academic achievements. But they can minimize the amount of humiliation that often accompanies relatively poor performance and they can minimize maladaptive, face-saving behaviors that inhibit learning. Teachers can also foster a feeling that their students' achievements are valued, and they can provide an educational environment that allows students to concentrate on developing skills and understanding rather than on avoiding "looking dumb." These are worthy goals. They lead to better learning and they make school a more pleasant and rewarding place for students.

TABLE 10-2 • Summary of Terms	
Terms	*Definition*
Proximal goals	Short-term goals, that can be achieved relatively quickly
Distal goals	Long-term goals that may involve several steps
Attribution retraining	Making explicit statements to change a child's perceptions of the cause of failure (usually from ability to effort or strategy)
Undifferentiated task structure	Students work on the same tasks at the same time, and the nature of tasks varies little from day to day
Differentiated task structure	Students work on different tasks at the same time and the nature of tasks varies from day to day
Unidimensional classroom	A classroom with an undifferentiated task structure in which valued performance outcomes are narrowly defined and social comparison information is salient
Multidimensional classroom	A classroom with a differentiated task structure in which many different kinds of performance are valued and social comparison information is not salient
Mastery learning	A program of instruction in which children move through the curriculum at their own pace, as a function of demonstrated mastery
Cooperative incentive structure	Students' rewards (e.g., grades) are based on their group's performance

11

COMMUNICATING EXPECTATIONS

Students' self-confidence in their ability to learn is affected by their teachers' expectations. To a very large degree, students expect to learn if their teachers expect them to. One of the most consistent findings in research on effective teachers is that children in classrooms in which the teacher expects all children to learn achieve at a higher level than children in classrooms in which the teacher does not hold uniformly high expectations (Edmonds, 1979; Madaus, Airasian, and Keileghan, 1980; Rutter, Maughan, Mortimore, Duston, and Smith, 1979).

Teacher expectations may concern the whole class, specific groups, or individual children. Expectations can be influenced by a teacher's stereotypes (e.g., boys have more trouble than girls learning to read; poor children learn more slowly than middle-class children), by students' siblings' performance, and by information from previous teachers, as well as from direct observations of students' behavior in the classroom. Teachers also have general beliefs about the malleability of students' abilities and about their own ability to effect desired change.

One effect of teacher expectations on student learning, referred to as the "self-fulfilling prophecy," has been demonstrated in experimental studies. In the original *Pygmalion* study by Rosenthal and Jacobson (1968), elementary-school teachers were told that some of the students in their class had demonstrated on a written test that they had remarkable potential for academic growth. The designated students had actually been selected randomly, but eight months later the students in the early grades for whom teachers were led to hold artificially high expectations showed greater gains in IQ than other students in the school. These students, in a sense, fulfilled their teachers' prophecies. This classic study has spawned virtually hundreds of studies on teachers' expectations (Dusek, 1975, 1985, for reviews).

The term "self-fulfilling prophecy" is apt because once an expectation develops, people often behave as if the belief were true. In so behaving they actually cause their expectancies to be fulfilled. Self-fulfilling prophecies involve three factors: (1) initial expectations, (2) behaviors that communicate those expectations, and (3) evidence that the initial expectation is confirmed. It is only a self-fulfilling prophecy if the original expectation was erroneous and a change was brought about in the student's behavior as a consequence of the expectation.

Inaccurate expectations are not always corrected because teachers create situations in which only confirming evidence is possible. For example, teachers sometimes develop strong "theories" about students and they structure the learning environment in a way that does not allow information contrary to their theory to emerge. I once observed a first-grader who had made no progress in six months of reading instruction. The child's mother had taken drugs while she was pregnant and the teacher was convinced that the drugs caused brain damage and the child was *unable* to learn to read. Because of her assumption the teacher made no effort to experiment with alternative approaches to reading instruction with him and, therefore, denied the child any opportunity to make progress in reading and to disconfirm her theory. The school psychologist eventually intervened and gave the child a sixth-grade student tutor. In two months he was reading at the same level as his classmates in the lowest reading group. He did not excel, but he did learn to read and he might not have if the teacher had continued to base curriculum decisions on her original theory.

A teacher might not notice information contrary to his or her theory, even if it is present. Classrooms are busy places. One teacher may have as many as 30 or more students to monitor, and Jackson (1968) claims that a single elementary-school teacher may engage in more than a thousand interpersonal exchanges a day with students. Under such conditions the teacher can hardly notice every student's behavior. Consequently, certain biases are likely to affect what the teacher does notice. For example, teachers are more likely to monitor closely children whom they expect to be fooling around rather than children whom they expect to be task-oriented. Consequently, they are more likely to notice the off-task behavior of the former than of the latter children, and therefore, to maintain their perception of the former children as easily distracted.

Expectations can also bias interpretations of students' behavior. If a child whom the teacher believes is very bright gives a wrong answer, the teacher is likely to attribute the wrong answer to a nonability-related cause, such as inattention. The same answer from a child perceived to be less bright may be interpreted as confirmation of the child's limited ability.

Teachers' expectations are, to a significant degree, based on students' past behavior and performance (West and Anderson, 1976). Nevertheless, because expectations bias opportunities for demonstrating certain kinds of behaviors and performance, and because they bias what teachers see and how they interpret what they see, inaccurate initial expectations are not always corrected. These inaccurate expectations sometimes affect teachers' behavior toward a student in ways that affect student learning.

For example, considerable evidence suggests that teachers treat students whom they consider bright differently from students they consider low in ability. Some of these differential behaviors have direct effects on learning. Students who are given more opportunities to learn, more clues, and who are called on more frequently should learn more than students who are given fewer opportunities to learn. Other teacher behaviors influence learning more indirectly by affecting students' beliefs about their competencies and their likelihood of success.

There are very good reasons for some kinds of differential behavior toward high and low achievers. Giving some children more difficult material than others is clearly necessary when there is variability in student skill level. Nevertheless, most of the teacher behaviors described below that have been shown to be associated with high versus low expectations cannot be defended on pedagogical grounds.

TEACHER BEHAVIOR TOWARD HIGH- AND LOW-EXPECTATION STUDENTS

Rosenthal (1974) divides teacher behavior associated with high or low expectations into four categories: (1) socio-emotional climate; (2) verbal inputs; (3) verbal outputs; and (4) affective feedback. Some of these differences in behavior are appropriate; many are unnecessary and harmful. Examples of each of the four categories are described below (Good, 1987):

Socio-emotional Climate

1. Smiles and nods at high-expectation students more than at low-expectation students;
2. Is friendlier toward high-expectation students;

Verbal Input

3. Seats low-expectation students farther from the teacher and interacts with them less;
4. Gives high-expectation students more information to learn, or more problems to complete;
5. Gives more difficult and more varied assignments to high-expectation students;

Verbal Output

6. Calls on high-expectation students more often;
7. Gives more clues and repeats or rephrases the question more often for high-expectation students;
8. Waits longer for high-expectation students to answer;
9. Provides high-expectation students with more detailed and more accurate feedback;

Affective Feedback

10. Criticizes low-expectation students more for incorrect responses;
11. Praises high-expectation students more frequently for correct responses;
12. Praises low-expectation students more for marginal or inadequate responses;
13. Expresses pity toward low-expectation students when they perform poorly, anger toward high-expectation students.

Emotional Displays

Some differential behavior, such as the display of emotions, can be extremely subtle but nevertheless important. Students often interpret teacher emotions as conveying information about the teacher's evaluation of their ability. This interpretation can affect the student's own perceptions of his or her ability.

Many studies have shown that individuals believe that emotional reactions reflect a person's perception of the cause of behavior [see Chapter 10 and Weiner (1986)]. Children as young as six years understand that anger is aroused when another's failure is attributed to controllable factors, such as lack of effort, and by about the age of nine years they understand that pity is aroused when another's failure is perceived to be caused by uncontrollable causes (Weiner et al., 1982; Graham, 1990).

Students, therefore, gain information about their teacher's beliefs regarding the cause of their performance outcomes by attending to the teacher's emotional reactions. Graham (1984b) describes a five-step process following failure. First, teachers make their own judgments about the cause of a child's failure; usually they attribute the outcome to either low ability or lack of effort. Second, the teacher communicates his or her own emotional reactions, such as sympathy or anger, respectively. Third, the student processes these emotional displays and uses them to infer the teacher's judgment about the cause of his or her failure. Fourth, the student utilizes the teacher's emotional cues to select, for him- or herself, the best explanation for failure. Fifth, the specific self-ascriptions influence other achievement-related cognitions such as expectancies for success.

Consider, for example, the teacher's likely response to Satisfied Sam when he turns in a math assignment that is only half completed. The teacher, knowing that Sam is capable of finishing the task, attributes the incomplete paper to his typical halfhearted effort. With exasperation in her voice the teacher threatens Sam with punishment: "If you don't finish your assignment tomorrow, you'll stay after school until it is finished." Sam knows that the teacher is angry because she thinks that he didn't try hard enough. Her anger also indicates to him that she assumes that he could have finished the assignment if he had tried. The teacher's emotional response, therefore, serves to reinforce his own confidence in his ability.

What if Hopeless Hannah turned in the same incomplete math assignment? The teacher is likely to assume that this was the best Hannah could do in the time she had. She might sympathetically tell Hannah that she was glad Hannah had done the best she could do. Hannah may interpret the teacher's sympathy as evidence of the teacher's low expectation and low perceptions of her competence. The teacher's response would consequently contribute to Hannah's own doubts about her ability to do the assigned work.

To be sure, I am not suggesting that teachers should express anger at children like Hannah who have difficulty with the regular curriculum. A much better solution would be to adjust the tasks so that Hannah could complete them. Rather, the example is to demonstrate that subtle, emotional responses contain important messages.

Graham (1984a) demonstrated the effect a teacher's emotional response can have on a student's self-perceptions. An experimenter expressed either mild anger or pity to children who had experienced failure. Children who had the sympathetic experimenter were more likely to attribute their failure to a lack of ability than children who had an angry experimenter. The latter were more likely to attribute their failure to a lack of effort. Children who received pity also had lower expectations for success in the future than children who received an angry response from the experimenter. By simply expressing an emotion, the experimenter affected children's perceptions of the cause of their failure and their expectations regarding future outcomes.

What is particularly important about Graham's (1984a) findings is that the consequences of the teacher's emotional response are not intended. For example, a teacher who responds with sympathy toward a failing student might be motivated by the desire to protect the student's self-esteem. Yet despite such good intentions, the effect can be exactly the opposite. The student can interpret the teacher's sympathy as evidence that the teacher believes she has low ability and could not do any better even if she tried. Anger is generally an emotion teachers try to avoid expressing. Ironically, anger may, under some circumstances, have a positive effect by communicating the message that the teacher believes the student's failure is due to lack of effort—a variable the student can control.

Praise

Another counterintuitive finding that has relevance for the classroom concerns the effect of praise on students' achievement-related beliefs. In some circumstances there appears to be negative side effects of praise, at least for older children and adults. As mentioned in Chapter 4, praise for successful performance on an easy task can be interpreted by a student as evidence that the teacher has a low perception of his or her ability. As a consequence, it can actually lower, rather than enhance, self-confidence. Criticism following a poor performance can, under some circumstances, be interpreted as an indication of the teacher's high perception of the student's ability.

Praise and criticism can have these paradoxical effects because of their link with effort attributions, and because individuals perceive effort and ability to be inversely related. If two students achieve the same outcome, the one who tried harder is judged as lower in ability (Nicholls and Miller, 1984a). Thus, if two children succeed and the teacher praises only one of them, the observer assumes that the praised child must have worked harder to achieve the same success as the other child, and therefore must be less able. If two children fail and only one is criticized, the observer assumes that the criticized child must not have worked as hard as the other child, and must therefore be higher in ability.

This analysis assumes a complex reasoning process, which, as indicated in Chapter 8, young children do not understand. Although children understand the relationship between praise and blame and make inferences about effort as young as age five (Harari and Covington, 1981; Weiner and Peter, 1973), they do not understand the inverse relationship between effort and ability until about the age of eleven (Nicholls and Miller, 1984a). Research has shown, therefore, that children above (but not below) about the age of eleven rate a child who is praised by the teacher as lower in ability than a child who was not praised, and they rate a child who is criticized as higher in ability than a child the teacher did not criticize (Barker and Graham, 1987).

The potential for negative effects of praise and positive effects of criticism on children's self-confidence is also illustrated in a study by Parsons, Kaczala, and Meece (1982). They found in the 20 fifth- to ninth-grade math classrooms they observed that frequent criticism of the quality of students' work was positively related to self-concept of math ability and future expectations among students. Praise was unrelated to math self-concept, although boys who were not praised believed that their teachers had high expectations for them. The researchers concluded that teachers who believe they should avoid criticism and give praise freely overlook the power of the context in determining the meaning of the message. They suggest that well-chosen criticism can convey as much positive information as praise.

Helping

Helping behavior can also give students a message that they are perceived as low in ability, and it can undermine the positive achievement-related emotions associated with success. Meyer (1982) describes a study by Conty in which the experimenter offered unrequested help either to the subject or to another individual in the room working on the same task. Subjects who were offered help claimed to feel negative emotions (incompetence, anger, worry, disappointment, distress, anxiety) more, and positive emotions (confidence, joy, pride, superiority, satisfaction) less, than subjects who observed another person being helped. Graham and Barker (1990) report that children as young as six who observed the teacher offering a student help rate that student as lower in ability than another student who was not offered help.

Again, an attributional analysis explains the effect of help on ability judgments and emotional reactions. Research has shown that in a variety of contexts individuals are more likely to help others when their need is perceived to be caused by uncontrollable factors, such as low ability, than when the need is attributed to controllable factors such as insufficient effort (Weiner, 1986). This was shown in a classroom study by Brophy and Rohrkemper (1981). They reported that teachers expressed a greater commitment to help "problem" students when the causes of need were uncontrollable factors, such as low ability or shyness, than when the problems were attributed to controllable factors, such as lack of effort.

There are many other ways teachers can unintentionally communicate low expectations. Good and Brophy (1978) describe the behavior of a physics professor who believed that females have difficulty with physics. To avoid embarrassing them, he never calls on them to answer a mathematical question or to explain difficult concepts. He also shows his concern by looking at one of the girls after he introduces a new point and asking, "Do you understand?" (p. 75). Such "helpful" behavior gives the females in the class a clear negative message about the teacher's perception of their competencies.

I have seen well-meaning teachers make devastating and not-so-subtle comments to students indicating low expectations. I observed a first-grade teacher exclaim to a child who had correctly solved a relatively easy arithmetic problem at the blackboard, "That's very good Jim, I didn't think you'd be able to get that one." A high school teacher once congratulated a friend of mine on a good grade in calculus, adding that he was particularly impressed because "girls don't usually do very well in math."

That such well-intentioned behavior can, in some circumstances, have negative effects on students' beliefs about their competence makes teaching all the more difficult. Teachers need to be extraordinarily attentive to their own behavior toward students and analyze the potential effects of this behavior. Since the same behavior can affect one student differently from another, teachers also need to consider the effect of their behavior on particular individuals. Thus, praise may build one student's self-confidence, whereas it may give another student in the same situation the message that the teacher has low expectations for him or her. The kind of analytic self-monitoring required is not easy in a classroom where teachers have as many as 1,000 exchanges with students in one day!

Teachers need to be especially conscious of potential differences in their behavior toward children from different ethnic groups. Graham (1990) believes that minority children may often be the targets of the subtle and well-meaning teacher behaviors (e.g., sympathy, praise, help) discussed above. She suggests that the low expectations that have been found for minority students (Dusek and Joseph, 1983; McCombs and Gay, 1988) may dispose teachers toward behaviors which, although well-meaning, actually undermine their self-confidence.

ABILITY GROUPING AND TRACKING

Many criticisms of within-class ability grouping and between-class tracking are directly related to concerns about the effects of teachers' expectations. One of the greatest dangers of ability grouping is that teachers begin to perceive all members of the group as equivalent despite the considerable variation usually found within groups (Rosenbaum, 1980). Thus, reading group placement has been shown to have a significant effect on ultimate performance. In one study Weinstein (1976) found that the reading group to which students were assigned contributed 25 percent to the prediction of midyear achievement over and above the students' initial readiness score. The independent effect of reading group placement on the gains children made in reading proficiency is explained, presumably, by differences in the nature and pace of instruction between groups and the teachers' failure to adjust instruction for children with different skill levels within groups. Ability grouping, which is used more frequently for reading than for math instruction, may explain why some studies find that teacher expectations have a stronger impact on reading achievement than on math achievement (Smith, 1980).

Researchers have also noted that teachers often structure high and low reading groups very differently (Borko and Eisenhart, in press; Hart, 1982; Hiebert, 1983). Reading lessons for high compared to low groups have been observed to be more loosely structured, to involve more meaningful questions and opportunities to connect reading to personal experiences, and to be more fun. Decoding skills, rather than meaning, are often stressed more with the "low" group (Hiebert, 1983; McDermott, 1987).

Although some pedagogical adjustments are appropriate for children reading at different levels, many of the differences are unnecessary and have negative effects on student learning. For example, opportunities to connect reading with personal experiences are no less important to children reading below grade level than they are to children reading above grade level. This kind of misperception of what relatively low-achieving students need interferes with effective instruction.

There is a great deal of evidence indicating that students in low tracks are taught differently than students in high tracks. Again, some differences, such as the pace of the curriculum, may reflect appropriate accommodations to students' learning. But many differences in teacher behavior toward students are unnecessary and inhibit the achievement of students in the low track. For example, Oakes (1990) analyzed survey data from 6,000 math and science classes in 1,200 U.S. elementary, junior high, and senior high schools, and found that, in contrast to other teachers, teachers of low-ability classes claimed to put less emphasis on students' own interests in math and science. They also put less emphasis on teaching basic science concepts, developing inquiry skills and problem solving, and in preparing students for further study in math and science. In a previous study she found that teachers of high-track classes more often included competence and autonomous thinking among the most important curricular goals for students (Oakes, 1985). Vanfossen, Jones, and Spade (1987) report from national survey data that college-track students were more likely than other students to describe their teachers as patient, respectful, clear in their presentations, and enjoying their work. These differential behaviors are not necessary and they exacerbate the existing differences between high- and low-achievers.

VALUE OF LOW VERSUS HIGH EXPECTATIONS

Although high expectations are generally assumed to have positive effects on students and low expectations to have negative effects, the opposite can also be true. Goldenberg (1989) points out that high expectations can inhibit teachers from providing needed instructional interventions or changes. He gives the example of a child in a first-grade classroom, Sylvia, who the teacher predicted would fare well in reading. All of the indicators, including reading-readiness scores, suggested that Sylvia would have no trouble mastering reading skills in first grade. Yet soon after the beginning of the year, Sylvia had some difficulty in completing her assignments. She fell farther and farther behind and, as a consequence, made little progress in learning to read. The teacher did not notice or did not reflect upon Sylvia's poor progress, maintained high expectations for her reading achievement, and therefore did not make efforts to adjust instruction. During the last two months of school, at the urging of an observer who had observed Sylvia's difficulties in reading, the teacher intervened, and Sylvia's reading improved at a much faster rate. But the intervention came too late. By the end of the year Sylvia was among the poorest readers in the class. Had the teacher adjusted her expectations and adapted instruction when Sylvia began to have problems, Sylvia might have finished the year with better reading skills.

Goldenberg (1989) provides another example of a teacher who adjusted her expectations appropriately, and by acting on them, contributed to significant improvement in a child's reading achievement. Marta began first grade with a poor prognosis. The first-grade teacher originally predicted that Marta's reading achievement would be among the lowest in the class, partly because of her attitude and behavioral problems. But after the first few months of school she noticed some improvement in Marta's behavior, and adjusted her expectations. Soon after Marta began showing signs of improved behavior, she was placed in a higher reading group. From the moment she was placed in the higher group her reading skills began to improve much more rapidly than they had before. Marta's case clearly demonstrates the value of careful teacher observation, of altering expectations as a function of those observations, and of adjusting educational interventions accordingly.

The point of these examples is that teachers interpret behaviors partly as a function of their expectations, and they base important instructional decisions on these interpretations. What is important is not whether expectations are high or low, but whether they are accurate and whether teachers are able to recognize and act on student behavior that is not consistent with their expectations.

GENDER DIFFERENCES IN TEACHERS' EXPECTATIONS

Gender has been shown to affect teachers' expectations (Good and Findley, 1985). Palardy (1969), for example, studied five first-grade teachers who thought that boys could learn to read just as successfully as girls, and five who thought that boys could not learn to read as successfully as girls. Although students were comparable on reading readiness scores taken in September, by March boys in classrooms in which teachers expected girls to read better than boys actually performed more poorly on a reading achievement test than girls; in the other classrooms no difference was found in boys' and girls' reading achievement scores.

Some researchers have suggested that differential teacher behavior toward girls and boys may explain a common finding that girls have lower perceptions of their competence and lower expectations for success than boys. Dweck and her colleagues proposed that girls may develop lower perceptions of competence, in part, because a larger proportion of their negative feedback concerns the quality of the academic performance. They observed in fourth- and fifth-grade classrooms that boys were criticized more than girls, but most of the criticism the boys received concerned conduct or failure to follow directions. In contrast to the boys, most of the small amount of criticism the girls received concerned the quality of their academic performance (Dweck et al., 1978). They suggested that boys may not view negative feedback as relevant to their intellectual abilities. Because a much larger proportion of the negative feedback girls received concerned their academic performance, they may have been less able to disregard the relevance of teacher feedback to their intellectual abilities.

The evidence on these proposals is not entirely consistent. Parsons, Kaczala, and Meece (1982) studied gender differences in teacher expectations and associated teacher-student interaction patterns in math classrooms in grades 5, 6, 7, and 9. They found that student gender was only modestly related to student-teacher interaction patterns, and not in the manner predicted by Dweck et al. (1978). In those classrooms in which girls had lower expectancies than boys, high-achieving girls were not praised as much as high-achieving boys. This study suggested that differential teacher praise, not criticism, was a more likely explanation of gender differences in achievement-related beliefs.

Much of the research on differential teacher behavior towards girls and boys has been done to explain females' low participation rates in science and math. Classroom observation studies suggest that differential treatment of girls and boys in math and science is more prominent in the upper than in the lower grades. Findings of studies of elementary- and middle-school children are mixed. A few studies have found that girls receive less academic contact than boys (Leinhardt, Seewald, and Engel, 1979), but other studies report few or no differences in the ways boys and girls are treated (Kimball, 1989). In contrast to the early grades, differences are consistently found in high school classes. Researchers have found that teachers talk to, call on, praise, and give more corrective feedback to boys than girls (Becker, 1981; Morse and Handley, 1985; Stallings, 1985). Becker observed, for example, that although there were no differences in student-initiated interactions with teachers in a sample of geometry classes, 63 percent of the teacher-initiated academic contacts were with boys. Girls received 30 percent of the encouraging comments and 84 percent of the discouraging comments. (See Kimball, 1989, for a review).

These differential behaviors are likely to affect boys' and girls' perceptions of competence and expectations, as well as their math learning. Researchers have been concerned about gender differences in achievement-related beliefs in math and science primarily because females take fewer high-level math and science courses than males, and females are underrepresented in math and science professions. Relatively low perceptions of competence and low expectations for success, along with differences in values associated with gender-stereotyping of academic domains and professions, are assumed to inhibit females from pursuing careers in math and science.

STUDENTS' PERCEPTIONS OF TEACHER EXPECTATIONS

Although teacher expectations are based primarily on children's performance, in some classrooms teacher expectancies have an independent effect on children's achievement-related beliefs and learning. Good and Brophy (1980) estimate that about one-third of the many teachers they had observed in several studies behaved in a way that appeared to exaggerate the initial deficiencies of low achievers.

Students are often aware of teachers' differential behavior toward themselves and their classmates, and their perceptions mediate the effects of teacher expectations on students' motivations (Weinstein, 1985, 1989). In one study children in grades one through six were asked to rate their teachers' behavior toward hypothetical male low and high achievers (Weinstein and Middlestadt, 1979). Students claimed that teachers differentiated high- and low-achieving students in the following ways:

1. The teacher goes out of her way to help low achievers.
2. The teacher asks other students to help low achievers.
3. The teacher does not explain what the rules are to low achievers.
4. High achievers are granted special privileges.
5. High achievers are allowed to make up their own projects.
6. The teacher is more concerned that low achievers learn something than enjoy themselves.
7. The teacher asks high achievers to suggest or direct activities.
8. The teacher lets high achievers do as they like as long as they complete the assigned work.
9. High achievers spend more time discussing outside student activities than class-related materials.
10. The teacher asks high achievers questions that demand facts for answers.
11. The teacher watches low achievers closely when they are working.
12. The teacher gives high achievers enough opportunity to respond before calling on someone else.
13. The teacher trusts high achievers.

14. The teacher collects work before low achievers have had a chance to finish.
15. Low achievers are not expected to complete their work.

The classrooms Weinstein and her colleagues have studied varied greatly in the degree to which the teacher was perceived as behaving differently toward high and low achievers (Weinstein, 1985, 1989), and the degree of differentiation has been shown to have implications for students' perceptions of how they are treated and for their own performance expectations. Brattesani, Weinstein, and Marshall (1984) asked students whether their teacher treated high- and low-achieving students differently and how the teacher treated them. In those classrooms in which students claimed that teachers behaved differently toward high and low achievers (high differential treatment classrooms), students' own expectations for their performance were associated with the teachers' expectations. In the "low differential treatment" classrooms, students' own expectations were not as strongly associated with their teachers' expectations. Children as young as first grade have demonstrated their awareness of teachers' differential behavior toward high- and low-achievers, but one study found that children in early elementary school were less likely to report negative treatment toward themselves, and their expectations for themselves conformed less to their teachers than was found for upper-elementary school-age children (Weinstein, Marshall, Sharp, and Botkin, 1987).

Additional evidence indicates that students' perceptions have some validity. In an observation study Mitman and Lash (1988) found that students' perceptions of their teacher's behavior toward them tended to conform to researchers' observations of their teacher's behavior. For example, both children and observers noted that low-achieving students received fewer teacher-initiated work contacts and more criticism of their work than high-achieving students.

AVOIDING THE NEGATIVE EFFECTS OF EXPECTATIONS

Good and Brophy (1986) describe three types of teachers with regard to expectations. The first group is *proactive*. Such teachers do not allow expectations to undermine effective interactions with children and appropriate instructional activities. The second group is *reactive*. They allow existing differences between high- and low-achievers to influence their own behavior. For example, high-achievers have more response opportunities simply because they raise their hands more often than low-achievers. In the third group, *overreactive* teachers provide qualitatively and quantitatively different instruction as a function of their expectations.

Some students are able to learn more advanced material and absorb it more quickly than other students. Such variability is unavoidable. Consequently, teachers need to make judgments about individual students' skill levels and learning rates in order to determine the appropriate difficulty level and pace of the curriculum for each student. Teachers' expectations are detrimental only if they are inaccurate, rigid, or are communicated to the student in ways that undermine his or her self-confidence and learning. Below are a few suggestions to help teachers avoid the negative consequences of teacher expectations.

Communicate High Expectations

In interactions with children, teachers can communicate positive beliefs, expectations, and attributions. They can do this explicitly, by telling students that they know they will be able to achieve a particular outcome, or more implicitly, by providing opportunities for working on challenging tasks, by being patient and encouraging when students have difficulties, by praising only performance that truly deserves praise, and in countless other subtle ways that convey confidence in children's abilities to achieve their goals.

Midgley, Feldlaufer, and Eccles (1989a) report a strong relationship between teachers' own beliefs about their efficacy (i.e., their abilities to motivate students and to positively influence achievement levels) and students' beliefs about their abilities and their likelihood of success in mathematics. Students who had low-efficacy teachers developed more negative beliefs as the school year progressed, whereas the beliefs of students who had high-efficacy teachers became more positive or showed less negative change from the beginning to the end of the school year.

Original impressions of children's skill level and learning ability should be based on valid and reliable information. Some educationists recommend that teachers purposefully remain ignorant of all past information on students' academic performance to avoid self-fulfilling prophecies. I would not make that recommendation because such information can be useful. Comments from previous teachers can help the new teacher initially structure an appropriate curriculum for a student. Test scores and other information in students' records can also be informative. But the new teacher should carefully assess the reliability of the previous teacher's perceptions. The new teacher must not interpret this information as the "truth." Rather, such information should be perceived as a *hypothesis* about the student that may or may not prove true, and could have changed. Furthermore, poor past performance information should be interpreted as a problem to be solved, not as an unalterable trait.

Teachers must also guard against allowing irrelevant information, such as race, social class, or sex, from influencing their expectations for a student. There is good evidence that such factors do affect some teachers' perceptions. Many experimental studies have shown, for example, that teachers often tend to have higher expectations for white than for black students (Baron, Tom, and Cooper, 1985). In some studies students are described in writing, and the race of the child is manipulated by using photography, a videotape of a black or white child, or an audiotape varying the dialect of the speaker. In most of these studies, teachers express higher expectations for the white child despite the fact that all relevant information is equivalent. Teachers must examine carefully the basis for their expectations of students and evaluate the validity of the factors influencing those perceptions.

Expectations Should Be Flexible

Even the teacher's own perceptions of a student's competencies should be thought of as hypotheses that need to be continually reevaluated. It is natural for expectations to bias what teachers see as well as their interpretation of what they see. Teachers, therefore, need to seek out disconfirming evidence in case their "working theory" is no longer accurate. This requires careful observation and some experimentation. For example, the teacher may move a child to a higher reading group on an experimental basis to find out whether the child is capable of mastering more difficult material than he or she has been given.

Sometimes teachers are not fully aware of the assumptions they make about students. It is helpful for teachers to make explicit the assumptions about individual students that are guiding their curriculum decisions. One method is for teachers to write down their assumptions for a particular child and consciously evaluate their validity. How good is the evidence for each assumption? Have alternative assumptions or explanations for the student's behavior been tested?

Do not differentiate behavior toward low- and high-performing students unless there are good reasons for doing so. Teachers should constantly monitor their own behavior and assess the degree to which they may be behaving differently toward different children. Rosenthal's list of behaviors in which teachers commonly differentiate high- and low-expectation students should be kept firmly in mind. There are no pedagogical reasons for most differentiated behavior toward low- and high-expectancy students. Good and Brophy (1986, p. 501) suggest asking questions such as those in Table 11-1 to help monitor behavior toward students varying in skill levels.

TABLE 11-1 • Questions for Teachers to Ask to Help Them Monitor Behavior Toward High- and Low-Achievers[1]

1. Am I as friendly with low-achieving students as I am with high-achieving students?

2. Do I praise or encourage "lows" when they initiate comments?

3. Do I stay with "lows" in failure situations?

4. Do I praise "lows" only for performance that is truly deserving of praise (i.e., that required real effort)?

5. Do I call on "lows" in public situations?

6. How often do "lows" have positive success experiences in public situations?

7. Are "lows" needlessly criticized for wrong answers or failures to respond?

8. Are "lows" placed in a "low group" and treated as group members rather than as individuals?

9. Do I ignore the minor inappropriate behavior of "lows," or do mild violations of classroom rules bring on strong reprimands?

10. Do I make assignments variable, interesting, and challenging for "lows"?

11. How frequently do "lows" have a chance to evaluate their own work and to make important decisions?

12. What are the work preferences of individual students—do they like to work in pairs—and how often are those work preferences honored?

13. Do I intervene with "highs" when they are having difficulty?

14. Do I praise "highs" regardless of their effort or the quality of their performance?

---

1. Adapted from Good and Brophy (1986, p. 501)

It is important to monitor subtle as well as more obvious differential behavior. This was demonstrated in Marshall and Weinstein's (1986; Weinstein, 1989) research. Comparisons of classrooms in which students perceived a high versus a low degree of teacher differential behavior suggested subtle differences in the ways teachers in high- versus low-differentiated classrooms behaved toward children. For example, teachers differed in the feedback provided (focus on mistakes as part of the learning process versus public display of student errors), in the responsibility given to students for evaluation, and in the warmth and humor the teacher used toward particular students.

It is not easy to manage a classroom and monitor one's own assumptions and subtle behavior simultaneously. Being aware of the potential ways in which one may communicate low expectations is an important first step. There are many strategies teachers can use to become more aware of their behavior. For example, it is sometimes useful to make a diagram of the seating in the classroom to check whether the high-expectancy students are more likely to be toward the front of the classroom than the low-expectancy students. It is also helpful to have another individual—an aide, a student teacher, or fellow teacher—observe and point out differential behavior that a teacher may not realize he or she is exhibiting.

Another method of evaluating teacher behavior toward high- and low-expectancy students is to directly assess the students' perceptions of differential behavior. Weinstein and her colleagues have developed a questionnaire that they have given to children in the upper-elementary grades.[1] Students' responses on the questionnaire provide information on the students' perceptions of how the teacher behaves toward high versus low achievers.

Never Give Up on a Child
Finally, although there are tremendous differences in the rate at which children learn, nearly all students who have not been identified as learning handicapped can master the basic curriculum. Some students do not, but it is not for lack of ability. Most students' failure to learn is caused by problems such as poor motivation or inappropriate instruction. The teacher who continues to expect each and every student in a class to learn will invariably be more successful in achieving that goal than the teacher who designates certain students as "impossible to teach."

ENDNOTE

1. A copy of the questionnaire can be obtained by writing Professor Rhona Weinstein, Psychology Department, University of California, Berkeley, CA 94720.

12

REAL STUDENTS

This book divided students into many psychological pieces. We have discussed, independently, various factors that influence children's behavior in achievement settings. But teachers must deal with whole children. Now, like all the king's horses and all the king's men, we must try to put the pieces back together. Let us return to the five children with motivation problems introduced in Chapter 1 and consider possible remedies for their problems.

Defensive Dick does everything that a student might do to avoid looking stupid. He relies on classmates for answers to assignments and he pretends that he can't find his assignments when he hasn't done them or when he believes that his own answers might be wrong. He has elaborate excuses for unfinished work or poor performance. He pays little attention to directions and sometimes flaunts his low level of effort.

Dick is a classic example of Covington and Beery's (1976) "failure-avoiding" student. He is not confident that he could actually achieve success by legitimate methods—such as learning the material and completing tasks on his own. He is, therefore, more motivated to avoid failure than to try to succeed. His behavior is logical in the sense that it achieves his short-term goal of not looking stupid. He is able to complete, more or less, many of the tasks without actually learning the material, and by not trying too hard, he prepares others to attribute his poor performance to his lack of effort rather than to a lack of ability. His behavior, however, is highly maladaptive in the sense that it does not result in any learning. Consequently, poor performance will become increasingly inevitable and difficult to explain away.

What does a teacher do with a student like Dick? Two things must be accomplished. First, the negative consequences of failure must be removed so that Dick can focus on achieving success rather than on avoiding failure. Second, Dick must begin to believe that he can achieve real success, *on his own*.

Making Dick believe that success is a realistic goal may require changing the definition of success. Dick will never expect to succeed if success is based on normative criteria. Success needs to be redefined, for him and probably for the entire class, in terms of personal improvement or in terms of achieving some predetermined, realistically achievable standard of excellence. Making success appear achievable may also require adapting tasks to address Dick's particular needs. Thus, if the standard for an "A" on a spelling test is 90 percent correct, the difficulty of the spelling words will need to be appropriate for Dick's skill level. In addition to increasing Dick's confidence in his ability to achieve success, he should be encouraged to attribute his successes to effort *and* ability. This can be accomplished, in part, by making explicit statements, such as, "You did really well on that; you worked hard and you really know how to do these problems."

To alleviate Dick's concerns about failure, the teacher needs to accept initial poor performance, to convince him that it is all right to make mistakes. If Dick gives a wrong answer in a public context (in a group or class discussion), the teacher needs to find something valuable in the answer. He should also have several opportunities to obtain a reasonably good grade. Thus, if he misses too many problems on a math test, he could be given a "preliminary" grade (in pencil) and an opportunity to study and retake the test until his performance is acceptable—to him and to the teacher.

It is not easy to increase the effort of a child like Dick, but finding solutions to the motivation problems presented by *Hopeless Hannah* is even more difficult. While Dick has not totally given up trying to look smart, Hannah is steadfastly convinced that she lacks ability and will inevitably fail. She has given up all hope, removing herself almost entirely from the reward system of the classroom.

Most of the Hannahs that I have seen have been a grade or more behind in the class. They have often been held back one year and are larger than the other children. They are usually out of the mainstream socially as well as academically. They are at the bottom of the lowest reading group and have difficulty with the easiest math problems. Because their reading skills are so poor, they are also unable to master the social studies curriculum.

Hannah needs considerable individual attention. It is impossible for a teacher of 25 to 35 students to provide an appropriate curriculum and the direct instruction a child like Hannah needs without help. I have seen creative use of older children, high-school students, and retired individuals in the community to help children like Hannah. If parents or older siblings are willing and able, they may also be enlisted to help Hannah at home. These "tutors" need to be given instructions—to be accepting and encouraging, and to make much of Hannah's successes, however modest they may be. They need to be supervised closely by the teacher.

Tasks need to be developed carefully so that they are appropriate for Hannah's skill level. Initially the material may need to be very easy, even for her, to provide her with the success experiences she needs to build her self-confidence. Increases in difficulty should be gradual because she is likely to become easily discouraged.

Obviously, an hour or two a day of individual tutoring is the most that can be realistically expected. Consequently, Hannah's teacher must also find ways to incorporate Hannah into the classroom. All of the suggestions made to help Defensive Dick would also be appropriate for Hannah, although the teacher may need to make an even greater effort to involve Hannah in classroom activities. Hannah could also be given responsibilities (e.g., leading the line to recess, taking the lunch money to the principal's office) to give her some social prestige and to demonstrate the teacher's faith in Hannah's ability to carry out a task.

Such superficial demonstrations of valuing Hannah, however, will not be effective unless she also experiences real improvement in her own skills. The best way to help a child like Hannah is to make sure that she learns. She may never perform well compared to her age-mates, but she can increase her skill level and therefore experience the same feelings of developing competencies that the other students experience. And she can enjoy social acceptance for exerting effort and making progress.

In contrast to Hannah, most teachers enjoy having students like *Safe Sally* in their classroom. Sally's elementary school teachers probably praised her for finishing her work early, put her many papers with 100 percent correct on the bulletin board, and gave her special privileges. Sally became hooked on these social rewards and is afraid to try anything that may threaten their continuation.

If Sally's teachers had praised her for attempting challenging tasks that required considerable effort and persistence rather than for getting all the answers right and finishing early, she might not have developed the belief that only perfect performance is acceptable. When Sally finished early, the teacher should have given her some more difficult problems to do, or a task (writing a short story, working on the computer, starting a class newspaper) that would stretch her knowledge and skills and develop creativity.

By high school it is difficult for teachers to eliminate Sally's obsession with good grades and her fear of situations in which she is not absolutely confident of success. But a school counselor can be obstinate about encouraging her to take challenging courses. And her teachers can discourage her interest in high grades by not emphasizing grades in their classrooms and by praising Sally for taking on difficult tasks rather than for optimal performance on unchallenging tasks.

Teachers can also model intrinsic interest. Students know early in the semester which of their teachers really love their subject. An animated and enthusiastic teacher is much more likely to engage the enthusiasm of his or her students than a teacher who presents the subject matter dryly and without expressing personal interest.

Teachers can also encourage students to engage in learning activities outside of the class requirements. Time can be set aside in an English class for students to discuss books they have read or plays they have seen. Teachers can provide opportunities for students to share their own journals or short stories or poems with their classmates. Newspaper articles can be discussed in social studies classes. In science classes students could share their own observations of scientific phenomena.

If Sally's teachers refer often to tests or grades as a means of evaluating students, Sally will continue to perceive external evaluation as the reason for working. But if her teachers discuss tests and grades in terms of the information they provide, and if they focus Sally's and her classmates' attention on the immediate intrinsic pleasure that can be derived from learning something new, Sally would, no doubt, begin to relax and allow herself to enjoy learning for its own sake, rather than seeing it as a means to a high grade and teacher admiration. And she might be willing to challenge herself.

Satisfied Sam is, in nearly every respect, the opposite of Safe Sally. He eagerly seeks out intellectual challenges and enjoys developing his skills. The problem is that the challenges he accepts and the skills he develops rarely coincide with the school curriculum. Indeed, nearly all of his intellectual activities (computers or science projects) occur outside of the classroom.

Sam is not motivated by grades. He is motivated to stay out of trouble and therefore to obtain minimally respectable grades, but certainly not to excel in school subjects. His threshold for acceptable grades is about a "C+"; he could easily be a straight-"A" student if he exerted some effort on school tasks.

Despite Sam's many intellectual achievements, he is not mastering material that wise adults believe is important to know in our society. Sam's teachers have a difficult task. They need to get Sam to attend to the school curriculum without dampening his curiosity and enthusiasm for intellectual challenge.

The first step is to gain some knowledge of Sam's own intellectual interests. The second step is to try to take advantage of these interests and to incorporate them into his school assignments. For example, if his English teacher is teaching students about biography, the teacher might encourage Sam to read a biography of a scientist, such as Charles Darwin. His geometry teacher might ask him to build a miniature city from another planet in which no buildings can have more than a certain pre-determined number of square inches and all buildings have to conform to certain unusual shapes. His interest in space and the pleasure he gets out of building things might make the mastery of geometry and measurement more meaningful and fun.

It is unrealistic to expect Sam's teachers to find creative ways to engage Sam's interest in every school task. But occasional attempts, such as the examples given above, might help convince Sam of the practical value of mastering the school curriculum.

In general, there are two principles that need to be kept in mind for students like Sam. First, teachers should give such students as much choice as possible. The more choices students have to select the specific tasks they do in order to master the school curriculum, the more likely they are to master it in a way that they find personally meaningful. Why assign the same biography to every student in the class, for example, when there are many excellent biographies that would appeal to students' diverse interests?

Second, an effort must be made to demonstrate the usefulness of "school knowledge." If students are learning composition skills, why not have them write personal journals, letters to the President, or stories for a school newsletter? Certainly these approaches to engaging the enthusiasm of a bright but uninterested student like Sam will be more effective than repeatedly warning him that he will receive a bad grade.

Finally, we come to *Anxious Amy*. Amy can learn the math concepts taught, but she has difficulty demonstrating her knowledge and she is extremely uncomfortable in math learning contexts. The solution to Amy's problem is clear—the risk of failure has to be eliminated from math.

There are several things a teacher can do to make math less threatening. Amy should probably not be asked to answer questions in public, at least not until she is more self-confident and less fearful of revealing her ignorance. The evaluative aspect of tests should not be stressed.

Tests should be presented as opportunities to find out what each student needs to study and what areas of instruction the teacher needs to pursue. Amy should be given all the time she needs to finish a test. It would also be helpful to give her a few sample problems to refer to or to allow her to refer to her textbook during a test. She needs to understand the concepts to be able to solve the test problems, but she can be reassured by having access to examples. She should also be given multiple opportunities to succeed. She obviously needs feedback to tell her which problems she missed, but initially no grade should be recorded. She should be able to retake a test, or to take a test with similar problems, as many times as she needs to in order to demonstrate mastery. The teacher should emphasize the importance of making personal progress and refrain from publicly rewarding certain children for their relatively high level of performance.

A child like Amy can often benefit from being put in the role of the teacher. She might be asked to help another student in her class or to tutor a sixth- or seventh-grader. As a consequence, her own understanding will be enhanced and she should gain some self-confidence.

The five students described in Chapter 1 do not enjoy school, and they do not benefit from school as much as they could. Perhaps Hannah suffers the most. Imagine spending day after day in an environment in which you feel powerless to achieve success, inferior to your peers, and publicly humiliated by your lack of achievement. It is not surprising that students who expect to perform relatively poorly often withdraw, misbehave, or, when they are old enough, leave school. School must also be an exceedingly threatening place for Dick and Amy. Dick is constantly fearful of revealing his ignorance and of losing his own sense of self-worth, which, evidently, is intimately bound up in academic success (as it is for most children). Amy is often in a state of anxiety and certainly does not enjoy her math class. Sam may not experience negative emotions in school, but he is probably bored. Sally, no doubt, enjoys school more than any of the other children described. But she certainly does not derive the kind of pleasure and excitement that learning can offer.

The suggestions made in this book for maximizing these and other students' learning and enjoyment are not easy to implement. Varying school tasks and making them fun requires a tremendous amount of time and energy. Maintaining order (which is essential for learning) in a classroom in which students are given some autonomy requires considerable skill. Knowing each student well and continually assessing each student's knowledge and interests in order to provide appropriate tasks requires an enormous amount of effort. Monitoring one's own behavior to avoid differential or ineffective behavior towards students is also extremely difficult while teaching students and managing a class-room.

Am I suggesting the impossible? I don't think so. I have seen many good teachers maintain children's enthusiasm for learning. I have seen many classrooms—from kindergarten to twelfth grade—in which students are enthusiastically and self-confidently engaged in learning activities. I am convinced that a high level of student motivation and pleasure in learning can be achieved in most classrooms.

Each of the many excellent teachers I have observed has a unique approach. Strategies that work effectively for one teacher and group of students can fail miserably in another classroom with another teacher and a different group of students. The principles of effective teaching and the suggestions made in this book, therefore, need to be adapted to each teacher's style and skills and to the specific characteristics of each group of students.

Teachers need to approach their profession as scientists. They should observe their students and generate hypotheses about motivational and learning problems and consider possible solutions. They must carefully test their hypotheses—by experimenting with different approaches and observing the effects—and revise their hypotheses when their observations do not confirm them. This is a never-ending, dynamic process which requires good observational skills and a willingness to experiment.

The task of maintaining students' enthusiasm to learn is, indeed, challenging. But according to motivational theory and research, individuals are most motivated when they have an opportunity to engage in challenging but not impossible tasks—tasks that can give them feelings of competency and accomplishment. The benefits of providing motivating instruction are immeasurable—for the teacher as well as the students.

REFERENCES

Aboud, F. (1985). The development of a social comparison process in children. *Child Development, 56,* 682–688.

Alberto, P., and Troutman, A. (1986). *Applied behavior analysis for teachers* (2nd edition). Columbus: Merrill.

Alschuler, A. (1968). *How to Increase Motivation Through Climate and Structure* (Working Paper No. 8–313). Cambridge, MA: Achievement Motivation Development Project, Graduate School of Education, Harvard University.

Amabile, T. (1983). *The Social Psychology of Creativity.* New York: Springer-Verlag.

Amabile, T., DeJong, W., and Lepper, M. (1976). Effects of externally imposed deadlines on subsequent intrinsic motivation. *Journal of Personality and Social Psychology, 34,* 92–98.

Ames, C. (1978). Children's achievement attributions and self-reinforcement: Effects of self-concept and competitive reward structure. *Journal of Educational Psychology, 70,* 345–355.

Ames, C. (1981). Competitive versus cooperative reward structure: The influence of individual and group performance factors on achievement attributions and affect. *American Educational Research Journal, 18,* 273–288.

Ames, C. (1984). Competitive, cooperative, and individualistic goal structures: A cognitive-motivational analysis. In R. Ames and C. Ames (Eds.), *Research on Motivation in Education: Vol. 1, Student Motivation* (pp. 177–207). New York: Academic Press.

Ames, C. (1986). Conceptions of motivation within competitive and noncompetitive goal structures. In R. Schwarzer (Ed.), *Self-related Cognitions in Anxiety and Motivation* (pp. 229–245). Hillsdale, NJ: Erlbaum.

Ames, C. and Ames, R. (1978). Thrill of victory and agony of defeat: Children's self and interpersonal evaluations in competitive and noncompetitive learning environments. *Journal of Research and Development in Education, 12,* 79–81.

Ames, C. and Ames, R. (1981). Competitive versus individualistic goal structures: The salience of past performance information for causal attributions and affect. *Journal of Educational Psychology, 73,* 411–418.

Ames, C. and Ames, R. (1984). Goal structures and motivation. *Elementary School Journal, 85,* 39–52.

Ames, C. and Ames, R. (1990). Motivation and effective teaching. In L. Friedman (Ed.), *Good Instruction: What Teachers Can Do in the Classroom.* North Central Regional Education Laboratory.

Ames, C., Ames, R., and Felker, D. (1977). Effects of competitive reward structure and valence outcome on children's achievement attributions. *Journal of Educational Psychology, 69,* 1–8.

Ames, C. and Archer, J. (1987). Mothers' beliefs about the role of ability and effort in school learning. *Journal of Educational Psychology, 79,* 409–414.

Ames, C. and Archer, J. (1988). Achievement goals in the classroom: Students' learning strategies and motivation processes. *Journal of Educational Psychology, 80,* 260–267.

Ames, C. and Felker, D. (1979). An examination of children's attribution and achievement-related evaluations in competitive, cooperative, and individualistic reward structures. *Journal of Educational Psychology, 71,* 413–420.

Ames, R. (1983). Help-seeking and achievement orientation: Perspectives from attribution theory. In B. DePaulo, A. Nadler, and J. Fisher (Eds.), *New Directions in Helping* (pp. 165–188). New York: Academic Press.

Anderson, L. (1981). Short-term students' responses to classroom instruction. *Elementary School Journal, 82,* 97–108.

Anderson, L. (1984). The environment of instruction: The function of seatwork in a commercially developed curriculum. In G. Duffy, L. Roehler, and J. Mason (Eds.), *Comprehensive Instruction: Perspectives and Suggestions* (pp. 93–103). New York: Longmans.

Anderson, L. and Burns, R. (1987). Values, evidence, and mastery learning. *Review of Educational Research, 57,* 215–223.

Anderson, L., Evertson, C., and Brophy, J. (1979). An experimental study of effective teaching in first-grade reading groups. *Elementary School Journal, 79,* 193–223.

Anderson, R., Manoogian, S., and Reznick, J. (1976). The undermining and enhancing of intrinsic motivation in preschool children. *Journal of Personality and Social Psychology, 34,* 915–922.

Anderson, R., Shirey, L., Wilson, P., and Fielding, L. (1987). Interestingness of children's reading material. In R. Snow and M. Farr (Eds.), *Aptitude, Learning, and Instruction: III. Conative and Affective Process Analyses* (pp. 287–299). Hillsdale, NJ: Erlbaum.

Apple, M. and King, N. (1978). What do schools teach? In G. Willis (Ed.), *Qualitative Evaluation: Concepts and Cases in Curriculum Criticism* (pp. 444–465). Berkeley, CA: McCutchan.

Arkes, H. (1978). Competence and the maintenance of behavior. *Motivation and Emotion, 2,* 201–211.

Aronfreed, J. (1969). The concept of internalization. In D. Goslin (Ed.), *Handbook of Socialization Theory and Research* (pp. 263–323). New York: Rand-McNally.

Aronson, E., Stephan, C., Sikes, J., Blaney, N., and Snapp, M. (1978). *The Jigsaw Classroom.* Beverly Hills, CA: Sage Publications.

Asher, S. (1981). Topic interest and children's reading comprehension. In R. Spiro, B. Bruce, and W. Brewer (Eds.), *Theoretical Issues in Reading Comprehension* (pp. 525–534). Hillsdale, NJ: Erlbaum.

Asher, S., Hymel, S., and Wigfield, A. (1978). Influence of topic interest on children's reading comprehension. *Journal of Reading Behavior, 10*, 35–47.

Atkinson, J. (1964). *An Introduction to Motivation.* Princeton, NJ: Van Nostrand.

Bachman, J. and O'Malley, P. (1986). Self-concepts, self-esteem and education experiences: The frog pond revisited (again). *Journal of Personality and Social Psychology, 50*, 35–46.

Bandura, A. (1965). Influence of models' reinforcement contingencies on the acquisition of imitative responses. *Journal of Personality and Social Psychology, 1*, 589–595.

Bandura, A. (1977a). Self-efficacy: Toward a unifying theory of behavioral change. *Psychological Review, 84*, 191–215.

Bandura, A. (1977b). *Social Learning Theory.* Englewood Cliffs, N.J.: Prentice Hall.

Bandura, A. (1981). Self-referent thought: A developmental analysis of self-efficacy. In J. Flavell and L. Ross (Eds.), *Social Cognitive Development: Frontiers and Possible Futures* (pp. 200–239). Cambridge: Cambridge University Press.

Bandura, A. (1982a). The self and mechanisms of agency. In J. Suls (Ed.), *Psychological Perspectives on the Self: Vol. 1* (pp. 3–39). Hillsdale, NJ: Erlbaum.

Bandura, A. (1982b). Self-efficacy mechanism in human agency. *American Psychologist, 37*, 122–147.

Bandura, A. (1986). *Social Foundations of Thought and Action: Social Cognitive Theory.* Englewood Cliffs, NJ: Prentice Hall.

Bandura, A. and Schunk, D. (1981). Cultivating competence, self-efficacy, and intrinsic interest through proximal self-motivation. *Journal of Personality and Social Psychology, 41*, 586–598.

Bandura, A. and Walters, R. (1963). *Social Learning and Personality Development.* New York: Holt, Rinehart, and Winston.

Barker, G. and Graham, S. (1987). Developmental study of praise and blame as attributional cues. *Journal of Educational Psychology, 79*, 62–66.

Baron, R., Tom, D. and Cooper, H. (1985). Social class, race, and teacher expectations. In J. Dusek (Ed.), *Teacher Expectations* (pp. 251–269). Hillsdale, NJ: Erlbaum.

Bates, J. (1979). Extrinsic reward and intrinsic motivation: A review with implications for the classroom. *Review of Educational Research, 49*, 557–576.

Becker, J. (1981). Differential treatment of females and males in mathematics classes. *Journal for Research in Mathematics Education, 12*, 40–53.

Benjamin, M., McKeachie, W., Lin, Y-G., and Holinger, D. (1981). Test anxiety: Deficits in information processing. *Journal of Educational Psychology, 73*, 816–824.

Benjamin, M., McKeachie, W., and Lin, Y-G. (1987). Two types of test anxious students: Support for an information processing model. *Journal of Educational Psychology, 59*, 128–132.

Benware, C. and Deci, E. (1984). Quality of learning with an active versus passive motivational set. *American Educational Research Journal, 21*, 755–765.

Berlyne, D. (1966). Curiosity and exploration. *Science, 153*, 25–33.

Blanck, P., Reis, H., and Jackson, L. (1984). The effects of verbal reinforcements on intrinsic motivation for sex-linked tasks. *Sex Roles, 10*, 369–387.

Block, J. (Ed.). (1974). *Schools, Society, and Mastery Learning*. New York: Holt, Rinehart, and Winston.

Block J. (1979). Mastery learning: The current state of the craft. *Educational Leadership, 37*, 114–117.

Block, J., Efthim, H., and Burns, R. (1989). *Building Effective Mastery Learning Schools*. New York: Longman.

Bloom, B. (1971). Mastery learning and its implications for curriculum development. In E. W. Eisner (Ed.), *Confronting Curriculum Reform* (pp. 17–55). Boston: Little, Brown.

Bloom, B. (1974). An introduction to mastery learning theory. In J. H. Block (Ed.), *Schools, Society, and Mastery Learning* (pp. 3–14). New York: Holt, Rinehart, and Winston.

Bloom, B. (1976). *Human Characteristics and School Learning*. New York: McGraw-Hill.

Bloom, B. (1981). *All Our Children Learning*. New York: McGraw-Hill.

Bloom, B., Hastings, J., and Madaus, G. (1971). *Handbook on Formative and Summative Evaluation of Student Learning*. New York: McGraw-Hill.

Blumenfeld, P., Hamilton, V., Bossert, S., Wessels, K., and Meece, J. (1983). Teacher talk and student thought: Socialization into the student role. In J. M. Levine and M. C. Wang (Eds.), *Teacher and Student Perceptions: Implications for Learning* (pp. 143–192). Hillsdale, NJ: Erlbaum.

Blumenfeld, P., Pintrich, P., and Hamilton, V. (1986). Children's concepts of ability, effort, and conduct. *American Educational Research Journal, 23*, 95–104.

Blumenfeld, P., Pintrich, P., Meece, J., and Wessels, K. (1982). The formation and role of self-perceptions of ability in elementary classrooms. *Elementary School Journal, 82*, 401–420.

Blumenfeld, P., Puro, P., and Mergendoller, J. (in press). Translating motivation into thoughtfulness. In H. Marshall (Ed.), *Redefining Student Learning: Roots of Educational Change*. Norwood, NJ: Ablex.

Blumenfeld, P., Soloway, E., Marx, R., Krajcik, J., Guzdial, M., and Palincsar, A. (in press). Motivating project-based learning: Sustaining the doing, supporting the learning. *Educational Psychologist*.

Boggiano, A., Main, D., and Katz, P. (1988). Children's preference for challenge: The role of perceived competence and control. *Journal of Personality and Social Psychology, 54*, 134–141.

Boggiano, A. and Ruble, D. (1979). Competence and the overjustification effect: A developmental study. *Journal of Personality and Social Psychology, 37,* 1462–1468.

Boggiano, A., Ruble, D., and Pittman, T. (1982). The mastery hypothesis and the overjustification effect. *Social Cognition, 1,* 38–49.

Borko, H. and Eisenhart, M. (in press). Students' conceptions of reading and their experiences in school. *Elementary School Journal.*

Borkowski, J., Weyhing, R., and Carr, M. (1988). Effects of attributional retraining on strategy-based reading comprehension in learning-disabled students. *Journal of Educational Psychology, 80,* 46–53.

Bornstein, P. and Quevillon, R. (1976). The effects of a self-instructional package on overactive preschool boys. *Journal of Applied Behavior Analysis, 9,* 179–188.

Bossert, S. (1979). *Tasks and Social Relationships in Classrooms.* (The Arnold and Caroline Rose Monograph Series of the American Sociological Association). Cambridge: Cambridge University Press.

Brattesani, K., Weinstein, R., and Marshall, H. (1984). Student perceptions of differential teacher treatment as moderators of teacher expectation effects. *Journal of Educational Psychology, 76,* 236–247.

Bricklin, B. and Bricklin, P. (1967). *Bright Child—Poor Grades.* New York: Dell.

Brockner, J. (1979). Self-esteem, self-consciousness, and task performance: Replications, extensions, and possible explanations. *Journal of Personality and Social Psychology, 37,* 447–461.

Brophy, J. (1981). Teacher praise: A functional analysis. *Review of Educational Research, 51,* 5–32.

Brophy, J. (1983). Fostering student learning and motivation in the elementary school classroom. In S. Paris, G. Olson, and H. Stevenson (Eds.), *Learning and Motivation in the Classroom* (pp. 283–305). Hillsdale, NJ: Erlbaum.

Brophy, J. (1986). *Socializing Student Motivation to Learn.* (Institute for Research Teaching Research Series No. 169). East Lansing, MI: Michigan State University.

Brophy, J. (1987a). On motivating students. In D. Berliner and B. Rosenshine (Eds.), *Talks to Teachers* (pp. 201–245). New York: Random House.

Brophy, J. (1987b). Socializing students' motivation to learn. In M. Maehr and D. Kleiber (Eds.), *Advances in Motivation and Achievement: Vol. 5, Enhancing Motivation* (pp. 181–210). Greenwich, CT: JAI Press.

Brophy, J. (1987c). Synthesis of research on strategies for motivating students to learn. *Educational Leadership, 45,* 40–48.

Brophy, J. and Evertson, C. (1978). Context variables in teaching. *Educational Psychologist, 12,* 310–316.

Brophy, J., Evertson, C., Anderson, L., Baum, M., and Crawford, J. (1976). *Student Personality and Teaching: Final Report of the Student Attribute Study.* Educational Resources Information Center (ERIC Document Reproduction Service No. ED 121 799).

Brophy, J. and Rohrkemper, M. (1981). The influence of problem ownership on teachers' perceptions of and strategies for coping with problem students. *Journal of Educational Psychology, 73*, 295–311.

Brophy, J., Rohrkemper, M., Rashid, H., and Goldberger, M. (1983). Relationships between teachers' presentations of classroom tasks and students' engagements in those tasks. *Journal of Educational Psychology, 75*, 544–552.

Brown, J. and Weiner, B. (1984). Affective consequences of ability versus effort ascriptions: Controversies, resolutions, and quandaries. *Journal of Educational Psychology, 76*, 146–158.

Bruch, M., Juster, H., and Kaflowitz, N. (1983). Relationships of cognitive components of test anxiety to test performance: Implications for assessment and treatment. *Journal of Counseling Psychology, 30*, 527–536.

Brush, L. (1979). *Why Women Avoid the Study of Mathematics: A Longitudinal Study.* Cambridge, MA: Abt Associates.

Buckholdt, D. and Wodarski, J. (1974). *The Effects of Different Reinforcement Systems on Cooperative Behaviors Exhibited by Children in Classroom Contexts.* Paper presented at the meeting of the American Psychological Association, New Orleans, LA.

Burns, M. (1987). *A Collection of Math Lessons: From Grades 3 Through 6.* New York: Cuisennaire.

Butkowsky, I. and Willows, D. (1980). Cognitive-motivational characteristics of children varying in reading ability: Evidence for learned helplessness in poor readers. *Journal of Educational Psychology, 72*, 408–422.

Butler, R. (1987). Task-involving and ego-involving properties of evaluation: Effects of different feedback conditions on motivational perceptions, interest, and performance. *Journal of Educational Psychology, 79*, 474–482.

Butler, R. (1988). Enhancing and undermining intrinsic motivation: The effects of task-involving and ego-involving evaluation on interest and performance. *British Journal of Educational Psychology, 58*, 1–14.

Butler, R. (1989). Mastery versus ability appraisal: A developmental study of children's observations of peers' work. *Child Development, 60*, 1350–1361.

Butler, R. and Nisan, M. (1986). Effects of no feedback, task-related comments, and grades on intrinsic motivation and performance. *Journal of Educational Psychology, 78*, 210–216.

Cain, K. and Dweck, C. (1989). The development of children's conceptions of intelligence: A theoretical framework. In R. Sternberg (Ed.), *Advances in the Psychology of Human Intelligence, Vol. 5* (pp. 47–82). Hillsdale, NJ: Erlbaum.

Carpenter, T., Corbitt, M., Kepner, H., Lindquist, M., and Reys, R. (1981). *Results from the Second Mathematics Assessment of the National Assessment of Educational Progress.* Reston, VA: National Council of Teachers of Mathematics.

Casady, M. (1975). The tricky business of giving rewards. *Psychology Today, 8*, 52.

Chan, K. and Keogh, B. (1974). Interpretation of task interruption and feelings of responsibility for failure. *Journal of Special Education, 8*, 175–178.

Chandler, T. (1980). Reversal peer tutoring effects on powerlessness in adolescents. *Adolescence, 15,* 715–722.

Chapman, M., Skinner, E., and Baltes, P. (1990). Interpreting correlations between children's perceived control and cognitive performance: Control, agency, or means-ends beliefs? *Developmental Psychology, 26,* 246–253.

Chen, C. and Uttal, D. (1988). Cultural values, parents' beliefs, and children's achievement in the United States and China. *Human Development, 31,* 351–358.

Clifford, M. (1984). Thoughts on a theory of constructive failure. *Educational Psychologist, 19,* 108–120.

Clifford, M. (1988). Failure tolerance and academic risk-taking in ten- to twelve-year-old students. *British Journal of Educational Psychology, 58,* 15–27.

Clifford, M. (in press). Risk taking: Theoretical, empirical, and educational considerations. *Educational Psychologist.*

Cohen, E. (1986). *Designing Groupwork.* New York: Teachers College Press.

Cohen, H. (1973). Behavior modification in socially deviant youth. In C. Thoresen (Ed.), *Behavior Modification in Education: Seventy-second Yearbook of the National Society for the Study of Education, 72, Part I* (pp. 291–314). Chicago: University of Chicago Press.

Collins, J. (1982, March). *Self-efficacy and Ability in Achievement Behavior.* Paper presented at the annual meeting of the American Educational Research Association, New York.

Connell, J. (1985). A new multidimensional measure of children's perceptions of control. *Child Development, 56,* 1018–1041.

Corno, L. (1989). Self-regulated learning: A volitional analysis. In B. Zimmerman and D. Schunk (Eds.), *Self-regulated Learning and Academic Achievement: Theory, Research, and Practice* (pp. 111–141). New York: Springer-Verlag.

Corno, L. and Rohrkemper, M. (1985). The intrinsic motivation to learn in classrooms. In C. Ames and R. Ames (Eds.), *Research on Motivation in Education, Vol. 2: The Classroom Milieu* (pp. 53–90). Orlando, FL: Academic Press.

Covington, M. (1984). The self-worth theory of achievement motivation: Findings and implications. *The Elementary School Journal, 85,* 5–20.

Covington, M. (1985). Strategic thinking and the fear of failure. In J. Segal, S. Chipman, and R. Glaser (Eds.), *Thinking and Learning Skills, Vol. 1: Relating Instruction to Research.* Hillsdale, NJ: Erlbaum.

Covington, M. and Beery, R. (1976). *Self-worth and School Learning.* New York: Holt, Rinehart & Winston.

Covington, M. and Omelich, C. (1979a). Effort: The double-edged sword in school achievement. *Journal of Educational Psychology, 71,* 169–182.

Covington, M. and Omelich, C. (1979b). It's best to be able and virtuous too: Student and teacher evaluative responses to successful effort. *Journal of Educational Psychology, 71,* 688–700.

Covington, M. and Omelich, C. (1981). As failures mount: Affective and cognitive consequences of ability demotion in the classroom. *Journal of Educational Psychology, 73*, 796–808.

Covington, M. and Omelich, C. (1984a). Controversies or consistencies? A reply to Brown and Weiner. *Journal of Educational Psychology, 76*, 159–168.

Covington, M. and Omelich, C. (1984b). An empirical examination of Weiner's critique of attribution research. *Journal of Educational Psychology, 76*, 1214–1225.

Covington, M. and Omelich, C. (1984c). Task-oriented versus competitive learning structures: Motivational and performance consequences. *Journal of Educational Psychology, 7*, 1038–1050.

Covington, M. and Omelich, C. (1988). Achievement dynamics: The interaction of motives, cognitions, and emotions over time. *Anxiety Research, 1*, 165–183.

Covington, M., Spratt, M., and Omelich, C. (1980). Is effort enough or does diligence count too? Student and teacher reactions to effort stability in failure. *Journal of Educational Psychology, 72*, 717–729.

Crandall, V. J. (1963). Achievement. In H. Stevenson (Ed.), *Child Psychology: Sixty-second Yearbook of the National Society for the Study of Education* (pp. 416–459). Chicago: University of Chicago Press.

Crandall, V. C. (1967). Achievement Behavior in Young Children. In W. W. Hartup and N. L. Smothergill (Eds.), *The Young Child* (pp. 165–185). Washington, DC: National Association for the Education of Young Children.

Crandall, V. C., Katkovsky, W., and Crandall, V. J. (1965). Children's beliefs in their own control of reinforcement in intellectual-academic achievement situations. *Child Development, 36*, 91–109.

Crandall, V. J., Katkovsky, W., and Preston, A. (1962). Motivational and ability determinants of young children's intellectual achievement behaviors. *Child Development, 33*, 643–661.

Crockenberg, S. and Bryant, B. (1978). Socialization: The "implicit curriculum" of learning environments. *Journal of Research Development in Education, 12*, 69–78.

Csikszentmihalyi, M. (1975). *Beyond Boredom and Anxiety*. San Francisco: Jossey Bass.

Culler, R. and Holahan, C. (1980). Test anxiety and academic performance: The effects of study-related behaviors. *Journal of Educational Psychology, 72*, 16–20.

Danner, F. and Lonky, E. (1981). A cognitive-developmental approach to the effects of rewards on intrinsic motivation. *Child Development, 52*, 1043–1052.

Deaux, K. (1976). Sex: A perspective on the attributional process. In J. Harvey, W. Ickes, and R. Kidd (Eds.), *New Directions in Attribution Research: Vol. 1* (pp. 335–352). Hillsdale, NJ: Erlbaum.

deCharms, R. (1976). *Enhancing Motivation*. New York: Irvington Publishers.

deCharms, R. (1983). Intrinsic motivation, peer tutoring, and cooperative learning: Practical maxims. In J. Levine and M. Wang (Eds.), *Teacher and Student Perceptions: Implications for Learning* (pp. 391–398). Hillsdale, NJ: Erlbaum.

deCharms, R. (1984). Motivating enhancement in educational settings. In R. Ames and C. Ames (Eds.), *Research on Motivation in Education, Vol. 1: Student Motivation* (pp. 275–310). New York: Academic Press.

Deci, E. (1971). The effects of externally mediated rewards on intrinsic motivation. *Journal of Personality and Social Psychology, 18*, 105–115.

Deci, E. (1972). Intrinsic motivation, extrinsic reinforcement, and inequity. *Journal of Personality and Social Psychology, 22*, 113–120.

Deci, E. (1975). *Intrinsic Motivation.* New York: Plenum Press.

Deci, E., Betley, G., Kahle, J., Abrams, L., and Porac, J. (1981). When trying to win: Competition and intrinsic motivation. *Personality and Social Psychology, 7*, 79–83.

Deci, E., Nezlek, J., and Sheinman, L. (1981). Characteristics of the rewarder and intrinsic motivation of the rewardee. *Journal of Personality and Social Psychology, 40*, 1–10.

Deci, E. and Ryan, R. (1985). *Intrinsic Motivation and Self-determination in Human Behavior.* New York: Plenum Press.

Deci, E. and Ryan, R. (1987). The support of autonomy and the control of behavior. *Journal of Personality and Social Psychology, 53*, 1024–1037.

Deci, E., Schwartz, A., Sheinman, L., and Ryan, R. (1981). An instrument to assess adults' orientations toward control versus autonomy with children: Reflections on intrinsic motivation and perceived competence. *Journal of Educational Psychology, 73*, 642–650.

Deci, E., Spiegel, N., Ryan, R., Koestner, R., and Kauffman, M. (1982). Effects of performance standards on teaching styles: Behavior of controlling teachers. *Journal of Educational Psychology, 74*, 852–859.

Deci, E., Vallerand, R., Pelletier, L., and Ryan, R. (in press). Motivation and education: The self-determination perspective. *The Educational Psychologist.*

Deffenbacher, J. (1980). Worry and emotionality in test anxiety. In I. Sarason (Ed.), *Test Anxiety: Theory, Research, and Applications* (pp. 111–128). Hillsdale, NJ: Erlbaum.

Desiderato, O. and Koskinen, P. (1969). Anxiety, study habits, and academic achievement. *Journal of Counseling Psychology, 16*, 162–165.

Diener, C. and Dweck, C. (1978). An analysis of learned helplessness: Continuous changes in performance, strategy, and achievement cognitions following failure. *Journal of Personality and Social Psychology, 36*, 451–462.

Diener, C. and Dweck, C. (1980). An analysis of learned helplessness: II. The processing of success. *Journal of Personality and Social Psychology, 39*, 940–952.

Doyle, W. (1983). Academic work. *Review of Educational Research, 53*, 287–312.

Dollinger, S. and Thelen, M. (1978). Overjustification and children's intrinsic motivation: Comparative effects of four rewards. *Journal of Personality and Social Psychology, 36*, 1259–1269.

Dulany, D. (1968). Awareness, rules, and propositional control: A confrontation with S-R behavior theory. In T. Dixon and D. Horton (Eds.), *Verbal Behavior and General Behavior Theory* (pp. 340–387). Englewood Cliffs, NJ: Prentice Hall.

Dusek, J. (1975). Do teachers bias children's learning? *Review of Educational Research, 45,* 661–684.

Dusek, J. (1980). The development of test anxiety in children. In I. Sarason (Ed.), *Test Anxiety: Theory, Research, and Applications* (pp. 87–110). Hillsdale, NJ: Erlbaum.

Dusek, J. (Ed.) (1985). *Teacher Expectancies.* Hillsdale, NJ: Erlbaum.

Dusek, J. and Joseph, G. (1983). The bases of teacher expectancies: A meta-analysis. *Journal of Educational Psychology, 75,* 327–346.

Dusek, J., Kermis, M., and Mergler, N. (1975). Information processing in low- and high-test-anxious children as a function of grade level and verbal labeling. *Developmental Psychology, 11,* 651–652.

Dusek, J., Mergler, N., and Kermis, M. (1976). Attention, encoding, and information processing in low- and high-test-anxious children. *Child Development, 47,* 201–207.

Dweck, C. (1975). The role of expectations and attributions in the alleviation of learned helplessness. *Journal of Personality and Social Psychology, 31,* 674–685.

Dweck, C. (1986). Motivational processes affecting learning. *American Psychologist, 41,* 1040–1048.

Dweck, C. and Bempechat, J. (1983). Children's theories of intelligence: Consequences for learning. In S. Paris, G. Olson, and H. Stevenson (Eds.), *Learning and Motivation in the Classroom* (pp. 239–255). Hillsdale, NJ: Erlbaum.

Dweck, C., Davidson, W., Nelson, S., and Enna B. (1978). Sex differences in learned helplessness, II: The contingencies of evaluative feedback in the classroom, and III: An experimental analysis. *Developmental Psychology, 14,* 268–276.

Dweck, C. and Elliott, E. (1983). Achievement motivation. In P. Mussen (Ed.), *Handbook of Child Psychology, Vol. IV: Socialization, Personality, and Social Development* (pp. 643–691). New York: Wiley.

Dweck, C. and Goetz, T. (1978). Attributions and learned helplessness. In W. Harvey and R. Kidd (Eds.), *New Directions in Attribution Research* (Vol. 2, pp. 157–179). Hillsdale, NJ: Erlbaum.

Dweck, C. and Leggett, E. (1988). A social-cognitive approach to motivation and personality. *Psychological Review, 95,* 256–273.

Dweck, C. and Reppucci, N. (1973). Learned helplessness and reinforcement responsibility in children. *Journal of Personality and Social Psychology, 25,* 109–116.

Eccles, J. (1980). Self-perceptions, task perceptions and academic choice: Origins and change. Final Report to National Institute of Education. Washington, D.C.

Eccles, J. (1983). Expectancies, values, and academic behavior. In J. T. Spence (Ed.), *Achievement and Achievement Motives: Psychological and Sociological Approaches* (pp. 77–146). San Francisco: Freeman.

Eccles, J. and Midgley, C. (1989). Stage environment fit: Developmentally appropriate classrooms for early adolescents. In R. Ames and C. Ames (Eds.), *Research on Motivation in Education (Vol. 3): Goals and Cognitions* (pp. 139–186). New York: Academic Press.

Eccles, J., Midgley, C., and Adler, T. (1984). Grade-related changes in the school environment: Effects on achievement motivation. In J. Nicholls (Ed.), *Advances in Motivation and Achievement, Vol. 3: The Development of Achievement Motivation* (pp. 283–331). Greenwich, CT: JAI Press.

Eder, D. (1983). Ability grouping and students' academic self-concepts: A case study. *The Elementary School Journal, 84,* 149–161.

Edmonds, R. (1979). Effective schools for the urban poor. *Educational Leadership, 37,* 15–18.

Elliott, E. and Dweck, C. (1988). Goals: An approach to motivation and achievement. *Journal of Personality and Social Psychology, 54,* 5–12.

Entwisle, D. and Hayduk, L. (1978). *Too Great Expectations: Young Children's Academic Outlook.* Baltimore, MD: Johns Hopkins University Press.

Enzle, M. and Ross, J. (1978). Increasing and decreasing intrinsic interest with contingent rewards: A test of cognitive evaluation theory. *Journal of Experimental Social Psychology, 14,* 588–597.

Eshel, Y. and Klein, Z. (1981). Development of academic self-concept of lower-class and middle-class primary school children. *Journal of Educational Psychology, 73,* 287–293.

Estes, W. (1972). Reinforcement in human behavior. *American Scientist, 60,* 723–729.

Eswara, H. (1972). Administration of reward and punishment in relation to ability, effort, and performance. *Journal of Social Psychology, 87,* 137–140.

Fagot, B. (1973). Influence of teacher behavior in the preschool. *Developmental Psychology, 9,* 196–206.

Farnham-Diggory, S. and Ramsey, B. (1971). Play persistence: Some effects of interruptions, social reinforcement, and defective toys. *Developmental Psychology, 4,* 297–298.

Feather, N. (1961). The relationship of persistence at a task to expectations for success and achievement-related motives. *Journal of Abnormal and Social Psychology, 63,* 552–561.

Feather, N. (1963). Persistence at a difficult task with an alternative task of intermediate difficulty. *Journal of Abnormal and Social Psychology, 66,* 604–609.

Feather, N. (1988). Values, valences, and course enrollment: Testing the role of personal values within an expectancy-valence framework. *Journal of Educational Psychology, 80,* 381–391.

Feld, S. and Lewis, J. (1969). The assessment of achievement anxieties in children. In C. P. Smith (Ed.), *Achievement-related Motives in Children* (pp. 151–199). New York: Russell Sage Foundation.

Feldlaufer, H., Midgley, C., and Eccles, J. S. (1988). Student, teacher, and observer perceptions of the classroom environment before and after the transition to junior high school. *Journal of Early Adolescence, 8,* 133–156.

Felson, R. and Reed, M. (1986). Reference groups and self-appraisals of academic ability and performance. *Social Psychology Quarterly, 49,* 103–109.

Fennema, E. and Peterson, P. (1985). Autonomous learning behavior: A possible explanation of gender-related differences in mathematics. In L. Wilkinson and C. Marrett (Eds.), *Gender Influences in Classroom Interaction* (pp. 17–35). New York: Academic Press.

Fincham, F., Hokoda, A., and Sanders, R. (1989). Learned helplessness, test anxiety, and academic achievement: A longitudinal analysis. *Child Development, 60,* 138–145.

Flink, C., Boggiano, A., and Barrett, M. (in press). Controlling teaching strategies: Undermining children's self-determination and performance. *Journal of Personality and Social Psychology.*

Forsterling, F. (1985). Attributional retraining: A review. *Psychological Bulletin, 98,* 495–512.

Frieze, I. (1975). Women's expectations for and causal attributions of success and failure. In M. Mednick, S. Tangri, and L. Hoffman (Eds.), *Women and Achievement* (pp. 158–171). New York: Wiley.

Fry, P. and Coe, K. (1980). Interaction among dimensions of academic motivation and classroom social climate: A study of the perceptions of junior high and high school pupils. *British Journal of Educational Psychology, 50,* 33–42.

Fyans, L. and Maehr, M. (1979). Attributional style, task selection, and achievement. *Journal of Educational Psychology, 71,* 499–507.

Gaa, J. (1973). Effects of individual goal-setting conferences on achievement, attitudes, and goal-setting behavior. *Journal of Experimental Education, 42,* 22–28.

Gaa, J. (1979). The effects of individual goal-setting conferences on academic achievement and modification of locus of control orientation. *Psychology in the Schools, 16,* 591–597.

Garbarino, J. (1975). The impact of anticipated rewards on cross-age tutoring. *Journal of Personality and Social Psychology, 32,* 421–428.

Garner, R., Alexander, P., Gillingham, M., Kulikowich, J., and Brown, R. (1991). Interest and learning from text. *American Educational Research Journal, 28,* 643–659.

Garner, R., Gillingham, M., and White, C. (1989). Effects of "seductive details" on macroprocessing and microprocessing in adults and children. *Cognition and Instruction, 6,* 41–57.

Gibbs, J. and Allen, A. (1978). *Tribes: A Process for Peer Involvement.* Oakland, CA: Center-Source Publications.

Gitelson, I., Petersen, A., and Tobin-Richards, M. (1982). Adolescents' expectancies of success, self-evaluations, and attributions about performance on spatial and verbal tasks. *Sex Roles, 8,* 411–419.

Glynn, E., Thomas, J., and Shee, S. (1973). Behavioral self-control of classroom behavior in an elementary classroom. *Journal of Applied Behavior Analysis, 6,* 105–113.

Goldberg, M., Passow, A., and Justman, J. (1966). *The Effects of Ability Grouping.* New York: Teachers College Press.

Goldenberg, C. (1987). Low-income Hispanic parents' contributions to their first-grade children's word-recognition skills. *Anthropology in Education Quarterly, 18,* 149–179.

Goldenberg, C. (1989). Making success a more common occurrence for children at risk for failure: Lessons from Hispanic first-graders learning to read. In J. Allen and J. Mason (Eds.), *Risk Makers, Risk Takers, Risk Breakers: Reducing the Risk for Young Literacy Learners* (pp. 48–78). Portsmouth, NJ: Heinemann.

Good, T. (1987). Teacher expectations. In D. Berliner and B. Rosenshine (Eds.), *Talks to Teachers* (pp. 159–200). New York: Random House.

Good, T. and Brophy, J. (1978). *Looking in Classrooms* (2nd edition). New York: Harper & Row.

Good, T. and Brophy, J. (1980). *Educational Psychology: A Realistic Approach* (2nd edition). New York: Holt, Rinehart, & Winston.

Good, T. and Brophy, J. (1986). *Educational Psychology* (3rd edition). White Plains, NY: Longman.

Good, T. and Findley, N. (1985). Sex role expectations and achievement. In J. Dusek (Ed.), *Teacher Expectations* (pp. 271–300). Hillsdale, NJ: Erlbaum.

Good, T., Slavings, R., Harel, K., and Emerson, H. (1987). Student passivity: A study of question asking in K-12 classrooms. *Sociology of Education, 60,* 181–199.

Goodlad, J. (1984). *A Place Called School.* New York: McGraw-Hill.

Gottfried, A. (1985). Academic intrinsic motivation in elementary and junior high school students. *Journal of Educational Psychology, 77,* 631–645.

Gottfried, A. (1986). *Children's Academic Intrinsic Motivation Inventory.* Odessa, FL: Psychological Assessment Resources.

Gottfried, A. (1990). Academic intrinsic motivation in young elementary school children. *Journal of Educational Psychology, 82,* 525–538.

Graham, S. (1984a). Communicating sympathy and anger to black and white children: The cognitive (attributional) consequences of affective cues. *The Journal of Personality and Social Psychology, 47,* 14–28.

Graham, S. (1984b). Teacher feelings and student thoughts: An attributional approach to affect in the classroom. *Elementary School Journal, 85,* 91–104.

Graham, S. (1990). Communicating low ability in the classroom: Bad things good teachers sometimes do. In S. Graham and V. Folkes (Eds.), *Attribution Theory: Applications to Achievement, Mental Health, and Interpersonal Conflict* (pp. 17–36). Hillsdale, NJ: Erlbaum.

Graham, S. (1991). A review of attribution theory in achievement contexts. *Educational Psychology Review, 3,* 5–39.

Graham, S. and Barker, G. (1990). The downside of help: An attributional-developmental analysis of helping behavior as a low ability cue. *Journal of Educational Psychology, 82,* 7–14.

Graham, S., Doubleday, C., and Guarino, P. (1984). The development of relations between perceived controllability and the emotions of pity, anger, and guilt. *Child Development, 55,* 561–565.

Graham, S. and Golan, S. (1991). Motivational influences on cognition: Task involvement, ego involvement, and depth of information processing. *Journal of Educational Psychology, 83,* 187–194.

Graves, D. (1983). *Writing: Teachers and Children at Work.* Portsmouth, NH: Heinemann.

Greene, J. C. (1985). Relationships among learning and attribution theory motivation variables. *American Educational Research Journal, 22,* 65–78.

Grolnick, W. and Ryan, R. (1987). Autonomy in children's learning: An experimental and individual difference investigation. *Journal of Personality and Social Psychology, 52,* 890–898.

Gross, T. and Mastenbrook, M. (1980). Examination of the effects of state anxiety on problem-solving efficiency under high and low memory conditions. *Journal of Educational Psychology, 72,* 605–609.

Gullickson, A. (1985). Student evaluation techniques and their relationship to grade and curriculum. *Journal of Educational Research, 79,* 96–100.

Guskey, T. (1985). *Implementing Mastery Learning.* Belmont, CA: Wadsworth.

Guskey, T. (1987). The essential elements of mastery learning. *Journal of Classroom Interaction, 22,* 19–22.

Guskey, T. (1990). Cooperative mastery learning strategies, *The Elementary School Journal, 91,* 33–42.

Guskey, T. and Pigott, T. (1988). Research on group-based mastery learning programs: A metaanalysis. *Journal of Educational Research, 8,* 197–216.

Hallahan, D. and Sapona, R. (1983). Self-monitoring of attention with learning-disabled children: Past research and current issues. *Journal of Learning Disabilities, 16,* 616–620.

Hallinan, M. and Sorensen, A. (1983). The formation and stability of instructional groups. *American Sociological Review, 48,* 838–851.

Hamilton, H. and Gordon, D. (1978). Teacher-child interactions in preschool and task persistence. *American Educational Research Journal, 15,* 459–466.

Harackiewicz, J. (1979). The effects of reward contingency and performance feedback on intrinsic motivation. *Journal of Personality and Social Psychology, 37,* 1352–1363.

Harackiewicz, J., Abrahams, S., and Wageman, R. (1987). Performance evaluation and intrinsic motivation: The effects of evaluative focus, rewards, and achievement orientation. *Journal of Personality and Social Psychology, 53,* 1015–1023.

Harari, O. and Covington, M. (1981). Reactions to achievement from a teacher and a student perspective: A developmental analysis. *American Educational Research Journal, 18,* 15–28.

Harnisch, D., Hill, K., and Fyans, L. (1980, April). *Development of a Shorter, More Reliable and More Valid Measure of Test Motivation.* Paper presented at the annual meeting of The National Council in Measurement in Education, Boston.

Hart, S. (1982). Analyzing the social organization for reading in one elementary school. In G. Spindler (Ed.), *Doing the Ethnography of Schooling* (pp. 410–438). New York: Holt, Rinehart, & Winston.

Harter, S. (1974). Pleasure derived from cognitive challenge and mastery. *Child Development, 45,* 661–669.

Harter, S. (1978a). Effectance motivation reconsidered: Toward a developmental model. *Human Development, 21,* 34–64.

Harter, S. (1978b). Pleasure derived from challenge and the effects of receiving grades on children's difficulty level choices. *Child Development, 49,* 788–799.

Harter, S. (1981a). A model of mastery motivation in children: Individual differences and developmental change. In W. Collins (Ed.), *Minnesota Symposia on Child Psychology Vol. 14* (pp. 215–255). Hillsdale, NJ: Erlbaum.

Harter, S. (1981b). A new self-report scale of intrinsic versus extrinsic orientation in the classroom: Motivational and informational components. *Developmental Psychology, 17,* 300–312.

Harter S. (1982). The perceived competence scale for children. *Child Development, 53,* 87–97.

Harter, S. (1987). The determinants and mediational role of global self-worth in children. In N. Eisenberg (Ed.), *Contemporary Topics in Developmental Psychology* (pp. 219–241). New York: Wiley & Sons.

Harter, S. (in press). The relationship between perceived competence, affect, and motivational orientation within the classroom: Process and patterns of change. In A. Boggiano and T. Pittman (Eds.), *Achievement and Motivation: A Social-developmental Perspective.* Cambridge: Cambridge University Press.

Harter, S. and Connell, J. (1984). A comparison of alternative models of the relationships between academic achievement and children's perceptions of competence, control, and motivational orientation. In J. Nicholls (Ed.), *The Development of Achievement-related Conditions and Behavior* (pp. 219–250). Greenwich, CT: JAI Press.

Harter, S. and Pike, R. (1984). The pictorial scale of perceived competence and social acceptance for young children. *Child Development, 55,* 1969–1982.

Hayes, S., Rosenfarb, I., Wolfert, E., Munt, E., Korn, Z., and Zettle, R. (1985). Self-reinforcement effects: An artifact of social standing setting? *Journal of Applied Behavior Analysis, 18,* 201–204.

Heckhausen, H. (1984). Emergent achievement behavior: Some early developments. In J. Nicholls (Ed.), *Advances in Motivation and Achievement: Vol. 3. The Development of Achievement Motivation* (pp. 1–32). Greenwich, CT: JAI.

Helmke, A. (1988). The role of classroom context factors for the achievement-impairing effect of test anxiety. *Anxiety Research, 1,* 37–52.

Hembree, R. (1988). Correlates, causes, effects, and treatment of test anxiety. *Review of Educational Research, 58,* 47–77.

Hembree, R. (1990). The nature, effects, and relief of mathematics anxiety. *Journal for Research in Mathematics Education, 21,* 33–46.

Hiebert, E. (1983). An examination of ability grouping in reading instruction. *Reading Research Quarterly, 18,* 231–255.

Higgins, E. and Parsons, J. (1983). Social cognition and the social life of the child. Stages as subcultures. In E. T. Higgins, D. N. Ruble, and W. W. Hartup (Eds.), *Social Cognition and Social Development: A Sociocultural Perspective* (pp. 15–62). New York: Cambridge University Press.

Hill, K. (1972). Anxiety in the evaluative context. In W. W. Hartup (Ed.), *The Young Child: Vol. 2* (pp. 225–283). Washington, DC: National Association for the Education of Young Children.

Hill, K. (1979). *Eliminating Motivational Testing Error by Developing Optimal Testing Procedures and Teaching Test-taking Skills.* Paper presented at the Educational Testing Service, Princeton, NJ.

Hill, K. (1980). Motivation, evaluation, and educational testing policy. In L. J. Fyans (Ed.), *Achievement Motivation: Recent Trends in Theory and Research* (pp. 34–95). New York: Plenum Press.

Hill, K. (1984). Debilitating motivation and testing: A major educational problem, possible solutions, and policy applications. In R. Ames and C. Ames (Eds.), *Research on Motivation in Education, Vol. 1: Student Motivation* (pp. 245–272). New York: Academic Press.

Hill, K. and Eaton, W. (1977). The interaction of test anxiety and success/failure experiences in determining children's arithmetic performance. *Developmental Psychology, 13,* 205–211.

Hill, K. and Horton, M. (1985, April). *Validation of a Classroom Curriculum Teaching Elementary School Students Test-taking Skills that Optimize Test Performance.* Paper presented at the annual meeting of the American Educational Research Association, Chicago.

Hill, K. and Sarason, S. (1966). The relation of test anxiety and defensiveness to test and school performance over the elementary-school years: A further longitudinal study. *Monographs of the Society for Research in Child Development, 104,* 31 (Whole No. 2).

Hill, K. and Wigfield, A. (1984). Test anxiety: A major educational problem and what can be done about it. *The Elementary School Journal, 85,* 105–126.

Holroyd, K. and Appel, M. (1980). Test anxiety and physiological responding. In I. Sarason (Ed.), *Test Anxiety: Theory, Research, and Applications* (pp. 129–151). Hillsdale, NJ: Erlbaum.

Holloway, S. (1988). Concepts of ability and effort in Japan and the United States. *Review of Educational Research, 58,* 327–345.

Holloway, S., Kashiwagi, K., Hess, R. D., and Azuma, H. (1986). Causal attributions by Japanese and American mothers and children about performance in mathematics. *International Journal of Psychology, 21,* 269–286.

Holt, J. (1964). *How Children Fail.* New York: Pitman.

Hom, H. and Murphy, M. (1985). Low-need achievers' performance: The positive impact of a self-determined goal. *Personality and Social Psychology Bulletin, 11,* 275–285.

Horwitz, R. (1979). Psychological effects of the "open-classroom." *Review of Educational Research, 49,* 71–86.

Hughes, B., Sullivan, H., and Mosley, M. (1985). External evaluation, task difficulty, and continuing motivation. *Journal of Educational Research, 78,* 210–215.

Hulton, R. and DeVries, D. (1976). *Team Competition and Group Practice: Effects on Student Achievement and Attitudes* (Report No. 212). Baltimore, MD: Johns Hopkins University, Center for Social Organization of Schools.

Humphrey, L., Karoly, P., and Kirschenbaum, D. (1978). Self-management in the classroom: Self-imposed response cost versus self-reward. *Behavior Therapy, 9,* 592–601.

Hunt, D. (1975). Person-environment interaction: A challenge found wanting before it was tried. *Review of Educational Research, 45,* 209–230.

Hunt, J. McV. (1965). Intrinsic motivation and its role in psychological development. In D. Levine (Ed.), *Nebraska Symposium on Motivation (Vol. 13)* (pp. 189–282). Lincoln, NE: University of Nebraska Press.

Hunter, M., Ames, D., and Koopman, R. (1983). Effects of stimulus complexity and familiarization time on infant preferences for novel and familiar stimuli. *Developmental Psychology, 19,* 338–352.

Jackson, P. (1968). *Life in Classrooms.* New York: Holt.

Jagacinski, C. and Nicholls, J. (1984). Conceptions of ability and related affects in task involvement and ego involvement. *Journal of Educational Psychology, 76,* 909–919.

Jagacinski, C. and Nicholls, J. (1990). Reducing effort to protect perceived ability: "They'd do it but I wouldn't." *Journal of Educational Psychology, 82,* 15–21.

Johnson, D. and Johnson, R. (1985a). The internal dynamics of cooperative learning groups. In R. Slavin, S. Sharan, S. Kagan, R. Lazawowitz, N. Webb, and R. Schmuck (Eds.), *Learning To Cooperate, Cooperating To Learn* (pp. 103–124). New York: Plenum Press.

Johnson, D. and Johnson, R. (1985b). Motivational processes in cooperative, competitive, and individualistic learning situations. In C. Ames and R. Ames (Eds.), *Research on Motivation in Education, Vol. 2: The Classroom Milieu* (pp. 249–286). Orlando FL: Academic Press.

Johnson, D. and Johnson, R. (1989). Toward a cooperative effort. *Educational Leadership, 46,* 80–81.

Johnson, D., Johnson, R., Holubec, E., and Roy, P. (1984). *Circles of Learning: Cooperation in the Classroom.* Alexandria, VA: Association for Supervision and Curriculum Development.

Kagan, J., Hertz-Lazarowitz, R., Webb, C., and Schmuck R. (Eds.), (1985). *Learning to Cooperate, Cooperating to Learn* (pp. 103–124). New York: Plenum Press.

Kagan, J. (1972). Motives and development. *Journal of Personality and Social Psychology, 22,* 51–66.

Kagan, S. (undated). *Cooperative Learning Resources for Teachers.* University of California, Riverside, CA

Kamii, C. (1984). Viewpoint: Obedience is not enough. *Young Children, 39,* 11–14.

Karabenick, S. and Knapp, J. (1988). Help-seeking and the need for academic assistance. *Journal of Educational Psychology, 80,* 406–408.

Karabenick, S. and Youssef, Z. (1968). Performance as a function of achievement motive level and perceived difficulty. *Journal of Personality and Social Psychology, 10,* 414–419.

Karniol, R. and Ross, M. (1977). The effect of performance-relevant and performance-irrelevant rewards on children's intrinsic motivation. *Child Development, 48,* 482–487.

Kauffman, J. and Hallahan, D. (1979). Learning disabilities and hyperactivity. In B. Lahey and A. Kazdin (Eds.), *Advances in Clinical Child Psychology: Vol. 2* (pp. 71–105). New York: Plenum Press.

Kazdin, A. (1974). Self-monitoring and behavior change. In M. Mahoney and C. Thoresen (Eds.), *Self-control: Power To the Person* (pp. 218–246). Monterey, CA: Brooks-Cole.

Kazdin, A. (1975). Recent advances in token economy research. In M. Hersen, R. Eisler, and P. Miller (Eds.), *Progress in Behavior Modification: Vol. 1* (pp. 233–274). New York: Academic Press.

Kazdin, A. and Bootzin, R. (1972). The token economy: An evaluative review. *Journal of Applied Behavior Analysis, 5,* 343–372.

Keller, F. (1968). Goodbye, teacher.... *Journal of Applied Behavior Analysis, 1,* 79–89.

Kelly, H. (1967). Attribution theory in social psychology. In D. Levine (Ed.), *Nebraska Symposium on Motivation* (pp. 192–238). Lincoln, NE: University of Nebraska Press.

Kimball, M. M. (1989). A new perspective on women's math achievement. *Psychological Bulletin, 105,* 198–214.

Kulik, J., Kulik, C-L., and Cohen, P. (1979). A metaanalysis of outcome studies of Keller's Personalized System of Instruction. *American Psychologist, 34,* 307–318.

Kulik, C-L., Kulik, J., and Bangert-Drowns, R. (1990a). Effectiveness of mastery learning programs: A meta-analysis. *Review of Educational Research, 60,* 265–299.

Kulik, J., Kulik, C-L., and Bangert-Drowns, R. (1990b). Is there better evidence on mastery learning? A response to Slavin. *Review of Educational Research, 60,* 303–307.

Lazarus, M. (1975, June 28). Rx for mathophobia. *Saturday Review, 2,* 46–48.

Lee, S., Ichikawa, V., and Stevenson, H. W. (1987). Beliefs and achievement in mathematics and reading: A cross-national study of Chinese, Japanese, and American children and their mothers. In M. Maehr and D. Kleiber (Eds.), *Advances in Motivation and Achievement: Vol. 5, Enhancing Motivation* (pp. 149–179). Greenwich, CT: JAI Press.

Lefcourt, H. (1976). *Locus of Control: Current Trends in Theory and Research.* Hillsdale, NJ: Erlbaum.

Leinhardt, G., Seewald, A., and Engel, M. (1979). Learning what's taught: Sex differences in instruction. *Journal of Educational Psychology, 71,* 432–439.

Lepper, M. (1973). Dissonance, self-perception, and honesty in children. *Journal of Personality and Social Psychology, 25,* 65–74.

Lepper, M. (1981). Intrinsic and extrinsic motivation in children: Detrimental effects of superfluous social controls. In A. Collins (Ed), *Aspects of the Development of Competence: The Minnesota Symposia on Child Psychology (Vol. 14* (pp. 155–214). Hillsdale, NJ: Erlbaum.

Lepper, M. (1983). Extrinsic reward and intrinsic motivation: Implications for the classroom. In J. Levine and M. Wang (Eds.), *Teacher and Student Perceptions: Implications for Learning* (pp. 281–317). Hillsdale, NJ: Erlbaum.

Lepper, M. (1985). Microcomputers in education. *American Psychologist, 40,* 1–18.

Lepper, M. (1988). Motivational considerations in the study of instruction. *Cognition and Instruction, 5,* 289–309.

Lepper, M., Aspinwall, L., Mumme, D., and Chabay, R. (1990). Self-perception and social-perception processes in tutoring: Subtle social control strategies of expert tutors. In J. Olson and M. Zanna (Eds.), *Self-inference Processes: The Ontario Symposium, Vol. 6* (pp. 217–237). Hillsdale, NJ: Erlbaum.

Lepper, M. and Greene, D. (1975). Turning play into work: Effects of adult surveillance and extrinsic rewards on children's intrinsic motivation. *Journal of Personality and Social Psychology, 31,* 479–486.

Lepper, M., Greene, D., and Nisbett, R. (1973). Undermining children's intrinsic interest with intrinsic rewards: A test of the overjustification hypothesis. *Journal of Personality and Social Psychology, 28,* 129–137.

Lepper, M. and Malone, T. (1987). Intrinsic motivation and instructional effectiveness in computer-based education. In R. Snow and M. Farr (Eds.), *Aptitude, Learning, and Instruction: III. Conative and Affective Process Analysis* (pp. 255–286). Hillsdale, NJ: Erlbaum.

Levine, J. (1983). Social comparison and education. In J. Levine and M. Wang (Eds.), *Teacher and Student Perceptions: Implications for Learning* (pp. 29–55). Hillsdale, NJ: Erlbaum.

Levine, J., Snyder, H., and Mendez-Caratini, G. (1982). Task performance and interpersonal attraction in children. *Child Development, 53,* 359–371.

Lewin, K., Lippitt R., and White, R. (1939). Pattern of aggressive behavior in experimentally created "social climates." *Journal of Social Psychology, 10,* 271–299.

Lewis, M., Wall, M., and Aronfreed, J. (1963). Developmental change in the relative values of social and nonsocial reinforcement. *Journal of Experimental Psychology, 66,* 133–137.

Licht, B. and Dweck, C. (1984). Determinants of academic achievement: The interaction of children's achievement orientations with skill area. *Developmental Psychology, 20,* 628–636.

Liebert, R. and Morris, L. (1967). Cognitive and emotional components of test anxiety: A distinction and some initial data. *Psychological Reports, 20,* 975–978.

Lipinski, D., Black, J., Nelson, R., and Ciminero, A. (1974). Influence of motivational variables on the reactivity and reliability of self-recording. *Journal of Consulting and Clinical Psychology, 42,* 118–123.

Litrownik, A. and Freitas, J. (1980). Self-monitoring in moderately retarded adolescents: Reactivity and accuracy as a function of valence. *Behavior Therapy, 11,* 245–255.

Locke, E., Frederick, E., Lee, C., and Bobko, P. (1984). Effect of self-efficacy, goals, and task strategies on task performance. *Journal of Applied Psychology, 69,* 241–251.

Locke, E., Shaw, K., Saari, L., and Latham, G. (1981). Goal setting and task performance: 1969–1980. *Psychological Bulletin, 90,* 125–152.

Luria, A. (1961). *The Role of Speech in the Regulation of Normal and Abnormal Behaviors.* New York: Liveright.

Mace, F., Belfiore, P., and Shea, M. (1989). Operant theory and research on self-regulation. In B. Zimmerman and D. Schunk (Eds.), *Self-regulated Learning and Academic Achievement: Theory, Research, and Practice* (pp. 27–50). New York: Springer-Verlag.

Mace, F. and Kratochwill, T. (1988). Self-monitoring. In J. Will, S. Elliott, and F. Gresham (Eds.), *Handbook of Behavior Therapy in Education* (pp. 489–522). New York: Plenum Press.

Mac Iver, D. (1987). Classroom factors and student characteristics predicting students' use of achievement standards during ability self-assessment. *Child Development, 58,* 1258–1271.

Mac Iver, D. (1988). Classroom environments and the stratification of pupils' ability perceptions. *Journal of Educational Psychology, 80,* 495–505.

Mac Iver, D. (1990). *A National Description of Report Card Entries in the Middle Grades* (Rep. No. 9). Baltimore, MD: Johns Hopkins University, Center for Research on Effective Schooling for Disadvantaged Students.

Mac Iver, D., Stipek, D., and Daniels, D. (1991). Explaining within-semester changes in student effort in junior high school and senior high school courses. *Journal of Educational Psychology, 83,* 201–211.

MacMillan, D. and Keogh, B. (1971). Normal and retarded children's expectancy for failure. *Developmental Psychology, 4,* 343–348.

Madaus, G., Airasian, P., and Kellaghan, T. (1980). *School Effectiveness: A Reassessment of the Evidence.* New York: McGraw Hill.

Maehr, M. (1982). *Motivational Factors in School Achievement.* Paper commissioned by the National Commission on Excellence in Education (NIE 400–81–0004, Task 10).

Maehr, M. (1984). Meaning and motivation: Toward a theory of personal investment. In R. Ames and C. Ames (Eds.), *Research on Motivation in Education, Vol. 1: Student Motivation* (pp. 115–144). Orlando, FL: Academic Press.

Maehr, M. and Stallings, W. (1972). Freedom from external evaluation. *Child Development, 43,* 117–185.

Malone, T. (1981a). Toward a theory of intrinsically motivating instruction. *Cognitive Science, 4,* 333–369.

Malone, T. (1981b). What makes computer games fun? *Byte, 6,* 258–277.

Malone, T. and Lepper, M. (1987). Making learning fun: A taxonomy of intrinsic motivation for learning. In R. Snow and M. Farr (Eds.), *Aptitude, Learning, and Instruction: III. Conative and Affective Process Analysis* (pp. 223–253). Hillsdale, NJ: Erlbaum.

Manderlink, G. and Harackiewicz, J. (1984). Proximal vs. distal goal setting and intrinsic motivation. *Journal of Personality and Social Psychology, 47,* 918–928.

Marsh, H. (1984a). Relations among dimensions of self-attribution, dimensions of self-concept, and academic achievement. *Journal of Educational Psychology, 76,* 3–32.

Marsh, H. (1984b). Self-concept, social comparison, and ability grouping: A reply to Kulik and Kulik. *American Educational Research Journal, 2,* 799–806.

Marsh, H. (1986). Verbal and math self-concepts: An internal/external frame of reference model. *American Educational Research Journal, 23,* 129–149.

Marsh, H. (1987). The big-fish—little-pond effect on academic self-concept. *Journal of Educational Psychology, 79,* 280–295.

Marsh, H., Barnes, J., Cairns, L., and Tidman, M. (1984). Self-description questionnaire: Age and sex effects in the structure and level of self-concept for preadolescent children. *Journal of Educational Psychology, 76,* 940–956.

Marsh, H., Byrne, B., and Shavelson, R. (1988). A multifaceted academic self-concept: Its hierarchical structure and its relation to academic achievement. *Journal of Educational Psychology, 80,* 366–380.

Marsh, H., Cairns, L., Relich, J., Barnes, J., and Debus, R. (1984). The relationship between dimensions of self-attribution and dimensions of self-concept. *Journal of Educational Psychology, 76,* 3–32.

Marsh, H. and Gouvernet, P. (1989). Multidimensional self-concepts and perceptions of control: Construct validation of responses by children. *Journal of Educational Psychology, 81,* 57–69.

Marsh, H. and Holmes, I. (1990). Multidimensional self-concepts: Construct validation of responses by children. *American Educational Research Journal, 27,* 89–117.

Marsh, H. and Parker, J. (1984). Determinants of student self-concept: Is it better to be a relatively large fish in a small pond even if you don't learn to swim as well. *Journal of Personality and Social Psychology, 47,* 213–231.

Marsh, H., Smith, I., and Barnes, J. (1983). Multitrait-multimethod analyses of the self-description questionnaire: Student-teacher agreement on multidimensional ratings of student self-concept. *American Educational Research Journal, 26,* 333–357.

Marshall, H. (1987). Motivational strategies of three fifth-grade teachers. *Elementary School Journal, 88,* 135–150.

Marshall, H. and Weinstein, R. (1984). Classroom factors affecting students' self-evaluation: An interactional model. *Review of Educational Research, 54,* 301–325.

Marshall, H. and Weinstein, R. (1986). Classroom context of student-perceived differential teacher treatment. *Journal of Educational Psychology, 78,* 441–453.

Mason, T. and Stipek, D. (1989). The stability of students' achievement-related thoughts and school performance from one grade to the next. *The Elementary School Journal, 90,* 57–67.

Masters, J., Furman, W., and Barden, R. (1977). Effects of achievement standards, tangible rewards, and self-dispensed achievement evaluations on children's task mastery. *Child Development, 48,* 217–224.

Masters, J. and Santrock, J. (1976). Studies in the self-regulation of behavior: Effects of contingent cognitive and affective events. *Developmental Psychology, 12,* 334–348.

Matheny, K. and Edwards, C. (1974). Academic improvement through an experimental classroom management system. *Journal of School Psychology, 12,* 222–232.

McClelland, D. (1961). *The Achieving Society.* New York: The Free Press.

McClelland, D. (1971). *Motivational Trends in Society.* New York: General Learning Press.

McClelland, D. (1978). Managing motivation to expand human freedom. *American Psychologist, 33,* 201–210.

McCombs, R. and Gay, J. (1988). Effects of race, class, and IQ information on judgments of parochial grade school teachers. *Journal of Social Psychology, 128,* 647–652.

McDermott, R. (1987). The explanation of minority school failure, again. *Anthropology and Education Quarterly, 18,* 361–364.

McGraw, K. and McCullers, J. (1979). Evidence of a detrimental effect of extrinsic incentives on breaking a mental set. *Journal of Experimental Social Psychology, 15,* 285–294.

McMullin, D. and Steffen, J. (1982). Intrinsic motivation and performance standards. *Social Behavior and Personality, 10,* 47–56.

Meece, J. (1991). The classroom context and students' motivational goals. In M. Maehr and P. Pintrich (Eds.), *Advances in Motivation and Achievement, Vol. 7* (pp. 261–285). Greenwich, CT: JAI Press.

Meece, J., Blumenfeld, P., and Hoyle, R. (1988). Students' goal orientations and cognitive engagement in classroom activities. *Journal of Educational Psychology, 80,* 514–523.

Meece, J., Blumenfeld, P., and Puro, P. (1989). A motivational analysis of elementary science learning environments. In M. Matyas, K. Tobin, and B. Fraser (Eds.), *Looking Into Windows: Qualitative Research in Science Education* (pp. 13–23). Washington D.C.: American Association for the Advancement of Science.

Meece, J., Wigfield, A., and Eccles, J. (1990). Predictors of math anxiety and its influence on young adolescents' course enrollment intentions and performance in mathematics. *Journal of Educational Psychology, 82,* 60–70.

Meichenbaum, D. (1977). *Cognitive Behavior Modification.* New York: Plenum Press.

Meichenbaum, D. and Asarnow, J. (1979). Cognitive-behavioral modification and metacognitive development: Implications for the classroom. In P. Kendall and S. Hollon (Eds.), *Cognitive-behavioral Interventions: Theory, Research, and Procedures* (pp. 11–35). New York: Academic Press.

Meid, E. (1971). *The Effects of Two Types of Success and Failure on Children's Discrimination Learning and Evaluation of Performance.* Doctoral dissertation, Yale University.

Meyer, J. (1970). High school effects on college intentions. *American Journal of Sociology, 76,* 59–70.

Meyer, W. (1982). Indirect communications about perceived ability estimates. *Journal of Educational Psychology, 74,* 888–897.

Meyer, W. (1987). Perceived ability and achievement-related behavior. In F. Halisch and J. Kuhl (Eds.), *Motivation, Intention, and Volition* (pp. 73–85). New York: Springer-Verlag.

Meyer, W., Bachmann, M., Biermann, V., Hempelmann, P., Ploger, F., and Spiller, H. (1979). The informational value of evaluative behavior: Influence of praise and blame on perceptions of ability. *Journal of Educational Psychology, 71,* 259–268.

Midgley, C., Feldlaufer, H., and Eccles, J. (1988). The transition to junior high school: Beliefs of pre- and posttransition teachers. *Journal of Youth and Adolescence, 17,* 543–562.

Midgley, C., Feldlaufer, H., and Eccles, J. (1989a). Change in teacher efficacy and student self- and task-related beliefs in mathematics during the transition to junior high school. *Journal of Educational Psychology, 81,* 247–258.

Midgley, C., Feldlaufer, H., and Eccles, J. (1989b). Student/teacher relations and attitudes toward mathematics before and after the transition to junior high school. *Child Development, 60,* 981–992.

Miller, A. (1985). A developmental study of the cognitive basis of performance impairment after failure. *Journal of Personality and Social Psychology, 4 9,* 529–538.

Miller, A. (1986). Performance impairment after failure: Mechanism and sex differences. *Journal of Educational Psychology, 78,* 486–491.

Miller, A. and Hom, H. (1990). Influence of extrinsic and ego incentive value on persistence after failure and continuing motivation. *Journal of Educational Psychology, 82,* 539–545.

Miller, D. and Ross, M. (1975). Self-serving bias in the attribution of causality: Fact or fiction? *Psychological Bulletin, 82,* 213–235.

Mitchell, K. and Ng, K. (1972). Effects of group counseling and behavior therapy on the academic achievement of test-anxious students. *Journal of Counseling Psychology, 19,* 491–497.

Mitman, A. and Lash, A. (1988). Students' perceptions of their academic standing and classroom behavior. *The Elementary School Journal, 89,* 55–68.

Montessori, M. (1964). *The Montessori Method.* New York: Schocken.

Morgan, M. (1984). Reward-induced decrements and increments in intrinsic motivation. *Review of Educational Research, 54,* 5–30.

Morris, L., Davis, M., and Hutchings, C. (1981). Cognitive and emotional components of anxiety: Literature review and a revised worry-emotionality scale. *Journal of Educational Psychology, 73,* 541–555.

Morris, W. and Nemcek, D. (1982). The development of social comparison motivation among preschoolers: Evidence of a stepwise progression. *Merrill-Palmer Quarterly, 28,* 413–425.

Morse, L. and Handley, H. (1985). Listening to adolescents: Gender differences in science classroom interaction. In L. Wilkinson and C. Marrett (Eds.), *Gender Influences in Classroom Interaction* (pp. 37–56). Orlando, FL: Academic Press.

Mosatche, H. and Bragonier, P. (1981). An observational study of social comparison in preschoolers. *Child Development, 52,* 376–378.

Mossholder, K. (1980). Effects of externally mediated goal setting on intrinsic motivation: A laboratory experiment. *Journal of Applied Psychology, 65,* 202–210.

Naveh-Benjamin, M., McKeachie, W., and Lin, Y-G. (1987). Two types of test-anxious students: Support for an information processing model. *Journal of Educational Psychology, 79,* 131–136.

Nelson-Le Gall, S. (1981). Help-seeking: An understudied problem-solving skill in children. *Developmental Review, 1,* 224–246.

Nelson-Le Gall, S. (1990). Classroom help-seeking behavior of African-American children. *Education and Urban Society, 24,* 27–40.

Nelson-Le Gall, S. (in press). Children's instrumental help seeking: Its role in the social acquisition of knowledge and skill. In R. Hertz-Lazarowitz and N. Miller (Eds.), *Interaction in Cooperative Groups: The Theoretical Anatomy of Group Learning.* New York: Cambridge University Press.

Newman, R. (1984). Children's achievement and self-evaluations in mathematics: A longitudinal study. *Journal of Educational Psychology, 76,* 857–873.

Newman, R. (1990). Children's reluctance to seek help with schoolwork. *Journal of Educational Psychology, 82,* 92–100.

Newman, R. (1991). Goals and self-regulated learning: What motivates children to seek academic help? In M. Maehr and P. Pintrich (Eds.), *Advances in Motivation and Achievement, Vol. 7* (pp. 151–183). Greenwich, CT: JAI Press.

Nicholls, J. (1975). Causal attributions and other achievement-related cognitions: Effects of task outcome, attainment value, and sex. *Journal of Educational Psychology, 31,* 379–389.

Nicholls, J. (1976a). Effort is virtuous, but it's better to have ability: Evaluative responses to perceptions of effort and ability. *Journal of Research in Personality, 10,* 306–315.

Nicholls, J. (1976b). When a scale measures more than its name denotes: The case of the test anxiety scale for children. *Journal of Consulting and Clinical Psychology, 44,* 976–985.

Nicholls, J. (1978). The development of the concepts of effort and ability, perception of own attainment, and the understanding that difficult tasks require more ability. *Child Development, 49,* 800–814.

Nicholls, J. (1979a). Development of perception of own attainment and causal attributions for success and failure in reading. *Journal of Educational Psychology, 71,* 94–99.

Nicholls, J. (1979b). Quality and equality in intellectual development: The role of motivation in education. *American Psychologist, 34,* 1071–1083.

Nicholls, J. (1980). A reexamination of boys' and girls' causal attributions for success and failure based on New Zealand data. In L. Fyans (Ed.), *Achievement Motivation: Recent Trends in Theory and Research* (pp. 266–288). New York: Plenum Press.

Nicholls, J. (1983). Conception of ability and achievement motivation: A theory and its implications for education. In S. Paris, G. Olson, and H. Stevenson (Eds.), *Learning and Motivation in the Classroom* (pp. 211–237). Hillsdale, NJ: Erlbaum.

Nicholls, J. (1984). Achievement motivation: Conceptions of ability, subjective experience, task choice, and performance. *Psychological Review, 9 1,* 328–346.

Nicholls, J. (1989). *The Competitive Ethos and Democratic Education.* Cambridge MA: Harvard University Press.

Nicholls, J. (1990). What is ability and why are we mindful of it? A developmental perspective. In R. Sternberg and J. Kolligian, Jr. (Eds.), *Competence Considered* (pp. 11–40). New Haven, CT: Yale University Press.

Nicholls, J., Cheung, P., Lauer, J., and Patashnick, M. (1989). Individual differences in academic motivation: Perceived ability, goals, beliefs, and values. *Learning and Individual Differences, 1,* 63–84.

Nicholls, J., Cobb, P., Wood, T., Yackel, E., and Patashnick, M. (1990). Assessing students' theories of success in mathematics: Individual and classroom differences. *Journal for Research in Mathematics Education, 21,* 109–122.

Nicholls, J., Cobb, P., Yackel, E., Wood, T., and Wheatley, G. (1990). Students' theories about mathematics and their mathematical knowledge: Multiple dimensions of assessment. In G. Kulm (Ed.), *Assessing Higher Order Thinking in Mathematics* (pp. 137–154). Washington, DC: American Association for the Advancement of Science.

Nicholls, J., Jagacinski, C., and Miller, A. (1986). Conceptions of ability in children and adults. In R. Schwarzer (Ed.), *Self-related Cognitions in Anxiety and Motivation* (pp. 265–284). Hillsdale, NJ: Erlbaum.

Nicholls, J. and Miller, A. (1984a). Development and its discontents: The differentiation of the concept of ability. In J. Nicholls (Ed.), *Advances in Motivation and Achievement, Vol. 3: The Development of Achievement Motivation* (pp. 185–218). Greenwich, CT: JAI Press.

Nicholls, J. and Miller, A. (1984b). Reasoning about the ability of self and others: A developmental study. *Child Development, 55,* 1990–1999.

Nottlemann, E. (1987). Competence and self-esteem during transition from childhood to adolescence. *Developmental Psychology, 23,* 441–450.

Nottelmann, E. and Hill, K. (1977). Test anxiety and off-task behavior in evaluative situations. *Child Development, 48,* 225–231.

Nolen, S. (1988). Reasons for studying: Motivational orientations and study strategies. *Cognition and Instruction, 5,* 269–287.

Notz, W. (1975). Work motivation and the negative effects of extrinsic rewards: A review with implications for theory and practice. *American Psychologist, 30,* 804–891.

Oakes, J. (1985). *Keeping Track: How Schools Structure Inequality.* New Haven, CT: Yale University Press.

Oakes, J. (1990). *Multiplying Inequalities: The Effects of Race, Social Class, and Tracking on Opportunities to Learn Math and Science.* Santa Monica, CA: Rand McNally.

O'Leary, K. (1978). The operant and social psychology of token systems. In A. Catania and T. Brigham (Eds.), *Handbook of Applied Behavior Analysis: Social and Instructional Processes* (pp. 179–207). New York: Irvington.

O'Leary, K. and Drabman, R. (1971). Token reinforcement programs in the classroom: A review. *Psychological Bulletin, 75,* 379–398.

O'Leary, S. and Dubey, D. (1979). Applications of self-control procedures by children: A review. *Journal of Applied Behavior Analysis, 12,* 449–465.

Parker, L. and Lepper, M. (in press). The effects of fantasy contexts on children's learning and motivation. *Journal of Personality and Social Psychology.*

Palardy, J. (1969). What teachers believe—what children achieve. *Elementary School Journal, 69,* 370–374.

Pallak, S., Costomiris, S., Sroka, S., and Pittman, T. (1982). School experience, reward characteristics, and intrinsic motivation. *Child Development, 53,* 1382–1391.

Parsons, J., Adler, T., and Kaczala, C. (1982). Socialization of achievement attitudes and beliefs: Parental influences. *Child Development, 53,* 310–339.

Parsons, J., Kaczala, C., and Meece, J. (1982). Socialization of achievement attitudes and beliefs: Classroom influences. *Child Development, 53,* 322–339.

Parsons, J., Meece, J., Adler, T., and Kaczala, C. (1982). Sex differences in attributions and learned helplessness. *Sex Roles, 8,* 431–432.

Pascarella, E., Walberg, H., Junker, L., and Haertel, G. (1981). Continuing motivation in science for early and late adolescents. *American Educational Research Journal, 18,* 439–452.

Pearlman, C. (1984). The effects of level of effectance motivation, IQ, and a penalty/reward contingency on the choice of problem difficulty. *Child Development, 55,* 537–542.

Pepitone, E. (1972). Comparison behavior in elementary school children. *American Educational Research Journal, 9,* 43–63.

Peterson, P. and Swing, S. (1982). Beyond time on task: Students' reports of their thought processes during classroom instruction. *The Elementary School Journal, 21*, 487–515.

Pelletier, L. and Vallerand, R. (1989). Behavioral confirmation in social interaction: Effects of teachers' expectancies on students' intrinsic motivation. *Canadian Psychology, 30*, 404.

Phillips, B. (1967). Anxiety as a function of early school experience. *Psychology in the Schools, 4*, 335–340.

Phillips, B., Martin, R., and Meyers, J. (1972). Interventions in relation to anxiety in school. In C. D. Spielberger (Ed.), *Anxiety: Current Trends in Theory and Research (Vol. 2)*. New York: Academic Press.

Phillips, B., Pitcher, G., Worsham, M., and Miller, S. (1980). Test anxiety and the school environment. In I. Sarason (Ed.), *Test Anxiety: Theory, Research, and Applications* (pp. 327–346). Hillsdale, NJ: Erlbaum.

Phillips, D. (1984). The illusion of incompetence among academically competent children. *Child Development, 55*, 2000–2016.

Phillips, D. and Zimmerman, M. (1990). The developmental course of perceived competence and incompetence among competent children. In J. Kolligian and R. Sternberg (Eds.), *Competence Considered* (pp. 41–66). New Haven, CT: Yale University Press.

Piaget, J. (1952). *The Origins of Intelligence in Children*. New York: W. W. Norton.

Pintrich, P. and Blumenfeld, P. (1985). Classroom experience and children's self-perceptions of ability, effort, and conduct. *Journal of Educational Psychology, 77*, 646–657.

Pintrich, P. and De Groot, E. (1990). Motivational and self-regulated learning components of classroom academic performance. *Journal of Educational Psychology, 82*, 33–40.

Pintrich, P. and Schrauben, B. (in press). Students' motivational beliefs and their cognitive engagement in classroom academic tasks. In D. Schunk and J. Meece (Eds.), *Student Perceptions in the Classroom: Causes and Consequences*. Hillsdale, NJ: Erlbaum.

Pittman, T., Boggiano, A., and Ruble, D. (1983). Intrinsic and extrinsic motivational orientations: Limiting conditions on the undermining and enhancing effects of reward on intrinsic motivation. In J. Levine and M. Wang (Eds.), *Teacher and Student Perceptions: Implications for Learning* (pp. 319–340). Hillsdale, NJ: Erlbaum.

Pittman, T., Davey, M., Alafat, K., Wetherill, K., and Kramer, N. (1980). Informational versus controlling verbal rewards. *Personality and Social Psychology Bulletin, 6*, 228–233.

Pittman, T., Emery, J., and Boggiano, A. (1982). Intrinsic and extrinsic motivational orientations: Reward-induced changes in preference for complexity. *Journal of Personality and Social Psychology, 42*, 789–797.

Plant, R. and Ryan, R. (1985). Intrinsic motivation and the effects of self-consciousness, self-awareness, ego-involvement: An investigation of internally-controlling styles. *Journal of Personality, 53*, 435-449.

Plass, J. and Hill, K. (1986). Children's achievement strategies and test performance: The role of time pressure, evaluation anxiety, and sex. *Developmental Psychology, 22*, 31–36.

Rainey, R. (1965). The effects of directed vs. nondirected laboratory work on high school chemistry achievement. *Journal of Research in Science Teaching, 3*, 286–292.

Reid, M. and Borkowski, J. (1987). Causal attributions of hyperactive children: Implications for teaching strategies and self-control. *Journal of Educational Psychology, 79*, 296–307.

Renick, J. and Harter, S. (1989). Impact of social comparisons on the developing self-perceptions of learning disabled students. *Journal of Educational Psychology, 81*, 631–638.

Rest, S., Nierenberg, R., Weiner, B., and Heckhausen, H. (1973). Further evidence concerning the effects of perceptions of effort and ability on achievement evaluation. *Journal of Personality and Social Psychology, 28*, 187–191.

Rheinberg, F. (1983). Achievement evaluation: A fundamental difference and its motivational consequences. *Studies in Educational Evaluation, 9*, 185–194.

Richardson, F. and Woolfolk, R. (1980). Mathematics anxiety. In I. Sarason (Ed.), *Test Anxiety: Theory, Research, and Applications* (pp. 271–288). Hillsdale, NJ: Erlbaum.

Robertson, D. and Keely, S. (1974). *Evaluation of a Mediational Training Program for Impulsive Children by a Multiple Case Study Design.* Paper presented at the annual meeting of the American Psychological Association. New Orleans, LA.

Rogers, C. (1951). *Client Centered Therapy.* New York: Houghton-Mifflin.

Rosen, B. and D'Andrade, R. C. (1959). The psychosocial origins of achievement motivation. *Sociometry, 22*, 185–218.

Rosenbaum, J. (1980). Social implications of educational grouping. In D. Berliner (Ed.), *Review of Research in Education: Vol. 8* (pp. 361–401). Washington, DC: American Educational Research Association.

Rosenbaum, M. and Drabman, R. (1979). Self-control training in the classroom: A review and critique. *Journal of Applied Behavior Analysis, 12*, 467–485.

Rosenberg, J. (1965). *Society and the Adolescent Self-image.* Princeton, NJ: Princeton University Press.

Rosenfield, D., Folger, R., and Adelman, H. (1980). When rewards reflect competence: A qualification of the over-justification effect. *Journal of Personality and Social Psychology, 39*, 368–376.

Rosenholtz, S. and Rosenholtz, S. (1981). Classroom organization and the perception of ability. *Sociology of Education, 54*, 132–140.

Rosenholtz, S. and Simpson, C. (1984a). Classroom organization and student stratification. *Elementary School Journal, 85*, 21–38.

Rosenholtz, S. and Simpson, C. (1984b). The formation of ability conceptions: Developmental trend or social construction? *Review of Educational Research, 54*, 31–63.

Rosenholtz, S. and Wilson, B. (1980). The effect of classroom structure on shared perceptions of ability. *American Educational Research Journal, 17,* 75–82.

Rosenthal, R. (1974). *On the Social Psychology of the Self-fulfilling Prophecy: Further Evidence for Pygmalion Effects and Their Mediating Mechanisms.* New York: MSS Modular Publications.

Rosenthal, R. and Jacobson, L. (1968). *Pygmalion in the Classroom: Teacher Expectation and Pupils' Intellectual Development.* New York: Holt, Rinehart & Winston.

Rothbaum, F., Weisz, J., and Snyder, S. (1982). Changing the world and changing the self: Two-process model of perceived control. *Journal of Personality and Social Psychology, 42,* 37.

Rotter, J. (1966). Generalized expectancies for internal versus external control of reinforcement. *Psychological Monographs, 1* (Whole No. 609).

Rotter, J. (1975). Some problems and misconceptions related to the construct of internal versus external control of reinforcement. *Journal of Consulting and Clinical Psychology, 43,* 56–67.

Roy, P. (Ed.). (1982). *Structuring Cooperative Learning: The 1982 Handbook.* Minneapolis, MN: Cooperative Network.

Ruble, D. (1983). The development of social comparison processes and their role in achievement-related self-socialization. In E. T. Higgins, D. N. Ruble, and W. W. Hartup (Eds.), *Social Cognition and Social Development: A Sociocultural Perspective* (pp. 134–157). New York: Cambridge University Press.

Ruble, D., Boggiano, A., Feldman, N., and Loebl, J. (1980). A developmental analysis of the role of social comparison in self-evaluation. *Developmental Psychology, 16,* 105–115.

Ruble, D., Feldman, N., and Boggiano, A. (1976). Social comparison between young children in achievement situations. *Developmental Psychology, 12,* 192–197.

Ruble, D. and Frey, K. (1991). Changing patterns of comparative behavior as skills are acquired: A functional model of self-evaluation. In J. Suls and T. Wills (Eds.), *Social Comparison: Contemporary Theory and Research* (pp. 79–113). Hillsdale, NJ: Erlbaum.

Ruble, D., Parsons, J., and Ross, J. (1976). Self-evaluative responses of children in an achievement setting. *Child Development, 47,* 990–997.

Rutter, M., Maughan, B., Mortimore, P., Duston, J., and Smith, A. (1979). *Fifteen Thousand Hours: Secondary Schools and Their Effects on Children.* Cambridge: Harvard University Press.

Ryan, R. (1982). Control and information in the intrapersonal sphere: An extension of cognitive evaluation theory. *Journal of Personality and Social Psychology, 43,* 450–461.

Ryan, R. and Connell, J. (1989). Perceived locus of causality and internalization: Examining reasons for acting in two domains. *Journal of Personality and Social Psychology, 57,* 749–761.

Ryan, R., Connell, J., and Deci, E. (1985). A motivational analysis of self-determination and self-regulation. In C. Ames and R. Ames (Eds.), *Research on*

Motivation in Education: Vol. 12, The Classroom (pp. 13–51). New York: Academic Press.

Ryan, R., Connell, J., and Plant, R. (1990). Emotions in nondirected text learning. *Learning and Individual Differences, 2,* 1–17.

Ryan, R. and Grolnick, W. (1986). Origins and pawns in the classroom: Self-report and projective assessments of individual differences in children's perceptions. *Journal of Personality and Social Psychology, 50,* 350–358.

Ryan, R., Mims, V., and Koestner, R. (1983). The relationship of reward contingency and interpersonal context to intrinsic motivation: A review and test using cognitive evaluation theory. *Journal of Personality and Social Psychology, 45,* 736–750.

Ryan, R. and Stiller, J. (1991). The social contexts of internalization: Parent and teacher influences on autonomy, motivation, and learning. In P. Pintrich and M. Maehr (Eds.), *Advanced in Motivation and Achievement: Vol. 7* (pp. 115–149). Greenwich, CT: JAI Press.

Ryckman, D. B. and Peckham, P. D. (1987). Gender differences in attributions for success and failure. *Journal of Early Adolescence, 7,* 47–63.

Salili, F., Maehr, M., Sorensen, R., and Fyans, L. (1976). A further consideration of the effects of evaluation on motivation. *American Educational Research Journal, 13,* 85–102.

Sarason, I. (1958). The effects of anxiety, reassurance, and meaningfulness of material to be learned, on verbal learning. *Journal of Experimental Psychology, 56,* 472–477.

Sarason, I. (1961). A note on anxiety, instructions, and word association performance. *Journal of Abnormal and Social Psychology, 62,* 153–154.

Sarason, I. (1973). Test anxiety and cognitive modeling. *Journal of Personality and Social Psychology, 28,* 58–61.

Sarason, I. (1975). Test anxiety, attention, and the general problem of anxiety. In I. Sarason and C. Spielberger (Eds.), *Stress and Anxiety: Vol. 1* (pp. 165–187). Washington, DC: Hemisphere.

Sarason, I. (1984). Stress, anxiety, and cognitive interference: Reactions to tests. *Journal of Personality and Social Psychology, 46,* 929–938.

Sarason, S., Davidson, K., Lighthall, F., Waite, R., and Ruebush, B. (1960). *Anxiety in Elementary School Children.* New York: Wiley.

Schunk, D. (1982). Effects of effort and attributional feedback on children's perceived self-efficacy and achievement. *Journal of Educational Psychology, 74,* 548–556.

Schunk, D. (1983a). Ability versus effort attributional feedback: Differential effects on self-efficacy an achievement. *Journal of Educational Psychology, 75,* 848–856.

Schunk, D. (1983b). Developing children's self-efficacy and skills: The roles of social comparative information and goal setting. *Contemporary Educational Psychology, 8,* 76–86.

Schunk, D. (1984a). Self-efficacy perspective on achievement behavior. *Educational Psychologist, 19,* 48–58.

Schunk, D. (1984b). Sequential attributional feedback and children's achievement behaviors. *Journal of Educational Psychology, 76,* 1159–1169.

Schunk, D. (1985). Participation in goal setting: Effects on self-efficacy and skills of learning-disabled children. *Journal of Special Education, 19,* 307–317.

Schunk, D. (1986). Children's social comparison and goal setting in achievement contexts. In L. Katz (Ed.), *Current Topics in Early Childhood Education* (pp. 62–84). Norwood, NJ: Ablex.

Schunk, D. (1989a). Self-efficacy and cognitive achievement: Implications for students with learning problems. *Journal of Learning Disabilities, 22,* 14–22.

Schunk, D. (1989b). Social cognitive theory and self-regulated learning. In B. Zimmerman and D. Schunk (Eds.), *Self-regulated Learning and Academic Achievement: Theory, Research and Practice* (pp. 83–110). New York: Springer-Verlag.

Schunk, D. (1990). Goal setting and self-efficacy during self-regulated learning. *Educational Psychologist, 25,* 71–86.

Schunk, D. (1991). Goal setting and self-evaluation: A social cognitive perspective on self-regulation. In M. Maehr and P. Pintrich (Eds.), *Advances in Motivation and Achievement: Vol. 7* (pp. 85–113). Greenwich, CT: JAI Press.

Schunk, D. (in press). Participation in goal setting: Effects on learning-disabled children's self-efficacy and skills. *Journal of Special Education.*

Schunk, D. and Hanson, A. (1985). Peer models: Influence on children's self-efficacy and achievement. *Journal of Educational Psychology, 77,* 313–322.

Schunk, D. and Rice, J. (1989). Learning goals and children's reading comprehension. *Journal of Reading Behavior, 21,* 279–293.

Sears, P. (1940). Level of aspiration in academically successful and unsuccessful children. *Journal of Abnormal and Social Psychology, 35,* 498–536.

Seligman, M. and Maier, S. (1967). Failure to escape traumatic shock. *Journal of Experimental Psychology, 74,* 1–9.

Shapira, Z. (1976). Expectancy determinants of intrinsically motivated behavior. *Journal of Personality and Social Psychology, 34,* 1235–1244.

Shapiro, E. (1984). Self-monitoring procedures. In T. Ollendick and M. Hersen (Eds.), *Child Behavioral Assessment: Principles and Procedures* (pp. 148–165). New York: Pergamon Press.

Sharan, S. (1980). Cooperative learning in small groups: Recent methods and effects on achievement, attitudes, and ethnic relations. *Review of Educational Research, 50,* 241–271.

Sherman, J. (1979). Predicting mathematics performance in high school girls and boys. *Journal of Educational Psychology, 71,* 242–249.

Shirey, L. and Reynolds, R. (1988). Effect of interest on attention and learning. *Journal of Educational Psychology, 80,* 159–166.

Shultz, T. and Zigler, E. (1970). Emotional concomitants of visual mastery in infants: The effects of stimulus movement on smiling and vocalizing. *Journal of Experimental Child Psychology, 10,* 390–402.

Sieber, J., O'Neil, H., Tobias, S. (1977). *Anxiety, Learning, and Instruction.* Hillsdale, NJ: Erlbaum.

Simpson, C. (1981). Classroom structure and the organization of ability. *Sociology of Education, 54,* 120–132.

Simpson, C. and Rosenholtz, S. (1986). Classroom structure and the social construction of ability. In J. Richardson (Ed.), *Handbook of Theory and Research for the Sociology of Education* (pp. 113–138). New York: Greenwood Press.

Skaalvik, E. and Rankin, R. (1990). Math, verbal, and general academic self-concept: The internal/external frame of reference model and gender differences in self-concept structure. *Journal of Educational Psychology, 82,* 546–554.

Skinner, B. (1974). *About Behaviorism.* New York: Knopf.

Skinner, E. (1990). Age differences in the dimensions of perceived control during middle childhood: Implications for developmental conceptualizations and research. *Child Development, 61,* 1882–1890.

Skinner, E., Chapman, M., and Baltes, P. (1988). Control, means-ends, and agency beliefs: A new conceptualization and its measurement during childhood. *Journal of Personality and Social Psychology, 54,* 117–133.

Slavin, R. (1977). Classroom reward structure: An analytic and practical review. *Review of Educational Research, 47,* 633–650.

Slavin, R. (1980a). Cooperative learning. *Review of Educational Research, 50,* 315–342.

Slavin, R. (1980b). *Using Student Team Learning* (rev. edition). Baltimore, MD: Johns Hopkins University, Center for Social Organization of Schools.

Slavin, R. (1983a). *Cooperative Learning.* New York: Longman.

Slavin, R. (1983b). When does cooperative learning increase student achievement? *Psychological Bulletin, 94,* 429–445.

Slavin, R. (1984). Students motivating students to excel: Cooperative incentives, cooperative tasks, and student achievement. *Elementary School Journal, 84,* 53–63.

Slavin, R. (1987a). Developmental and motivational perspectives on cooperative learning: A reconciliation. *Child Development, 58,* 1161–1167.

Slavin, R. (1987b). Mastery learning reconsidered. *Review of Educational Research, 57,* 175–213.

Slavin, R. (1988). *Student Team Learning: An Overview and Practical Guide.* Washington, D.C.: National Education Association.

Slavin, R. (1990). Mastery learning re-reconsidered. *Review of Educational Research, 60,* 300–302.

Slavin, R., Sharan, S., Kagan, S., Hertz-Lazarowitz, N., Webb, N., and Schmuck, R. (1985). *Learning to Cooperate, Cooperating to Learn.* New York: Plenum Press.

Smith, M. (1980). Metaanalysis of research on teacher expectations. *Evaluation in Education, 4,* 53–55.

Sohn, D. (1977). Affect-generating powers of effort and ability: Self-attributions of academic success and failure. *Journal of Educational Psychology, 69,* 500–505.

Sohn, D. (1982). Sex differences in achievement self-attributions: An effect-size analysis. *Sex Roles, 8,* 345–357.

Spear, P. and Armstrong, S. (1978). Effects of performance expectancies created by peer comparison as related to social reinforcement, task difficulty, and age of child. *Journal of Experimental and Child Psychology, 25*, 254–266.

Speidel, G. and Tharp, R. (1980). What does self-reinforcement reinforce? An empirical analysis of the contingencies in self-determined reinforcement. *Child Behavior Therapy, 2*, 1–22.

Spielberger, C. (1972). Anxiety as an emotional state. In C. Spielberger (Ed.), *Anxiety: Current Trends in Theory and Research*: Vol. 1 (p. 23–49). New York: Academic Press.

Stallings, J. (1985). School, classroom, and home influences on women's decisions to enroll in advanced mathematics courses. In S. Chipman, L. Brush, and D. Wilson (Eds.), *Women and Mathematics: Balancing the Equation* (pp. 199–223). Hillsdale, NJ: Erlbaum.

Stevenson, H., Lee, S., and Stigler, J. (1986). Mathematics achievement of Chinese, Japanese, and American children. *Science, 231*, 693–699.

Stevenson, H. and Newman, R. (1986). Long-term prediction of achievement and attitudes in mathematics and reading. *Child Development, 57*, 646–659.

Stevenson, H. and Stigler, J. (1992). *The Learning Gap*. New York: Summit Books.

Stigler, J. and Stevenson, H. (1991). How Asian teachers polish each lesson to perfection. *American Educator, 15*, 12–20.

Stipek, D. (1981). Children's perceptions of their own and their classmates' ability. *Journal of Educational Psychology, 73*, 404–410.

Stipek, D. (1984a). Developmental aspects of motivation in children. In R. Ames and C. Ames (Eds.), *Research on Motivation in Education: Vol. 1. Student Motivation* (pp. 145–174). New York: Academic Press.

Stipek, D. (1984b). Young children's performance expectations: Logical analysis or wishful thinking? In J. Nicholls (Ed.), *The Development of Achievement Motivation* (pp. 33–56). Greenwich, CT: JAI Press.

Stipek, D. (1984c). Sex differences in children's attributions for success and failure on math and spelling tests. *Sex Roles, 11*, 969–981.

Stipek, D. and Daniels, D. (1990). Children's use of dispositional attributions in predicting the performance and behavior of classmates. *Journal of Applied Developmental Psychology, 11*, 13–28.

Stipek, D. and Gralinski, H. (1991). Gender differences in children's achievement-related beliefs and emotional responses to success and failure in math. *Journal of Educational Psychology, 83*, 361–371.

Stipek, D. and Hoffman, J. (1980). Children's achievement-related expectancies as a function of academic performance histories and sex. *Journal of Educational Psychology, 72*, 861–865.

Stipek, D. and Kowalski, P. (1989). Learned helplessness in task-orienting versus performance-orienting testing conditions. *Journal of Educational Psychology, 81*, 384–391.

Stipek, D. and Mac Iver, D. (1989). Developmental change in children's assessment of intellectual competence. *Child Development, 60*, 521–538.

Stipek, D. and Sanborn, M. (1985). Preschool teachers' task-related interactions with handicapped and nonhandicapped boys and girls. *Merrill-Palmer Quarterly, 31*, 285–300.

Stipek, D. and Tannatt, L. (1984). Children's judgments of their own and their peers' academic competence. *Journal of Educational Psychology, 76*, 75–84.

Stipek, D. and Weisz, J. (1981). Perceived personal control and academic achievement. *Review of Educational Research, 51*, 101–137.

Stodolsky, S. (1985). Telling math: Origins of math aversion and anxiety. *Educational Psychologist, 20*, 125–133.

Suinn, R. (1970). *The Application of Short-term Videotape Therapy for the Treatment of Test Anxiety of College Students.* Progress Report. Fort Collins, CO: Colorado State University.

Sulzer-Azaroff, B. and Mayer, G. (1986). *Achieving Educational Excellence.* New York: Holt, Rinehart & Winston.

Swann, W. and Pittman, T. (1977). Initiating play activity of children: The moderating influence of verbal cues on intrinsic motivation. *Child Development, 48*, 1128–1132.

Swanson, H. and Scarpati, S. (1985). Self-instruction training to increase academic performance of educationally handicapped children. *Child and Family Behavior Therapy, 6*, 23–39.

Thoresen, C. and Mahoney, M. (1974). *Behavioral Self-control.* New York: Holt, Rinehart, & Winston.

Thorndike, E. (1898). Animal intelligence: An experimental study of the associative processes in animals. *Psychological Review Monograph Supplements, 2* (No. 4).

Tobias, S. (1977). A model for research on the effect of anxiety on instruction. In J. Sieber, H. O'Neil, and S. Tobias (Eds.), *Anxiety, Learning, and Instruction* (pp. 223–240). Hillsdale, NJ: Erlbaum.

Tobias, S. (1980). Anxiety and instruction. In I. Sarason (Ed.), *Test Anxiety: Theory, Research, and Applications* (pp. 289–309). Hillsdale, NJ: Erlbaum.

Tobias, S. (1986). Anxiety and cognitive processing of instruction. In R. Schwarzer (Ed.), *Self-related Cognitions in Anxiety and Motivation* (p. 35–54). Hillsdale, NJ: Erlbaum.

Tobias, S. and Weissbrod, C. (1980). Anxiety and mathematics: An update. *Harvard Educational Review, 50*, 63–70.

Tollefson, N., Tracy, D., Johnsen, E., Farmer, A., and Buenning, M. (1984). Goal setting and personal responsibility training for LD adolescents. *Psychology in the Schools, 21*, 224–233.

Trudewind, C. (1982). The development of achievement motivation and individual differences: Ecological determinants. In W. Hartup (Ed.), *Review of Child Development Research, Vol. 6* (pp. 669–703). Chicago: University of Chicago Press.

Tryon, G. (1980). The measurement and treatment of test anxiety. *Review of Educational Research, 50*, 343–372.

Vallerand, R., Gauvin, L., and Halliwell, W. (1986). Negative effects of competition on children's intrinsic motivation. *Journal of Social Psychology, 126*, 649–657.

Vanfossen, B., Jones, J., and Spade, J. (1987). Curriculum tracking and status maintenance. *Sociology of Education, 60*, 104–122.

Vygotsky, L. (1962). *Thought and Language.* Cambridge, MA: MIT Press.

Vygotsky, L. (1978). *Mind in Society: The Development of Higher Psychological Processes.* Cambridge, MA: Harvard University Press.

Wall, S. (1983). Children's self-determination of standards in reinforcement contingencies: A reexamination. *Journal of School Psychology, 21*, 123–131.

Wang, M. (Ed.) (1976). *The Self-schedule System for Instructional-learning Management in Adaptive School Learning Environments* (LRDC Publication 1976/9). Pittsburgh, PA: University of Pittsburgh, Learning Research and Development Center.

Wang, M. (1980). Adaptive instruction: Building on diversity. *Theory into Practice, 19*, 122–128.

Wang, M. (1983). Development and consequences of students' sense of personal control. In J. Levine and M. Wang (Eds.), *Teacher and Student Perceptions: Implications for Learning* (pp. 213–247). Hillsdale. NJ: Erlbaum.

Wang, M. and Stiles, B. (1976). An investigation of children's concept of self-responsibility for their school learning. *American Educational Research Journal, 13*, 159–179.

Webb, N. (1984). Student interaction and learning in small-group and whole-class settings. In P. Peterson, L. Wilkinson, and M. Hallinan (Eds.), *The Social Context of Instruction: Group Organization and Group Processes* (pp. 153–170). Orlando, FL: Academic Press.

Webb, N. (1985). Student interaction and learning in small groups: A research summary. In R. Slavin, S. Sharan, S. Kagan, R. Hertz-Lazarowitz, N.Webb, and R. Schmuck (Eds.), *Learning to Cooperate, Cooperating to Learn* (pp. 147–172). New York: Plenum Press.

Weiner, B. (1979). A theory of motivation for some classroom experiences. *Journal of Educational Psychology, 71*, 3–25.

Weiner, B. (1980a). *Human Motivation.* New York: Holt, Rinehart, & Winston.

Weiner, B. (1980b). The role of affect in rational (attributional) approaches to human motivation. *Educational Researcher, 9*, 4–11.

Weiner, B. (1983). Some methodological pitfalls in attributional research. *Journal of Educational Psychology, 75*, 530–543.

Weiner, B. (1985). An attributional theory of achievement motivation and emotion. *Psychological Review, 92*, 548–573.

Weiner, B. (1986). *An Attributional Theory of Motivation and Emotion.* New York: Springer-Verlag.

Weiner, B. and Brown, J. (1984). All's well that ends. *Journal of Educational Psychology, 76*, 169–171.

Weiner, B., Graham, S., Stern, P., and Lawson, M. (1982). Using affective cues to infer causal thoughts. *Developmental Psychology, 18*, 278–286.

Weiner, B. and Peter, N. (1973). A cognitive-developmental analysis of achievement and moral judgments. *Developmental Psychology, 9*, 290–309.

Weiner, B., Russell, D., and Lerman, D. (1978). Affective consequences of causal ascriptions. In J. Harvey, W. Ickes, and R. Kidd (Eds.), *New Directions in Attribution Research: Vol. 2* (pp. 59–90). Hillsdale, NJ: Erlbaum.

Weiner, B., Russell, D., and Lerman, D. (1979). The cognition-motion process in achievement-related contexts. *Journal of Personality and Social Psychology, 37*, 1211–1220.

Weinstein, R. (1976). Reading group membership in first grade: Teacher behaviors and pupil experience over time. *Journal of Educational Psychology, 68*, 103–116.

Weinstein, R. (1985). Student mediation of classroom expectancy effects. In J. Dusek (Ed.), *Teacher Expectancies* (pp. 329–350). Hillsdale, NJ: Erlbaum.

Weinstein, R. (1989). Perceptions of classroom processes and student motivation: Children's views of self-fulfilling prophecies. In C. Ames and R. Ames (Eds.), *Research on Motivation in Education, Vol. 3: Goals and Cognitions* (pp. 187–221). New York: Academic Press.

Weinstein, R., Marshall, H., Sharp, L., and Botkin, M. (1987). Pygmalion and the student: Age and classroom differences in children's awareness of teacher expectations. *Child Development, 58*, 1079–1093.

Weinstein, R. and Middlestadt, S. (1979). Student perceptions of teacher interactions with male high and low achievers. *Journal of Educational Psychology, 71*, 421–431.

Weisz, J. (1979). Perceived control and learned helplessness among mentally retarded and nonretarded children: A developmental analysis. *Developmental Psychology, 15*, 311–319.

Weisz, J. (1986). Understanding the developing understanding of control. In M. Perlmutter (Ed.), *Cognitive Perspectives on Children's Social and Behavioral Development: The Minnesota Symposia on Child Psychology, Vol. 18* (pp. 219–278). Hillsdale, NJ: Erlbaum.

Weisz, J. (1990). Development of control-related beliefs, goals, and styles in childhood and adolescence: A clinical perspective. In K. Schaie, J. Rodin, and C. Schooler (Eds.), *Self-directedness: Causes and Effects Throughout the Life Course* (pp. 103–145). Hillsdale, NJ: Erlbaum.

Weisz, J., Rothbaum, F., and Blackburn, T. (1984a). Standing out and standing in: The psychology of control in America and Japan. *American Psychologist, 39*, 955–969.

Weisz, J., Rothbaum, R., and Blackburn, T. (1984b). Swapping recipes for control. *American Psychologist, 39*, 974–975.

Weisz, J. and Stipek, D. (1982). Competence, contingency, and the development of perceived control. *Human Development, 25*, 250–281.

Wentzel, K. (1989). Adolescent classroom goals, standards for performance, and academic achievement: An interactionist perspective. *Journal of Educational Psychology, 81*, 131–142.

Wentzel, K. (1991). Social and academic goals at school: Motivation and achievement in context. In M. Maehr and P. Pintrich (Eds.), *Advances in Motivation and Achievement, Vol. 7* (pp. 185–212). Greenwich, CT: JAI Press.

West, C. and Anderson, T. (1976). The question of preponderant causation in teacher expectancy research. *Review of Educational Research, 46,* 185–213.

Wentzel, K. (1989). Adolescent classroom goals, standards for performance, and academic achievement: An interactionist perspective. *Journal of Educational Psychology, 81,* 131–142.

Wentzel, K. (1991). Social and academic goals at school: Motivation and achievement in context. In M. Maehr and P. Pintrich (Eds.), *Advances in Motivation and Achievement, Vol. 7* (pp. 185–212). Greenwich, CT: JAI Press.

White, R. (1959). Motivation reconsidered: The concept of competence. *Psychological Review, 66,* 297–333.

Wigfield, A. and Eccles, J. (1989). Test anxiety in elementary and secondary school students. *Educational Psychologist, 24,* 159–183.

Wigfield, A., Eccles, J., Mac Iver, D., Reuman, D., and Midgley, C. (1991). Transitions during early adolescence: Changes in children's domain-specific self-perceptions and general self-esteem across the transition to junior high school. *Developmental Psychology, 27,* 552–565.

Wigfield, A. and Meece, J. (1988). Math anxiety in elementary and secondary school students. *Journal of Educational Psychology, 80,* 210–216.

Wine, J. (1980). Cognitive-attentional theory of test anxiety. In I. Sarason (Ed.), *Test Anxiety: Theory, Research, and Applications* (pp. 349–384). Hillsdale, NJ: Erlbaum.

Winterbottom, M. (1958). The relation of need for achievement to learning experiences in independence and mastery. In J. Atkinson (Ed.), *Motives in Fantasy, Action, and Society.* Princeton, NJ: Van Nostrand Reinhold.

Wittmaier, B. (1972). Test anxiety and study habits. *Journal of Educational Research, 65,* 352–354.

Wlodkowski, R. (1986). *Motivation and Teaching: A Practical Guide.* Washington, D C: National Education Association.

Wlodkowski, R. and Jaynes, J. (1990). *Eager to Learn: Helping Children Become Motivated and Love Learning.* San Francisco: Jossey-Bass.

Yussen, S. and Kane, P. (1985). Children's conception of intelligence. In S. R. Yussen (Ed.), *The Growth of Reflection in Children* (pp. 207–241). Orlando, FL: Academic Press.

Zatz, S. and Chassin, L. (1985). Cognitions of test-anxious children under naturalistic test-taking conditions. *Journal of Consulting and Clinical Psychology, 53,* 393–401.

Zigler, E. and Harter, S. (1969). The socialization of the mentally retarded. In D. Goslin (Ed.), *Handbook of Socialization Theory and Research* (pp. 1065–1102). Chicago: Rand McNally.

Zuckerman, M., Porac, J., Lathin, D., Smith, R., and Deci, E. (1978). On the importance of self-determination for intrinsically motivated behavior. *Personality and Social Psychology Bulletin, 4,* 443–466.

APPENDIX 2–A

IDENTIFYING MOTIVATION PROBLEMS

INSTRUCTIONS

1. Observe students for a few days before completing the form. To make some of these judgments you may need to try new teaching practices—e.g., give choices in assignments with different difficulty levels; give some ungraded assignments; provide some opportunities to work on unassigned tasks.
2. Select several students who appear to have relatively serious motivation problems and rate their behavior in different subject areas or for different types of tasks or learning contexts.
3. If there are two adults in the classroom (e.g., a teacher and an aide) it is instructive for both to fill out the form for the same student. Differences can reveal biases in the teacher's or the aide's perceptions of a student, or context effects on behavior (because the teacher and aide see the student in different contexts).

SCORING

Create scores by adding together all of the +1's and –1's in each of the three categories ("W" = work orientation; "C"= confidence; "I" = intrinsic interest in schoolwork). A score close to or below 0 on any of these three dimensions suggest a problem.

Child's Name _____

Put a number before each behavior:
–1 = not usually true; 0 = sometimes true; +1 = usually true

1 (W) _____ Pays attention to the teacher

2 (W) _____ Begins work on tasks immediately

3 (W) _____ Follows directions on tasks

4 (W) _____ Maintains attention until tasks are completed

5 (W) _____ Completes work

6 (W) _____ Turns assignments in on time

7 (C) _____ Persists rather than gives up when problems appear difficult

8 (C) _____ Works autonomously

9 (C) _____ Volunteers answers in class

10 (C) _____ Test performance reflects skill level demonstrated on assignments

11 (C) _____ Seeks help when it is needed

12 (C) _____ Not upset by initial errors or difficulties

13 (C) _____ Enjoys challenging work

14 (I) _____ Works intensely

15 (I) _____ Asks questions to expand knowledge beyond immediate lesson

16 (I) _____ Engages in learning activities that are not required

17 (I) _____ Is reluctant to stop working on tasks when highly engaged

18 (I) _____ Engages in learning activities after assignments are completed

19 (I) _____ Appears happy, proud, enthusiastic and eager

20 (I) _____ Strives to improve skills, even when performing well relative to classmates

21 (I) _____ Initiates challenging learning activities on own

22 (I) _____ Works hard on ungraded tasks

EXTERNAL REINFORCEMENT
Teacher Self Reports

INSTRUCTIONS

This form is designed to help you reflect upon your use of external rewards and punishment. After completing the form, examine your responses for inconsistencies between your values and goals and your behaviors.

1. What reinforcements do you use?

		never	occasionally	often
(a)	social reinforcement (praise)	_____	_____	_____
(b)	symbolic rewards (e.g., stickers)	_____	_____	_____
(c)	good grades	_____	_____	_____
(d)	material rewards (e.g., food, prizes, trinkets)	_____	_____	_____
(e)	public recognition (e. g., paper on bulletin board)	_____	_____	_____
(f)	privileges (e.g., play with special materials)	_____	_____	_____
(g)	responsibilities (e.g., take roll, errand to the office)	_____	_____	_____

2. What punishments do you use?

(a)	private criticism	_____	_____	_____
(b)	public criticism	_____	_____	_____
(c)	bad grades	_____	_____	_____

	never	occasionally	often
(d) "time out" (social isolation)			
	_____	_____	_____
(e) loss of privileges (e.g., no recess)	_____	_____	_____
(f) other:	_____	_____	_____

3. What behaviors or outcomes is reinforcement contingent upon?

	never	occasionally	often
(a) high effort/attention	_____	_____	_____
(b) absolute performance (e.g., few errors)	_____	_____	_____
(c) relative performance (e.g., fewer errors than most other students	_____	_____	_____
(d) improved performance (i.e., for a particular child)	_____	_____	_____
(e) following instructions	_____	_____	_____
(f) finishing	_____	_____	_____
(g) creativity	_____	_____	_____
(h) personal initiative	_____	_____	_____
(i) helpfulness (e. g., to another child)	_____	_____	_____
(j) other	_____	_____	_____

4. What behaviors or outcomes is punishment contingent upon?

	never	occasionally	often
(a) low effort/ inattention	_____	_____	_____
(b) absolute performance (e. g., many errors)	_____	_____	_____
(c) relative performance (e. g., more errors than most other students)	_____	_____	_____
(d) no improvement	_____	_____	_____
(e) not following directions	_____	_____	_____
(f) not finishing	_____	_____	_____
(g) lack of personal initiative	_____	_____	_____

	never	occasionally	often
(h) dependency (asking for help needlessly)	_____	_____	_____
(i) refusal to help	_____	_____	_____
(j) misbehavior	_____	_____	_____
(k) other	_____	_____	_____

5. Are there any children in your class who are frequently rewarded (e.g., with good grades, praise, recognition) for outcomes that did not require much effort (i.e., were fairly easily achieved)?

6. Are there any children in your class who are not rewarded (e.g., with good grades, praise, or recognition), even when they try?

7. Are the rewards in your classroom realistically available to all children?

APPENDIX 4–A

OBSERVATIONS OF TEACHERS' USE OF PRAISE

INSTRUCTIONS

Each time the teacher uses verbal praise, an observer indicates whether the praise was "effective" or "ineffective" according to a set of criteria. Effective praise is described to the left of the slash; ineffective praise is either described on the right of the slash or it is the absence of the effective criterion. Put a "+" if the praise was effective according to a particular criterion, a "–" if the praise was ineffective according to the criterion, or nothing, if you are not sure if the criterion is not applicable. Observers should fill out this form in a variety of situations in which the teacher is likely to praise students (e. g., during reading groups, during whole-class or small-group question-and-answer periods). Examine criteria in which there are a large number of minuses. These provide specific information regarding ways in which praise might be used more effectively.

Motivation to Learn: From Theory to Practice	1	2	3	4	5	6	7	8
(+) contingent on behavior or outcome/(–) random, unsystematic								
(+) specific particulars of accomplishment/(–) global								
(+) spontaneous, credible/(–) bland, perfunctory								
(+) specifies performance (or effort) criteria/(–)								
(+) provides information about competence/(–)								
(+) stresses students' own behavior/(–) social comparison								
(+) focuses on improvement/(–) focuses on relative performance								
(+) focuses on effort or personal meaning of accomplishment/(–)								
(+) attributes success to effort and ability/(–) to ability or external factors								
(+) fosters endogenous attributions/(–) exogenous attributions								
(+) focuses on students' task behavior/(–) on teacher's authority								
(+) focuses on task behavior/(–) distracts attention from task behavior								

APPENDIX 6–A

RATINGS OF THE INTRINSIC VALUE OF TASKS

INSTRUCTIONS

For two typical days rate all of the tasks students are given (include small-group and whole-class question-and-answer periods in addition to written tasks). Circle the "–" if the task is best described on the left, "+" if it is best described on the right, and a "0" if it is somewhere in between or the description is not applicable to the task.

Task: _____

presented blandly	–	0	+	presented with enthusiasm
no mention of value of task or skill	–	0	+	intrinsic or other value mentioned
routine; minor variation on typical task	–	0	+	novel; different from typical task
simple (one step)	–	0	+	complex
evaluation of outcome stressed	–	0	+	no mention of external evaluation
extrinsic reward or punishment	–	0	+	no extrinsic reward or punishment
no student choice (how or when)	–	0	+	some student choice
passive student role	–	0	+	active student role
no feedback on skill or understanding	–	0	+	feedback during or soon after task is completed
student cannot discern improvement	–	0	+	improvement likely and discernible
mechanical	–	0	+	opportunities for creativity, problem solving
disconnected from child's life outside of classroom	–	0	+	directly related to personal experience
isolated knowledge (not connected to other school learning)	–	0	+	connected to other parts of the curriculum
task goals vague	–	0	+	task goals clear
task is too easy or too difficult for some	–	0	+	task requires effort but success achievable
no peer interaction allowed	–	0	+	peer cooperation encouraged
performance stressed	–	0	+	learning, understanding stressed

TEACHER RATINGS OF STUDENT HELPLESSNESS

INSTRUCTIONS

Rate children who are not exerting much effort on school tasks and appear to be performing below their capacity. Create scores (1) by summing all ratings and computing the average, or (2) by counting the number of "4's" and "5's." An average of 3 or above, or more than about 5 ratings of 4 or 5 suggest that the child lacks confidence in his or her ability to succeed and has given up trying.

Student's Name _____

		never				often
1.	Says "I can't"	1	2	3	4	5
2.	Doesn't pay attention to the teacher's instructions	1	2	3	4	5
3.	Doesn't ask for help, even when she/he needs it	1	2	3	4	5
4.	Does nothing (e. g., stares out the window)	1	2	3	4	5
5.	Doesn't show pride in successes	1	2	3	4	5
6.	Appears bored, uninterested	1	2	3	4	5
7.	Is unresponsive to teacher's exhortations to try	1	2	3	4	5
8.	Is easily discouraged	1	2	3	4	5
9.	Doesn't volunteer answers to teacher's questions	1	2	3	4	5
10.	Doesn't interact socially with classmates	1	2	3	4	5

AUTHOR INDEX

Koskinen, P., 169
Kowalski, P., 186
Krajcik, J., 93
Kramer, N., 70
Kratochwill, T., 47, 48
Kulik, C-L., 201
Kulik, J., 201
Kulikowich, J., 95

Lash, A., 222
Latham, G., 184
Lathin, D., 107
Lauer, J., 182
Lawson, M., 137, 213
Lazarus, M., 173, 174
Lee, C., 148
Lee, S., 131
Lefcourt, H., 123
Leggett, E., 15, 142
Leinhardt, G., 220
Lepper, M., 15, 67, 68, 69, 70, 74, 93, 97, 188, 197
Lerman, D., 136
Levine, J., 157, 202
Lewin, K., 106, 108, 112
Lewis, J., 167
Lewis, M., 155
Licht, B., 134, 135
Liebert, R., 166
Lighthall, F., 165
Lin, Y-G., 169
Lindquist, M., 173
Lipinski, D., 49
Lippitt, R., 106
Litrownik, A., 48
Locke, E., 148, 184
Loebl, J., 156
Lonky, E., 62
Luria, A., 51

Mac Iver, D., 64, 80, 155, 158, 174, 191, 193
Mace, F., 47, 48
MacMillan, D., 131
Madaus, G., 200, 209
Maehr, M., 11, 15, 70, 100, 112
Mahoney, M., 48
Maier, S., 133
Main, D., 64, 80
Malone, T., 93, 97
Manderlink, G., 70
Manoogian, S., 71
Marsh, H., 131, 155, 161
Marshall, H., 222
Martin, R., 171
Marx, R., 93
Mason, T., 182
Mastenbrook, M., 178

Masters, J., 49, 50
Matheny, K., 107
Maughan, B., 209
Mayer, G., 28
McClelland, D., 9, 118
McCombs, R., 216
McCullers, J., 82
McDermott, R., 217
McGraw, K., 82
McKeachie, W., 169, 175
McMullin, D., 62, 86
Meece, J., 15, 17, 83, 90, 91, 107, 131, 149, 155, 158, 174, 175, 215, 220
Meichenbaum, D., 46, 51
Meid, E., 54
Mendez-Caratini, G., 157
Mergendoller, J., 91
Mergler, N., 169
Meyer, J., 132, 159
Meyer, W., 53, 54, 141, 215
Meyers, J., 171
Middlestadt, S., 221
Midgley, C., 80, 114, 143, 157, 158, 159, 174, 223
Miller, A., 135, 143, 144, 148, 153, 156, 178, 214, 215
Miller, D., 148
Miller, S., 179
Mims, V., 70
Mitchell, K., 169
Mitman, A., 222
Montessori, M., 53
Morgan, M., 68
Morris, L., 166
Morris, W., 157, 159
Morse, L., 220
Mortimore, P., 209
Mosatche, H., 156
Mosley, M., 70
Mossholder, K., 70
Mumme, D., 188, 197
Munt, E., 50
Murphy, M., 184

Naveh-Benjamin, M., 169
Nelson, R., 49
Nelson, S., 132, 220
Nemcek, D., 157
Newman, R., 24, 155, 185
Nezlek, J., 107
Ng, K., 169
Nicholls, J., 15, 16, 17, 18, 19, 83, 131, 143, 144, 145, 149, 151, 155, 156, 166, 170, 182, 214, 215
Nierenberg, R., 149
Nisan, M., 82, 101
Nisbett, R., 67
Nolen, S., 17

SUBJECT INDEX